The Ecology of Nations

POLITICS AND CULTURE

James Davison Hunter and John M. Owen IV, Series Editors

The Ecology
of Nations

American Democracy in a
Fragile World Order

JOHN M. OWEN IV

Yale UNIVERSITY PRESS

New Haven and London

Published with the assistance of the Institute for
Advanced Studies in Culture, University of Virginia, and from
the foundation established in memory of Calvin Chapin of the
Class of 1788, Yale College.

Yale University Press books may be purchased in quantity for
educational, business, or promotional use. For information,
please e-mail sales.press@yale.edu (U.S. office) or sales@
yaleup.co.uk (U.K. office).

Set in Minion type by Integrated Publishing Solutions.
Printed in the United States of America.

Library of Congress Control Number: 2022951001
ISBN 978-0-300-26073-1 (hardcover : alk. paper)

A catalogue record for this book is available from the British
Library.

This paper meets the requirements of ANSI/NISO Z39.48-1992
(Permanence of Paper).

10 9 8 7 6 5 4 3 2 1

To my teachers and mentors

Nay; but we will have a king over us; that we also may be like all the nations; and that our king may judge us, and go out before us, and fight our battles.

—1 SAMUEL 8:20

Contents

Preface

Democracy and autocracy, the current U.S. president often asserts, are in a global competition. The winner will shape the twenty-first century. Is this true? China's government does not like such talk, and routinely ascribes it to a backward-looking "Cold War mentality."

Mr. Biden's assertion is plausible, at least for people of a certain age, people who do remember the Cold War. But it is not only the Chinese who question whether he has it right. The United States and China—two great powers—compete, to be sure. So do America and Russia. Perhaps Mr. Biden is trying to drape noble attire on America's struggle to remain the world's superpower? And even if democracy and autocracy are contending in some way, why should people who live in democracies care? How does it affect Americans if democracy is pushed back in Eastern Europe or Southeast Asia? Is the tug-of-war between two regimes just about bragging rights? Are citizens of democracies so fragile that they need constant reassurance from the rest of the world that their regime is best?

Reassurance and even bragging rights do matter, it turns out, but only as details of a much larger picture. This book argues that constitutional self-government and authoritarianism are indeed in a worldwide contest, that the contest is a matter of national interest for the great powers, and that it is not going well for democracy.

Great powers assuredly do compete for power and influence. But each great power competes as a particular type of country—as a democracy or an autocracy. Most American leaders (and most citizens) want two things very badly: for their country to be internationally competitive, and for it to be a democracy. Chinese leaders want their country to be competitive and for it to be authoritarian, or "socialist with Chinese characteristics." No one in this picture wants to have to choose between national power and domestic regime.

To see why this leads to a global contest between regime types, we can borrow from biological evolution. Great powers share an international environment that selects for various traits in states, including particular domestic regimes. Just as a snowy clime selects for animals with white fur, a certain kind of international environment can select for democratic states. On top of that, some organisms turn things around and modify their environment to the point where it actually selects for different traits than it otherwise would. Scientists call this "ecosystem engineering" or "niche construction."

Great powers try to engineer their ecosystems to favor their regime type. That is why democracy and autocracy are in a great and lengthy contest. Great powers do this so that they can avoid what I call the "regime-power dilemma," which says that if you want to be competitive, you must adapt your regime; and if you want to keep your regime, you must become less competitive. To relieve this dilemma, a democracy will do what it can, within reason, to make its environment friendlier to democracy. An autocracy faces a mirror-image version of the dilemma, and so will try to engineer the ecosystem to favor authoritarianism.

All of that is abstract, and in this book I make clear that

the international environment consists of three components: the balance of power among regimes (more democracies, and more powerful democracies, means a friendlier environment); international rules and practices (trading rules that punish more opaque economies are friendlier to democracies); and information about which regime type works best. These components all affect one another. I show the United States, China, and Russia all trying to shape this environment to favor their own type.

Democracy is in trouble in the United States and elsewhere partly because it is not doing very well in this competition. The international environment is no longer selecting for constitutional self-government. The following pages unfold two large reasons why. First, the United States, along with other wealthy democracies, has made the environment more liberal since World War II, but the kind of liberalism Washington has pushed into that environment lately is no longer working. Liberalism is the political doctrine that upholds individual freedom as the highest political good. It has been through three historic stages; the third, which I call "open liberalism," has served a few people very well, but its economic and cultural faces have alienated countless communities, polarized populations, and fed anti-liberal populism. Liberalism needs reform.

Second, the two authoritarian giants of China and Russia are infusing the international environment with content more supportive of their regimes. They have put up with the liberal international order for decades, and China has done well by it. But they know that it handicaps them so long as they retain their authoritarian regimes. Beijing and Moscow both believe that to be great powers, their countries must be authoritarian. The ecosystem that America has built is rigged to keep them down. In matters such as trade, cyberspace, human rights, and foreign intervention, they are laboring to turn the environment to favor their regime type.

The contest is on, then. That does not mean great-power war. It does mean that international cooperation will always be limited by the conflicting goals each side has for international order—goals that relate not just to ideals but to the national interest of each great power. The contest could become a long-term stalemate over the kind of international order we will have. Or, it could mean the emergence of two separate but overlapping international orders, one favoring liberal democracy, the other favoring authoritarian capitalism. But remedying the crisis of democracy requires recognizing the contest and waging it prudently.

I am grateful to many people and several institutions for helping me think all of this through and make it into a book. I spent the 2015–16 academic year in Berlin, funded by a Humboldt Research Award from the Alexander von Humboldt Foundation of Bonn. During that year I read extensively into evolutionary theory, convinced that it could help me pull together a number of ideas about states, regime types, and the international system. For criticism and conversation, I thank Thomas Risse and colleagues at the Otto Suhr Institute at the Free University of Berlin, and Michael Zürn and colleagues in the Global Governance program at the WZB Berlin Social Science Research Center. The Dahrendorf Forum at the Hertie School in Berlin and the London School of Economics commissioned a paper that became an early version of my argument about liberalism; the paper was published in *Global Policy* in 2017. I thank Helmut Anheier, Robert Falkner, and Peter Trubowitz for involving me in that project. I presented papers on coevolution and international relations to the German Institute for Global and Area Studies (GIGA) in Hamburg, the Peace Research Institute Frankfurt (HSFK), and the Swedish Institute of International Affairs (UI) in Stockholm. I thank my colleagues in each of these places—Patrick Köllner, Nicola Nymalm, Oliver Turner, Stein Tønnesson, Harald Müller, and others—for their comments and hospitality.

I drafted this book on another sabbatical five years later, at the University of British Columbia (UBC) in Vancouver, during the worst of the COVID-19 pandemic. I thank Dick Price and colleagues in Political Science at UBC for their comments on pieces of this work. I presented my article "Two Emerging International Orders?," later published by *International Affairs,* to groups at UBC and George Washington University, and the International Studies Association annual meeting. I thank Xiaojun Li, Julie Thompson-Gomez, Alex Downes, Amoz Hor, Alex Lennon, Sverrir Steinsson, Henry Hale, T. V. Paul, and Markus Kornprobst for comments. I thank the Ambassador Henry J. and Mrs. Marion R. Taylor Chair at the University of Virginia, as well as UVa's College and Graduate School of Arts and Sciences, for helping to fund my sabbaticals and my research more generally.

The two sabbaticals bookended a period in which democracy in the United States and other Western countries went from bad to worse. For pressing me to pull everything together into a set of cohesive arguments that could speak to audiences outside of my scholarly guild, I thank Jay Tolson, the intrepid editor of the *Hedgehog Review.* Writing and delivering the Winston Churchill Memorial Lecture at the Institute of Politics at the Catholic University of Portugal in September 2018 helped me assemble more of the puzzle; I thank João Carlos Espada, Bill Hasselberger, and other colleagues in Lisbon.

James Davison Hunter, Executive Director of the Institute for Advanced Studies in Culture (IASC), was most encouraging while I worked on this project. The IASC hosted a manuscript workshop in October 2021. I am deeply grateful to each participant for reading the manuscript so carefully and providing such productive feedback: James, John Ikenberry, John Mearsheimer, Dan Nexon, Harry Harding, Shirley Lin, Sid Milkis, Isaac Reed, Jay Tolson, and Kyle Williams. Nick Lowe's hopeful power pop hit from 1979, "Cruel to Be Kind," was an earworm for months afterward. I'm grateful to Dale Copeland, David Leblang, Melvyn Leffler, Arri Eisen, Olivier Zunz, and Seva Gunitsky for comments on the arguments.

For invaluable research assistance I thank Malloy Owen, Estelle McKinney, and especially the stalwart Howe Whitman. For all he has done to shepherd this book, including persuading me to add a chapter on Russia, I thank Bill Frucht at Yale University Press.

I thank my wife, Trish, for her rare combination of unstinting support, curiosity, patience, and perspective. For perpetual inspiration, I thank our children, Malloy, Frances, and Alice.

With enduring gratitude, I dedicate this book to the teachers and mentors, from high school through college, graduate school, and beyond, living and dead, who have helped me understand that politics is a moral science, and its study a worthy calling.

The Ecology of Nations

1

Democracy under Pressure

For some time it has been clear that American democracy is in trouble. It is also evident that Americans do not know what to do about it. The clumsy yet deadly serious assault on the U.S. Capitol on January 6, 2021—an attack on the country's constitutional order—was not the sort of thing that was supposed to happen in the United States. Long accustomed to thinking of their system of government as natural and permanent, Americans have had to come to terms with the possibility that it is mortal after all. Centuries of certainty about its capacity for innovation and self-correction have given way to fears that it is not up to the challenges that the twenty-first century is throwing at it.

January 6 was only the lowest point (thus far) of a low period in U.S. politics, a dramatization of the lengthy grinding down of the norms and habits, the toleration and forbearance, the trust and respect and belief in fairness on which democracy depends.[1] The Trumpification of the American Right befuddled so many because it entailed the unwilling, even unwitting, cooperation of the Left, in a cycle we call "polarization." One side goads the other, which obliges by reacting with outrage, which outrage goads (and gratifies) the first side, and so on. Indeed, the energy of Right and Left has come to reside with ambitious "influencers" for whom public service consists not of addressing difficult national problems but of gaining attention by competitively baiting and reacting to the other side. Our media business models are built on polarization, not locating or building consensus. Democratic virtues no longer pay.

The Trump years aggravated the polarization and sectarianism that had been growing since the late 1980s. It was in 1991 that the phrase "culture wars" appeared, as sociologist James Davison Hunter identified a new divide in the country's politics between traditionalists and progressives.[2] Polarization has a long history in the United States, and the country has managed it in the past, sometimes at great cost.[3] In the third decade of the twenty-first century, however, it seems out of control. Polarization persists partly because it hides its tracks so well: it causes people on each side to become extremist while making it appear to the other that they were extremist all along. It makes people you disagree with look dangerous to you, and thereby can make you dangerous to them.[4] It has made talk of secession and civil war more common than at any time since the 1860s.[5]

At the same time, when Americans look up from their country's carnival politics and survey the surrounding world, their sense of dread only grows. Only a generation ago, democracy bestrode the planet. The West had won the Cold War; communism was collapsing; there seemed no alternative to market-based constitutional democracy. Today, two facts about the world are clear: autocracy is back, and it is on the move.

Russia has defied confident Western pronouncements that it must democratize. It has in fact become more autocratic internally and pushed its autocracy outward, launching the largest military action in Europe since 1945 to crush Ukraine's struggling democracy and annex part of the country. Russia has grown closer to an even greater authoritarian giant, China. Not long ago, Western politicians and merchants hailed the spectacular rise of this immense, enterprising country as more evidence that democratic capitalism was the only viable way to order society in the modern world. China's openness to the world—economic, scientific, educational, cultural—was bound to lead to political liberalization. That thesis sits in the dustbin of history, atop other decomposing teleologies. China has become more authoritarian in recent years while in many ways outshining the United States. It is flexing its muscles off its coast and extending its influence throughout the Southern Hemisphere and into Europe.

Then, too, self-government is in trouble in other wealthy, mature democracies. Nothing as dramatic as January 6, 2021, has happened in Europe, but populist parties and politicians have risen in the twenty-first century, have gained power in some states, show no sign of fading, and indeed gathered strength during the COVID-19 pandemic of the early 2020s. Populists present themselves as the true democrats dedicated to rescuing their countries from parasitic elites. From the Right, Trump's Republicans, the National Front in France, the Alternative for Germany party, the Fidesz party in Hungary, and from the Left, Podemos in Spain and the Five Star movement in Italy—all say they are working to sweep away the self-appointed grandees of society, with their rigged systems, their complex rules, and their unpatriotic policies, and to restore the rule of the real people.

Beyond the North Atlantic area, democracy has been in a global crisis for a number of years. Younger democracies such as India and Brazil have stepped toward authoritarianism. Year after year, think tanks and research groups that assess the state of self-government in countries around the world issue gloomy reports. Not long ago, democracy was expanding and autoc-

racy contracting. Today, autocrats display the confidence re-
served for liberals a generation ago. Books from the 1990s and
2000s such as *The End of History and the Last Man* and *The
Ideas that Conquered the World* have become period pieces.
Now we read sobering titles such as *How Democracies Die, The
Road to Unfreedom,* and *How Fascism Works.*[6]

Many Americans sense that these international and domestic trends are all connected in some way. Their intuition is
correct. Modern history shows that democracy tends both to
advance and to recede in waves over regions and even the entire world. In 1991 political scientist Samuel Huntington identified three international historical waves of democracy. The
third wave began in 1974 with democratization in Greece and
Portugal. Huntington also noted two "reverse waves."[7] A third
reversal began in the early twenty-first century as Russia, Turkey, Venezuela, and other countries became more authoritarian.

Why democracy tends to wax and wane across entire
regions is a topic much studied by social scientists. In this
book I look at some of that research because it touches on my
main concern: *how to protect democracy in the United States.* I
focus on American democracy not out of indifference to self-
government and human rights in other countries. Quite the
contrary: I hope to make clear that Americans who care about
the condition of their country's domestic regime should care
about populism in Europe and about the global democratic
recession. Many Americans tend to think strictly nationally
about democracy. American Exceptionalism is a bipartisan
thesis. When asked what endangers their democracy, Americans of Right or Left will say some person or group or trend or
decision within the country: it is this or that politician or party
or court decision; it is Wall Street or white evangelicalism or
"wokeism."

But much of what ails American democracy is coming at

it from without. Like all countries, the United States exists in an international environment that affects not only its actions but its domestic politics. Some may like to think that America can carry on as a democracy without worrying about the rest of the world, but it is not so. No country is isolated from other countries and their ways of life, from international rules and institutions, or from information about the world. These are the basic elements of the international environment, and they can gradually work to buttress or undermine constitutional self-government in the United States. U.S. leaders have understood this since the country's founding and have refused to remain passive, simply acted upon by their country's environment, but rather have chosen to act upon it, to shape it.

When I say that America needs to protect its democracy from the outside, I do not mean it needs to encase itself in armor against foreign enemies, much less to hunt them down and fight them. Biologists teach that something is only part of an organism's environment if the organism interacts with it. So it is with a country: its environment consists of elements that it affects even as they affect it. America's leaders have understood this too. From George Washington to James Monroe to Franklin Roosevelt to Ronald Reagan and beyond, they have taken steps to try to adapt to and shape the international environment so as to enable the country to thrive while keeping intact its cherished domestic institutions.

Note the complexity of the problem: not only to be a powerful and wealthy country such as Napoleonic France, or to be a self-governing one such as Switzerland, but to be both at once. Professors of international relations and diplomatic history typically create a false dichotomy between these two goals. They assert that any country, including the United States, can ultimately care about either power or principle, but not both. (In academic arguments, power usually wins.) But the professors oversimplify and assume away the real problem: not how to maximize power or security, but rather how to optimize between two things most countries and most leaders want, namely national power *and* regime preservation. There is not a dichotomy but rather a dilemma, one I call the *regime-power dilemma*. For powerful countries such as the United States, the goal is to minimize the trade-offs between international competitiveness (power and prosperity), on the one hand, and liberal democracy, on the other. It is to have as much of both of these good things as possible. The way to do that is to shape the international environment so that it favors democracy over alternative, competing regimes.

Franklin Roosevelt stated the dilemma clearly in 1940: if the Axis ruled Europe and Asia, the United States "would have to embark upon a course of action which would subject our producers, consumers, and foreign traders, and ultimately the entire nation, to the regimentation of a totalitarian system." America "could not become a lone island in a world dominated by the philosophy of force."[8] Thus it had to take active steps to relieve itself of this Hobson's choice.

America has managed to pull off this trick and minimize the regime-power dilemma, to have it both ways, for much of its history—to influence its surroundings so that it can be a secure and rich democratic republic. But in recent years its shaping efforts have become self-defeating. It remains wealthy and powerful, but its wealth and power seem somehow to be pummeling its democracy. At the same time, China and Russia have begun to use their power to shape the international environment as well, trying to enable them to flourish while retaining their domestic regime of authoritarian capitalism.

The back-and-forth, the country-environment dynamic, requires some attention. It is an example of what biologists call "coevolution." In the natural world, organisms are not passive in the face of their environment. They alter it to their advantage, to the point where they can unintentionally steer the evolution of their own species and others. Long-toothed, sociable beavers build dams to trap the food they need; having more food gives them a reproductive advantage over short-toothed, antisocial beavers; over time, the beaver population is dominated by long-toothed, sociable ones.

Thinking about coevolution can help us address an old question that scholars, politicians, and citizens have argued about for many years. Do states care about power or purpose? Do they pursue gain or principle? The correct answer is that they do both: most of them want more control over their environment and also to keep their domestic system of government. Much statecraft aims to arrange matters so that states can have their cake and eat it—both avoid becoming less competitive while clinging to their cherished domestic order and also shifting toward a different domestic order, so as to become more competitive.

Coevolutionary thinking can also help us understand two large challenges, separate but related, that endanger democracy in America (and elsewhere). First, for more than seven decades, America has safeguarded its internal regime partly through a grand strategy called "liberal internationalism." The strategy has entailed the protection of other wealthy democracies through self-binding multilateral military, political, and economic institutions. Liberal internationalism was never only about what America did to other states or the "international system"; it was always about, at bottom, manipulating what the international system did to America, because U.S. leaders knew that there was no escaping that system. Until the 1970s, the strategy helped sustain democracy in the United States by allowing it and its democratic allies enough leeway to keep their economies and societies stable—to avoid the crises of the 1930s that nearly killed off democracy.

In the 1970s and 1980s, however, under pressure from new challenges, liberalism was transformed from an ideology of economic stability to an ideology of efficiency and individual self-determination. The change from *welfare liberalism* to *open liberalism* helped spread democracy into other parts of the world at the end of the twentieth century, and it played a role in the end of the Cold War. In the current century, however, open liberal internationalism has begun to backfire on the world and America itself. Its unanticipated economic and cultural costs have alienated millions, hollowing out communities, polarizing entire populations, and calling forth dark forces from the political extremities. Open liberalism has shown itself an ideology that rewards the elite and betrays everyone else.

The second challenge is moving more slowly, and its effects are only beginning to be felt. Its main source is the People's Republic of China, a superpower-in-waiting whose power and influence have grown at an astonishing rate in recent decades. Under the rule of its Communist Party, China began participating in liberal internationalism during the 1980s. Had it not done so, it would not be where it is today. Jessica Chen Weiss and Jeremy Wallace note that China is not trying to remake the world in its image; it is not aggressively exporting the "China model." But it is nonetheless trying to make the world safe for autocracy.[9] Its ruling party has long resented and feared the "liberal" of liberal internationalism—the advantages that the U.S.-shaped system gives to democracies and the handicaps it imposes upon authoritarian states. That intrinsic bias presses the regime-power dilemma on China's rulers: adapt by becoming more democratic, or discover a low ceiling to your own rise. For China to become a great power, its leaders believe, it must be authoritarian, under the rule of the party. Hence it must break out of the regime-power dilemma. In the late twentieth century, the Communist Party defied pressure to democratize by keeping a low profile. In the current century, China has begun to try to reverse the pressure by reshaping the international environment to favor its own system.

This second challenge has another source, the Russian Federation, chief heir to the long-deceased Soviet Union. In the early 1990s, Russia was dominated by liberals who aimed to make the country a Western-style, wealthy liberal democracy. That cruel decade nearly picked Russia apart, however. As weakened postrevolutionary states have done many times in history, Russia turned for help to a man on horseback. Vladimir Putin, who took power in 1999, first thought Russia could thrive in the liberal international order by doing what was necessary to stabilize its politics and economy. He brought to heel corrupt oligarchs who were stealing the nation's wealth and waged a savage war to suppress unrest and terrorism in its republic of Chechnya. But Putin soon perceived Western hostility to his regime and began to look for ways to push back against liberal internationalism as well. Their differences and conflicting interests notwithstanding, Russia and China have cooperated more and more closely in recent years in seeking to replace the liberal-democratic bias in the international environment with an authoritarian-capitalist bias. The two are having some successes in the economic, diplomatic, human rights, and cyber realms.[10]

These two challenges—the West's own loss of confidence in the order it built, and the solidifying authoritarian-capitalist alternative international order—are large, and many books and articles have been published about each. Most treat them separately. But the two challenges are related. We can make sense of them and see how they fit together if we think about the back-and-forth between large, powerful countries that dearly want to preserve their domestic regimes by shaping the international environment. How the competitive coevolution of the United States, on the one hand, and China and Russia, on the other, plays out will to a large degree tell the story of democracy in this century.

Democracy

By "democracy," I mean what political scientists call *liberal democracy,* a marriage of majority rule and individual rights. The rights generally include freedoms of speech, religion, assembly, and the press, as well as rights against arbitrary coercion by the state. Another term for this regime is *constitutional democracy,* which points to the constraints that law places on the popular will. Like any good marriage, liberal democracy entails some compromise. Democracy gives up a bit because the majority cannot get whatever it wants whenever it wants it. It cannot, for example, violate the rights of members of minority groups. The "liberal" part is not completely sovereign either, but is accountable to the majority. The law must be interpreted by judges and enforced by officials, all of whose power traces back to the will of the majority.

If either majority rule or individual rights dominates, you no longer have liberal democracy. In the eighteenth and nineteenth centuries, Great Britain was fairly liberal but not very democratic, and, as elaborated in Chapter 3, most English liberals believed democracy to be incompatible with individual freedom. On the other hand, today, Hungary's prime minister, Viktor Orbán, declares that his country is an "illiberal democracy"—ruled by the majority but embodying Christian rather than liberal principles (which he takes to be incompatible).[11]

The liberal-democratic marriage takes different forms in different countries. Some countries are presidential, with a chief executive elected separately from the legislative or law-making body. Some are parliamentary, with a chief executive the leader of her party in the legislature. Some have electoral rules that encourage two parties, while others' rules encourage multiple parties. Some are constitutional monarchies, others republics. To many citizens in democracies, these differences are not trivial. But both governments and political scientists accept that the similarities are even more important and that liberal democracy, in all of its variety, is a meaningful category.[12]

Across the world, liberal democracies vary in other ways. Some are more socialistic, with a robust welfare state and a heavily regulated economy. Others are more capitalistic, allowing markets a greater role in distributing goods.[13] It is fair to say that all liberal democracies have mixed economies. None is completely laissez-faire, none completely socialist. Scholars do not completely agree on why this is, but most do agree that a democracy needs to have a market-based economy so as to deny the state the power it could use to wreck democracy. Note, then, that we are not employing a "substantive" notion of democracy, for example, social democracy or libertarian democracy. Finland's strong social safety net does not, in and of itself, make it more or less democratic than the United States. Where to end up with respect to these questions of political economy is a matter for a democracy to decide for itself—although, as this book will make clear, there are times when greater or less state influence over the economy is more supportive of self-government.

But if democracy is about rules and procedures, it is not only about those things. Like any set of institutions, it must be supported by a culture or set of norms, practices, and habits. The cultural burden on democracy is heavier than that on au-

thoritarianism because state coercion in democracies is so limited. For the system of self-government to work, a majority of
the people must believe in it, value it, and defend it, if need
be, at great cost. They must internalize the habits of democratic life—default settings of trust, fairness, compromise, respect, and equality.[14] The people must see the laws as meriting
obedience because, in a real sense, they made those laws. A
democratic culture and democratic laws are so intertwined that
it can be difficult to tell them apart.[15]

The Democratic Recession

The symptoms of democracy's disease in the United States
have been analyzed endlessly. A recent study by the Institute
for Advanced Studies in Culture reports that public confidence
in politicians and government has dropped in recent years. In
1996, 64 percent had little or no confidence that government
officials tell the truth; in 2020 the figure had risen to 74 percent. In 1996, 79 percent believed that politicians cared more
about winning elections than doing the right thing; in 2020
that figure was 92 percent.[16] We normally think of agreement
about the nature of a problem as leading to cooperation on a
remedy, but Americans perceive too little in common to rally
together to repair the system. They are deeply polarized, unable to agree on who or what is causing the problem or even a
common language to describe it. The Trump years only worsened the polarization that had been set in train decades earlier.
The two poles show ideological differences, to be sure. Democrats see racism, inequality, and climate change as the greatest
threats to the country, while Republicans see media distor-
tions, China, and crime as the greatest threats.[17] In the 2020
U.S. election, Democratic-voting districts were further to the
Left than they had been in 2016.[18]

But it appears that political tribe has swallowed up ideology. It is group identity, not ideas, that determines most people's positions on the questions of the day. Experiments show that Americans who favor a policy will turn against it when told that the other party favors it. Some social scientists label the phenomenon "political sectarianism," comparable to the situation among contesting religious groups. Polarization is less an intensification of preferences along a few political issues and more a spreading homogenization of preferences across more and more issues; it is less a wall getting higher than an oil spill spreading outward.[19] The situation has become so severe that each side reports more loathing of the other side than affection for its own.[20] Conservatives apply words such as "arrogant and pretentious," "un-Christian," "intolerant," and "socialist" to progressives. Progressives return the favor with words such as "closed-minded," "racist," "authoritarian," and "undereducated."[21]

A moderate degree of polarization is healthy for democracy. Complete societal harmony would be a sure sign that the rights and interests of some people are being submerged. In the past, the cause of justice has been furthered in the United States by dissonance that forced majorities to confront bigotry, poverty, and other social ills. But a healthy polarization is complex, featuring what political scientists call "cross-cutting cleavages."[22] Simple, binary polarization is dangerous for liberal democracy because it means people on either side perceive few if any common interests and values with people on the other side. Binary polarization damages trust among political opponents and can be used to justify violations of the rule of law. It generates illiberalism, in other words. If the other side cheats, my side would be foolish to play by the rules. If the other side is dangerous, then we may need to violate constitutional principles now to save the Constitution for posterity.[23]

All is fair in war. Anyone on my side who is willing to compromise is either a dupe or a traitor, to be made an example of.

What can make polarization so robust is its self-aggravating quality. It exhibits what social scientists call "positive feedback." When one side regards the other as a threat, it tends to exhibit more internal solidarity, and its members communicate more intensely with each other than with outsiders. Members try to outbid one another in depicting the other group's words and actions as malevolent. Reactions to these mirror-image depictions move each side toward the extreme and fulfills the other group's worst prophecies about it.[24] The problem is exacerbated when people and institutions invest in polarization for their own gain. Political and media entrepreneurs multiply the issues along which the tribes differ—not just politics but geography, food, fashion, entertainment, religion—and make it more difficult to build bridges across the tribes. That is how polarization can lead to populist leaders and movements, who have contempt for constitutional restraints, portraying them as elitist ruses to thwart the will of the "real people."[25]

Severe polarization can throw even clever analysts off the trail, precisely because those analysts tend to belong to one of the poles themselves and thus to misunderstand their side's role in driving the other side to extremes. Thinking they are wounding the beast, they end up feeding it. It is to America's enduring shame that racism remains a source of serious and widespread injustice, while excuses remain more common than remedies. Yet racist attitudes, acts, and social structures have varied over time and space: the American story is not one of stagnant bigotry; some times and places have been better than others. Overt racism has increased in recent years. Some of that, however, is itself a product of polarization. White, working-class, rural Americans, never the most powerful group in the country, have been assured over many years by the political

Left (comprising mostly upper-middle-class whites) that they are declining demographically and losing power. The message has sunk in, and the white working class is reacting. What looks to many to be essential—long-hidden racism now revealed—is, in many cases, contingent—racism embraced because of polarization.[26]

Polarization is found in other industrial democracies too, and so are growing populist movements and politicians. As of 2020 in Europe, more than a quarter of voters cast ballots for populist-authoritarian parties in their country's most recent election.[27] Indeed, populism and encroachments on constitutionalism have become distressingly common in much of the world. Freedom House, the Washington-based institution that has reported on democracy across the world since the 1940s, reported in 2021 the fifteenth consecutive year of "decline in global freedom." This decline steepened in 2020, with the democracy rating of seventy-three countries declining and that of only twenty-eight improving.[28] The findings of the 2021 report of the Varieties of Democracy (V-Dem) project, from the University of Gothenburg in Sweden, were similar. Whereas in 2010, 52 percent of the world's population lived in democracies, in 2020 the figure was only 32 percent. The level of democracy enjoyed by the average citizen in the world in 2020 was roughly the same as it was in 1990, the end of the Cold War.[29] In 2020 the London-based Economist Intelligence Unit reported the lowest global democracy score since it began its reports in 2006. Only 8.4 percent of the world's population lived in what the researchers labeled a "full democracy." Forty-one percent—including the U.S. population—lived in a "flawed democracy," and the remaining half of the world lived in "hybrid" or "authoritarian" regimes. Among the other backsliders were France and Portugal.[30]

Democracy's loss is autocracy's gain. V-Dem reported that

"autocratization" continued to accelerate across many countries while democratization slowed to a trickle.[31] The most visible authoritarian regimes go from strength to strength, defying long-standing Western prophecies of their demise. China's ruling party removed term limits for its president, allowing Xi Jinping to remain in office indefinitely. In 2021 Russia followed suit, passing a law that would permit Vladimir Putin to be president until 2036.

The global democratic recession is in plain sight. Populist leaders and parties have won elections and entered governments, chipped away at constitutional restraints, and met with the approval of large proportions of their citizens (and the opposition of others) for doing so. Populists present themselves as democratic but seek to erode constitutional restraints so as to enact the will of some subset of the population.[32] Narendra Modi in India, Jair Bolsonaro in Brazil, Viktor Orbán in Hungary, and R. T. Erdogan in Turkey are among the most prominent members of the club. Most European countries have populist parties, and many of them have the wind at their backs in the twenty-first century.

At the same time, esteem for democracy has been dropping around the world. Since 1980 the World Values Surveys have been asking people in ninety-nine countries what they think of democracy. As depicted by the curve in Figure 1.1, in 1994 average support for democracy was around 52 percent. By 2018 it had dropped to 36 percent. (Each dot represents the probability the average citizen of a country will hold democracy in high regard.) The decline shows up in democracies themselves, where people's discontent with their own form of government has risen steadily since 2008 in every region of the world apart from South and Southeast Asia. In the wealthy democracies, dissatisfaction increased from under 40 percent to 49 percent. In the Anglo-Saxon democracies—Great Britain,

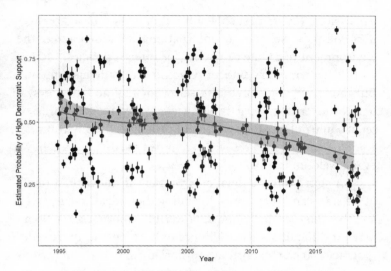

Figure 1.1. Global support for democracy, 1994–2018.
(Source: Joshua Alley and John Owen, "Trump and Public Support for Democracy Abroad" [working paper, University of Virginia, June 2021], using World Values Survey data, https://www.worldvaluessurvey.org/wvs.jsp.)

the United States, Canada, Australia, and New Zealand—it shot up from 25 percent in 2005 to 52 percent in 2020.[33]

The Argument

The global democratic recession and the poor state of American democracy are related. During what Samuel Huntington called the world's "second reverse wave of democracy," in the 1930s, democracy was entering a crisis in the United States as well.[34] Then, as now, something "out there" was also "in here" powering us-versus-them politics and corroding the rule of law.

In some ways, states are like organisms living in a complex environment that selects for some traits rather than others. Biology teaches that the environment of a population of organ-

isms selects for traits such as fur color, height, or aggressive-
ness. As most scholars of international relations agree, the
environment of a state can select for foreign policies, such as
increasing a military budget or joining a trade agreement.[35]
But the environment can also select for regime types or systems of government, partly because most regime types are better at some policies than others. In principle, the environment
could be neutral with respect to regime type. In practice, however, it seldom is.[36]

A state's international environment includes, first of all,
other states and their traits, including their ideas, their power,
and their physical locations. A powerful authoritarian state can
make it difficult for its neighbors to become and remain democracies. It can "export" authoritarianism to them in various
ways, including by cultivating friendly individuals and groups,
undermining unfriendly ones, fostering economic penetration
and dependence, and outright imposition. Second, a state's environment consists of rules, norms, and institutions that regulate its actions abroad and at home. When some states cut foreign trade and begin to build empires, they can make it hard
for other states to continue free trade and even to become and
remain liberal democracies; when powerful states violate human
rights, it becomes easier for smaller states to do the same.

Finally, the international environment contains information about which policies and regime types perform better,
information that can alter the way elites across the world—
politicians, lawyers, military officers, businesspeople, journalists, and intellectuals—think about systems of government, the
national interest, and their own interests. When a mob forces
its way into the U.S. Capitol to stop Congress from performing
a fundamental constitutional task, doubts about democracy
extend well beyond the United States. Questions about the ef-
ficacy of autocracy grow when China's ruling Communist Party

maintains its "zero COVID" strategy with its relentless lock-downs that slow economic growth and generate widespread protests across several cities. Large events of that sort put new information in the international environment that is digested by political elites everywhere, information about which systems of government work in today's world and which do not.

These elements of the international environment—other states, rules, and information—are not isolated from one another. They interact, each affecting the other two, building and reinforcing virtuous or vicious cycles. When a democratic great power wins a long struggle against an authoritarian rival, it becomes more likely that other states will democratize and open their economies, which in turn further strengthens the democratic great power. When an authoritarian giant sustains higher economic growth than its democratic counterparts for decades, it becomes more likely that other states will become and remain authoritarian, which makes it more likely that international human rights norms will become relativistic, which further buttresses authoritarianism in some countries.

The back-and-forth between states and their environment tells us that ecological selection for democracy or authoritarianism is only half of the picture. The environment is not a force bestowed by nature that acts on passive countries. It is built, maintained, and modified by governments as they interact with it. The governments of powerful and rich states have a larger effect on the environment than weak and poor states. Biologists refer to "keystone" species that have outsized influence over their habitats. The same is true of powerful states: they can respond to the selection pressure by pushing against it and redirecting it. In a word, states and their environments *coevolve:* the environment puts a kind of selection pressure on states to have one domestic regime rather than another, and states in turn engage in ecological engineering, altering—

intentionally and otherwise—the direction of that selection pressure, steering it toward or away from democracy.

Today, it is evident that the international environment does not select for democracy. It clearly does not favor liberal democracy in the United States, my primary focus in this book. The polarization-populism spiral that is pulling the country further and further down and loosening commitments to the institutions of democracy is in part a product of America's interaction with its international environment. That environment has borne America's own imprint for generations: the United States is a cause of the antidemocratic pressure its environment places on it. Policies and norms that America has been implanting in the international environment have boomeranged on it and aggravated the polarization that is endangering American democracy.

The international environment also contains a chronic problem for U.S. democracy, in the form of powerful authoritarian-capitalist states that, contrary to the expectations of optimistic liberals until recently, are not moving toward democracy. One of these is Russia, underestimated by a haughty West since the 1990s, increasingly audacious in its bid to reclaim its former influence.[37] The other is China, the greater long-term challenge to democracy in America and around the world. China has grown rich and powerful by participating in the U.S.-shaped international environment, but its ruling party been very careful not to adapt in such a way as to put its domestic regime at risk. In the early twenty-first century, the Chinese Communist Party began its own efforts to shape the international environment to make the world safe for authoritarianism.

Understanding both of these large problems—the United States' own missteps, and the rise of the authoritarians—requires that we understand how governments act strategically to safeguard the domestic regimes under and through which they govern. Democratic and authoritarian governments alike do this.

Democratic institutions and culture face continuous threats from inside and outside countries, and they need protecting. Sometimes the threats become so great and intractable that a government engages in a strategic shift in policy and philosophy, what I call "fundamental reform." Such reform amounts not to regime change, but to regime preservation. In the 1930s, American democracy was beset at home and from abroad by the Great Depression and the political extremism it fed. Franklin Roosevelt and his administration decided that the old basic policy orientation, classical liberalism, was no longer adequate—indeed, was effectively eroding liberal democracy. FDR's experiments in repair amounted to the New Deal, an early edition of what became known as the "welfare state." The welfare state was not itself democracy. It was a carapace to protect democracy, designed to make it work to the satisfaction of enough ordinary citizens and elites once again.

Other industrial democracies began to build welfare states as well. In the next decade, the United States and these others effectively pressed welfare liberalism outward and upward. America and its partners constructed an international order that contained institutions and information derived from this innovative, second-stage liberalism. Great powers—states with the military, economic, and social resources to wield outsized international influence—often do this more generally. When, for complex reasons, success at home depends on the participation of other states, great powers do not confine their institutional and policy reforms to themselves. As discussed in Chapter 3, such was the case at the end of World War II: the success of American self-government depended on self-government's success in Canada, Western Europe, and Japan.

We can think of efforts such as the liberal international order as what evolutionary biologists call *ecosystem engineering*.[38] Ant species that build anthills do so because some of their ancestors had mutated the ability to do so. Those ants came to predominate because their anthills gave them reproductive advantages—for example, in keeping nests warm and predators away. The altered environment fed back into the evolution of the ant species, leading to the disappearance of ants who could not build hills; hence, coevolution. An engineered ecosystem of this sort can be stable, at least for a time.

Ants do not intend to affect their population's gene pool; they simply want advantageous housing. Governments, being made up of human beings, can be more self-conscious and strategic about what they are doing. A democratic country can take steps not only to help itself operate more efficiently, but to protect its democratic institutions from external and internal threats. It can alter its surroundings by new economic, social, and foreign policies along with a justifying narrative that tells how the policies are true to the principles of liberal democracy. By helping the country flourish amid challenges and threats, the modified ecosystem can help reinforce the legitimacy of its liberal-democratic institutions.

Liberal internationalism, writes John Ikenberry, aims "to shape the political-institutional and normative environment— the international ecosystem—in which liberal democracies operate."[39] The original liberal international order was an ecosystem engineered to save democracy by adapting it to new conditions. Fundamental reform that works well and gains the support of enough people and groups becomes entrenched. Social scientists call this "path-dependence": reform made at a critical juncture, such as a regime-threatening crisis, effectively binds future decision makers to keep the reform in place.[40] It becomes institutionalized to the point where people think of it as part and parcel of the regime itself. For several decades in the United States, the New Deal seemed simply part of the country's democracy, as many regarded it as the natural development of the country's founding principles and could not imagine the country without it. The same was true of the welfare state in other industrial democracies. Constitutional self-government in all of these countries was reinforced by the liberal international order.

In the middle 1970s, U.S. leaders found that welfare liberalism had run its course and was itself undermining liberal democracy. They began to dismantle it and reengineer the international ecosystem with a new set of fundamental reforms that add up to what I call *open liberalism*. Open liberalism is a hybrid of what is often called "social liberalism," coming out of the cultural changes of the 1960s, and "neoliberalism," or small government and free markets. Welfare liberalism was chiefly concerned with securing economic stability and full employment. Open liberalism values the emancipation of all individuals— the elimination of barriers to individual choice. The greatest barrier to individual emancipation, for open liberals, is traditional institutions and cultures. The United States has led other mature democracies in injecting the international environment with open liberalism by reducing the economic and cultural importance of national borders.

American and other elites intended open liberal internationalism to be a lever to pry open the world and widen opportunity for individuals everywhere, not out of altruism but because they believed an open world supported liberal democracy in their own countries. For its first few decades, this novel form of internationalism enjoyed broad success. Its notion of the good life as one unencumbered by old boundaries and norms did help end the Cold War and raise incomes in much of the world. More recently, however, open liberalism has come to favor only smaller, more enclosed and exclusive groups within democracies, particularly the United States. The local communities on which U.S. democracy has always depended have proved especially vulnerable to the risks that open liberalism brings. Its economic policies have skewed the distribution of wealth to the very upper tier, degrading the ability of everyone else to self-organize.[41] Its culture has elbowed aside the local and the bottom-up and placed in its stead the authority of a kind of cosmopolitan individualism. John Mearsheimer calls it "unbounded liberalism," and it has created what John Ikenberry calls a "crisis of social purpose."[42] Open liberalism is not the only driver of polarization. Automation has eliminated manufacturing jobs. The internet and social media exacerbate the polarization that is making Americans enemies of one another. But the kind of liberalism that has predominated in the West for two generations has made extravagant promises that a particular version of the good life is within everyone's reach. For most, it has decidedly failed to deliver.

Authoritarian governments, too, engineer international ecosystems to protect their domestic regimes from threats.[43] China's ruling Communist Party began a set of experimental reforms in 1978, abandoning the disasters of Maoism for a mixture of market and socialist economics and international openness. Deng Xiaoping and other reformers never intended for China to become a multiparty liberal democracy. Quite the opposite: they wanted China to rise and flourish while keeping its Leninist political system, which Deng called "socialism with Chinese characteristics." Aware of the coevolutionary nature of states and the international environment, party leaders for the first two decades after 1978 both exposed China to liberal-democratic pressure and sheltered China from that pressure.

In the twenty-first century, the party has shifted tactics and is now doing some ecosystem engineering of its own. Xi

Jinping and his circle seek not to destroy and replace the order that America and its wealthy allies have maintained; after all, China has done quite well by that system. Rather, China's rulers seek to remove the U.S.-imposed liberal bias from that environment and replace it as much as possible with a bias that will allow China to thrive and continue to gain power and influence *as an authoritarian-capitalist state,* without the pressure to become more liberal and democratic. In the long run, the more the party leaders succeed in altering the international environment, the harder it will be for the United States to compete as a liberal democracy. China will effectively impose the dilemma on America that America once imposed on China.

China has assistance from Russia, a country that has become increasingly autocratic since its reemergence as a sovereign state and aspiring democracy in 1991. Vladimir Putin, now apparently Russia's president-for-life, and his ruling circle evidently are convinced that their country must be ruled by a heavily coercive central state if it is to be a great power again. They cannot accept the regime-power dilemma that the liberal international environment imposes upon Russia. They believe that their attempts to work with the United States and the West have met with nothing but abuse and betrayal. The wealthy democracies, they have concluded, want a liberal, weak, compliant Russia. That is why the Europeans and Americans have pushed regime change and NATO expansion to Russia's western borders. So Russia must take things in hand and reclaim territory that will help restore its great-power status, territory they believe rightly belongs to it, in any case. Russia and China have cooperated to reshape the international environment— not to make the entire world authoritarian, but to serve their entwined goals of protecting their own authoritarian regimes and making their countries more competitive internationally.

U.S. politicians and journalists often assert that the United

States and other mature democracies are in a contest with China and Russia over which regime type, democracy or autocracy, will become predominant in the twenty-first century. The intuition behind these statements is sound, but the reasoning is seldom spelled out. The coevolution of regime types and the international environment provides that reasoning. The United States, China, Russia, and the other countries of the world are not operating in isolation. They share an environment that can favor liberal democracy or authoritarian capitalism, but not both. There are other ways to think about contests over international order, such as the competition over who will sit atop the global hierarchy.[44] This book focuses on efforts of great powers to steer regime evolution in their direction.

What States Want

Some serious analysts, including academic realists who study international relations, are skeptical about this kind of argument. Structural realism separates a country's quest for power and security from its domestic regime. Domestic politics is one thing, international politics another entirely; because there is no world government to ensure peace and enforce agreements, democracies are forced to act like authoritarian states. It is a fundamental mistake of liberalism, say realists, to assert that there are connections between the two realms—to say, for example, that democracies are less likely to go to war with one another or more likely to cooperate. John Mearsheimer's *The Great Delusion* is an outstanding recent statement of this position. Mearsheimer argues forcefully that Americans are courting trouble when they try to make the international system more liberal.[45]

Realists certainly are correct that many U.S. attempts to spread democracy by force have failed and even done more harm than good, not least to America itself. But what Mearsheimer and other realists miss is that the international system and American democracy cannot be pried apart. Most Americans—certainly most U.S. leaders—want to keep their republic *and* keep it competitive. The leaders of China and Russia want their countries to be powerful and secure *and* to be authoritarian. The international system can select for democracy or authoritarianism. The United States, China, and Russia can all affect which regime it selects for. If you want to keep the republic, your foreign policy must be concerned about much more than guarding the homeland from foreign attack or blackmail.

Another school of thought within realism, the hegemonic school, is closer to the argument of this book. It presents a more complex international system, one with rules and institutions as well as material power.[46] The United States after World War II is the archetypal hegemon: for dozens of states, it set and enforced the rules of many types of international interaction and was the main supplier of public or club goods such as freedom of navigation, a global currency for financial transactions, and lending to heavily indebted governments. Hegemons do these things because it is to their advantage. The chief subject of this book is not simple hegemony, however. It is how to maintain America's international position and its democracy at the same time.

The contest over the content of international order—liberal *versus* authoritarian—does not doom the United States to fight Russia or China. China and America can evade what Graham Allison calls the "Thucydides Trap" that can ensnare great powers in a bipolar system.[47] The contest does mean that cooperation between the democracies and the authoritarian sides over common interests will necessarily be limited, because each side must be concerned with denying the other's domestic system an advantage. Democracy versus authoritarianism is not just about ideals or symbols or bragging rights. In a real sense, it is about the ability of the United States to remain at once a liberal democracy and a wealthy, powerful, influential country. It is about whether the country can avoid choosing between those two things.

Plan of the Book

Because constitutional self-government in the United States is related to the same system in other countries, particularly other mature, industrial (or postindustrial) countries, the book pays a great deal of attention to other countries, both democracies and autocracies, and even more to the medium in which the United States and all of these countries move and relate to one another.

Chapter 2 lays out in more detail the book's argument about coevolution. It discusses what liberal democracy and authoritarian capitalism are and why governments normally care so deeply about regime type. It notes how regimes can change either against a government's will (via revolution or coup d'état) or at the direction of a government (via what political scientists call "autocratization"), and how a state's environment can make either process more or less likely. The chapter explains what the relevant components of a state's environment are and precisely how each can select for democracy or autocracy. Borrowing from biology the concept of "ecosystem engineering," it explains how governments, deliberately or not, can alter the state's environment so as to bias regime selection.

Chapters 3 and 4 tell the story of how the ecosystem that the United States and other liberal democracies have engineered and sustained has changed over time. After decades of experimentation and success, the ecosystem today is no longer selecting for democracy. The changes have come because the content of liberalism itself has evolved. Liberalism has always been about individual liberty and has always been an international project, but as time has passed liberals have filled in the concepts differently and mounted different international programs. First-stage or classical liberalism saw the despotic state as the chief threat to liberty, and limited government as the remedy. Liberal internationalism was limited to bilateral trade treaties and efforts to strengthen international law. Second-stage or welfare liberalism declared unregulated markets the main hazard to individual freedom, and the welfare state as the solution. It was welfare liberalism that constructed the matrix of multilateral institutions after World War II. Third-stage or open liberalism, predominant today, has retained the international institutions but filled them in with rules and policies that have continued to foster growth while leaving millions of citizens behind, polarizing the country (and many other mature democracies), and threatening constitutional self-government.

Chapters 5, 6, and 7 consider the slower, less obvious threat to democracy: the authoritarian-capitalist giants China and Russia, which are laboring to reengineer the international ecosystem so as to rid it of its liberal bias and make it friendlier to their own regime type. For years Western leaders hoped that China would become a "responsible stakeholder" in the liberal international order—a state that would leave intact its liberal principles. Such a goal was never feasible so long as China retained its domestic regime. The Chinese Communist Party is determined to hold on to its monopoly on political power in China and is convinced that the country must continue to have economic access to most of the world for raw materials, technology, and markets. But Xi Jinping and the party leadership are equally convinced that China must retain "socialism with Chinese characteristics," including party-state ownership of large firms in sectors such as energy and banking, and also controlling influence in privately owned firms. Party leaders also believe that the international environment is biased against their domestic regime, hobbling China's continuing rise, and are taking active measures to alter that bias in their direction, particularly in human rights, trade, and global internet governance.

When the liberal ecosystem pressed so hard on the Soviet Union that it collapsed in 1991, liberals had high hopes that Russia would develop into a free-market liberal democracy. Bad luck and bad policy—in the West as well as Russia—set the country on a path back to authoritarianism and aggressive revanchism in states that were once part of the old Russian empire. Vladimir Putin and his ruling circle are convinced that for Russia to be a great power, it must centralize power in a strong state, and that when the West presses human rights and democracy in Russia and its western neighborhood, it is really just trying to keep Russia down and boost American imperialism. The color revolutions of the early twenty-first century, and NATO and European Union expansion, form dots that the Kremlin easily connects into a conspiracy run out of Washington. Putin is trying to reengineer the ecosystem, preeminently by promoting and preserving autocracy in Ukraine and countries to Russia's west and southwest, but also by working with China and other like-minded states to make international institutions and practices less liberal, to show that liberal democracy has had its day, and to make "sovereign democracy" the global norm.

Chapter 8 offers some ways to think about how to remedy the challenges of today's boomeranging liberal internationalism and the authoritarian challenge. It calls on Americans and others to reconceive liberalism yet again, in ways to meet the conditions of late modern culture and postindustrial society. What I call "pluralistic liberalism" would not present the good life as one of perpetual change and choice, but would recognize that many individuals want a democracy that does not penalize them for making long-term commitments to people, communities, and institutions. Regarding China and Russia, I argue that they may persist in ongoing competition with the West over the content of global order; that would probably minimize the threat of great-power conflict but would also place democracy at greater risk. Or we could already be living in the emergence of two separate but overlapping orders—a liberal international order (LIO) and an authoritarian-capitalist international order (ACIO). A world of two international orders might allow the great powers to minimize pressure on their domestic regimes but might also intensify competition in Asia, Africa, and Latin America for members, and hence might produce a severe cold war.

My ultimate concern is not America's geopolitical competition with China or preserving or restoring U.S. global supremacy. It is not how to restore or reform the liberal or rule-based international order. It is not how to slow or reverse the shift in wealth and power from west to east. It is not avoiding or ending a Sino-American cold war. All of those topics are related to our subject.[48] But the ultimate focus of this book is how to maintain the ability of the United States to *remain competitive in the world as a constitutional self-governing country*—that is, without having to sacrifice civil liberties or democracy.

2

Coevolution
Domestic Regimes and the
International Environment

Protecting the Republic from the Outside, 1823

Two centuries ago, the customs surrounding the U.S. president's State of the Union address were nothing like those of today. The president did not process into the House of Representatives like a monarch. No phalanx of outthrust hands greeted him. Rote partisan eruptions did not halt his speech every minute or so. In the gallery sat no ordinary citizens waiting for their seconds of fame as presidential props. In that more republican era, the president did not go to the Capitol at all, but sat at the White House while a courier carried the written text down Pennsylvania Avenue, to be read to the assembled houses of Congress by a Senate clerk.

The clerk who read President James Monroe's address to Congress on December 2, 1823, found himself covering the usual questions of the day: national boundaries, public finance, the state of the Army and Navy, piracy in the Caribbean, the Post Office, and infrastructure. It was at the end that Monroe's message considered the recent, unexpected turn of events in

Europe. Two years earlier, liberal uprisings in various southern European states had pressed monarchs to give up absolute
power and submit to constitutions. In his message a year earlier, Monroe had noted these events with approval. In April
1823, however, things in Europe had taken a bad turn. A French
army of one hundred thousand had invaded Spain to overthrow the constitutional regime and restore the old absolute
monarchy. Now, in December, the Senate clerk read out Monroe's warning to the monarchs of Europe not to take similar
action in the Western Hemisphere.

Monroe wanted to protect the infant republics of Central
and South America. Since 1810 a chain of dominoes in Latin
America had fallen, as one Spanish colony after another declared independence. Now, many Americans wondered whether
France's invasion of Spain was a precursor to European invasions of these Latin American republics to restore Spanish
monarchy there. A few years earlier, after crushing Napoleon
Bonaparte and restoring the old Bourbon monarchy in France,
the absolutist great powers of Europe—Austria, Russia, and
Prussia—had established the Holy Alliance. Called a "political
system" by Monroe, the Holy Alliance announced its right to
quash liberal revolutions.[1] "The political system of the allied
Powers [in Europe] is essentially different, in this respect, from
that of America," read Monroe's message. "This difference proceeds from that which exists in their respective Governments."[2]

Monroe went on to caution the European powers that
"we should consider any attempt on their part to extend their
system to any portion of this hemisphere, as dangerous to our
peace and safety." The United States would not interfere with
any European colony and would be neutral in any wars of co-
lonial independence. But it would not allow the monarchs of
Europe to roll back republicanism in the New World. "It is
impossible that the allied Powers should extend their political

system to any portion of either continent, without endangering our peace and happiness; nor can any one believe that our Southern brethren, if left to themselves, would adopt it of their own accord."[3]

What later became known as the Monroe Doctrine was a bluff. The U.S. Navy was too small to defend the Latin American republics from Europe's navies. In the event, the Holy Alliance left Latin America alone, in part because the British Royal Navy, the world's largest, ended up enforcing the doctrine.[4] British governments had their own reasons for keeping European rivals out of the New World, and Britain was besides a constitutional monarchy that saw itself as essentially different from the absolute monarchies of Europe.

Monroe bluffed, but his doctrine aimed to protect something important. It was an attempt to safeguard the United States' own domestic regime. For Monroe and John Quincy Adams, his secretary of state who drafted this portion of Monroe's speech, the United States was not simply a piece of territory, its inhabitants, and their property. It was an independent republic that the preceding generation of patriots had established at great cost. As Daniel Deudney has put it, the young American republic "was explicitly designed to prevent North America from becoming a Westphalian system of hierarchic units lodged in anarchy."[5] Republicanism in North America would not be safe, these leaders thought, if absolute monarchy were to spread in Central and South America. With monarchy would come the "political system" of the European powers—the set of norms and institutions that authorized the monarchs to intervene in Spain and other weaker states fighting for their liberty. Republicans saw monarchies as rapacious and imperialistic. Indeed, for some U.S. politicians such as Representative Henry Clay, the Monroe Doctrine was too timid.[6]

Never mind that Monroe's own republic, the United States,

itself had a voracious appetite for territory that belonged to Native Americans. Monroe and Adams were gesturing toward a more general theory: a republic surrounded by monarchies is in a precarious position. That kind of environment is bound to be hostile. In private correspondence, Monroe wrote that if the Europeans did reimpose monarchy in Latin America, he fully expected that "they would, in the next instance, invade us."[7] From the time of its own independence from Britain up to only a few years earlier, the young United States had been surrounded by colonies of European monarchies, from the Arctic Circle to the southern tip of South America. Now, in 1823, it saw a string of young republics to its south. The Western Hemisphere, then, was becoming friendlier to the American regime. In warning off the European monarchies, Monroe was trying to keep it that way.

This chapter explains why it can make sense for governments to do what Monroe did. The international environment can make it easier or harder for a country to thrive and compete under its current regime. A hostile environment can impose a dilemma upon a state, which we can call the *regime-power dilemma*: conform your regime to your surroundings, or subject your country to more risk and find its international position deteriorating. Governments that understand this dilemma can try to shape that international environment so as to favor their own regimes. They may or may not do it well. But in doing it, they contradict foundational claims of both realism and liberalism in international relations. Realism expects states, at bottom, to care about material power and security, not about institutions or ideas. Liberalism expects states, at least democracies, to care about extending liberty for its own sake. Each school of thought gets only half of the story right. Governments want their states to be secure and to have a particular domestic regime; they optimize between these two goods and want to minimize the trade-offs they have to make between them. That is why they try to manipulate their international environment.

There are three relevant components of an international environment: the balance of power among regime types—for example, how many democracies and autocracies are in the world, how powerful they are, and where they are located; information about how various domestic regimes perform; and states' predominant rules and practices. A biased international environment favors states of the right regime type and handicaps states with the wrong one. It presses the latter states to change their policies, possibly in ways that would weaken their domestic regime and, at a maximum, lead to regime change.

I use an analogy from evolutionary biology to discuss briefly the mechanics of how this back-and-forth, state-environment process works. I discuss what domestic regimes such as liberal democracy are and why they matter to governments. I look specifically at how governments can and do shape the international environment and redirect selection pressure to favor their own regime type—for example, how a government can make it easier for itself (and other countries) to remain democracies.

States, Governments, and Regime Change

In 1823 Monroe and Adams did not have modern social science at their disposal, but they grasped an important fact about international relations: certain features of a state's external environment can affect the health and survival of its domestic regime. In 1978 political scientist Peter Gourevitch published "The Second Image Reversed" in a leading academic journal of international relations. The "second image" refers to a set of theories that explains international events, such as wars, by looking to states' domestic features—whether they are democracies, for example. Reversing the second image meant flipping the causal arrow to argue that the international could help explain the domestic. Gourevitch presented some "outside-in" social science that argued that a perpetual high threat of war pushes states to develop authoritarian regimes, whereas countries that are relatively secure externally tend to become more democratic. He went on to identify other international factors that could affect states' domestic regimes, including the international economy, the international states system, military intervention, and "meddling."[8]

More recently, separate studies have found that the more great powers in the world are democratic, the more democracy tends to spread.[9] Whether a country becomes a democracy, or remains one, is not completely up to its population or even its own powerful elites. Countries exist in a social environment that presents them with constraints and opportunities. The environment can make it easy for them to become and remain democracies and hard for them to become and remain authoritarian. Or it can do the opposite. What evolutionary theory calls a "selection logic" is at work in states' interactions with their surroundings.

There is a great deal to a state's environment, of course. In biological evolution, scientists use "environment" to mean only those elements of an organism's surroundings with which it interacts.[10] For a population of foxes, the snow and ice on the ground are part of the environment much of the year, but a meteorite passing overhead is not. The meteorite does not affect the foxes, nor the foxes the meteorite. The snow and ice do impinge on the foxes in many ways, however—for example, by making it easier or harder for them to hide from predators and prey, depending on their color. Snow grants an advantage to white foxes by concealing them; it imposes a disadvantage on

red and gray foxes by revealing them. Over time, the population of foxes in Arctic areas came to be dominated by white
ones because the environment selects for white fur.

Much international relations scholarship uses evolutionary frameworks and mechanisms, sometimes only implicitly.
Scholars have used Darwinian logic to explain the emergence
of international rules and practices, of globalization, of sovereign states, and of world politics itself.[11] Evolutionary logic can
help us understand how events outside a state affect whether
the state is a democracy or not.

A state's domestic regime is one of its traits, analogous to
an animal's fur color. The immediate cause of fur color (phe-
notype) is genetic material (genotype). The immediate cause
of a regime type is sufficient domestic support for it among the
country's elites and public. States are not organisms, of course;
they are social constructs, not natural things. Still more important, in biological evolution change occurs in a population
over time, as individual organisms are born, reproduce, and
die. By contrast, an individual state can change its regime and
retain the new regime if it helps the state (or at least its elites)
thrive. Yet, environmental pressure affects the traits of states as
it does the traits of populations of organisms. (For the hardy
band of readers who care about evolutionary theory, the version this book uses to explain states' domestic regimes is as
much Lamarckian as neo-Darwinian.)[12]

But states affect the same environments that affect them,
and here biology offers international relations an even more
powerful concept: *coevolution*. Social scientists sometimes use
that term loosely, to mean something like "evolving together."
Following biologists, I have a more precise meaning in mind: a
state and its environment coevolve when a state alters its international environment in such a way that the state itself evolves
differently from how it otherwise would.[13] When the environ-

ment is pressing the state to become authoritarian, but the state manipulates its environment so that instead it can remain democratic, it engages in what evolutionary ecologists call "ecosystem engineering," and coevolution happens. For many decades, the United States has been engineering its ecosystem. It has molded the international system to reinforce its own domestic regime of democratic capitalism.

I am far from the first to draw attention to this back-and-forth dynamic between states and their environments. In other social sciences, theorists have offered the concept of "structuration"—in which agents and structures constitute one another over time. International relations scholars have applied structuration to states and the international system.[14] On liberal internationalism specifically, John Ikenberry writes: "The essential goals of liberal states' order building have not changed: creating an environment—a sort of cooperative eco-system—in which liberal democracies can operate by providing tools and capacities for their governments to manage economic and security interdependence, balance their often conflicting values and principles, and secure rights and protections for their societies."[15] Ikenberry and Daniel Nexon note that the domestic politics of hegemonic states are affected by the international orders that they build.[16] Both America and its environment are different from what they would have been without this molding. So are scores of other countries in the world. Coevolution has happened.[17]

Many elements of a state's surroundings can affect its domestic regime. I focus on three. First is the *balance of power among regime types,* including how many states have each regime type and how powerful those states are. A second element of a state's environment includes *international rules, institutions, and practices*—how much the powerful respect the sovereignty of the weak, whether economies are more or less open, how institutionalized international cooperation is, and so on. Third is *information* about which regimes work well and are considered acceptable by powerful actors.

Domestic Regimes and Regime Change

Before elaborating on how these three elements can select for democracy, we need to clarify what domestic regimes are and how regime changes happens—how democracies can autocratize, and autocracies democratize. Political scientist David Eastman and his colleagues define a regime as a country's "institutions, operational rules of the game, and ideologies (goals, preferred rules, and preferred arrangements among political institutions)."[18] Regimes are not policies or ordinary laws; they are the matrix of basic institutions, norms, and practices that enables a society to have the government that makes those laws and policies.

In some countries, such as dictatorships, the regime *is* the government. Political scientists call a fusion of government and regime *personalist*. Germany's Nazi regime and Iraq's Baathist regime were personalist; the death or deposition of the leader meant the end of the regime. For most countries, however, the regime is not the same as the government; the regime is what enables the government to exist and govern. The regime sets the terms for the government's operation, and also outlives the government. Such regimes are called *institutionalist*. Joe Biden's administration governs under and through America's liberal-democratic regime. Xi Jinping's government governs under China's authoritarian-capitalist regime.[19]

No two states have precisely the same regime. Canada is a constitutional monarchy with a parliamentary system; the United States is a republic with a presidential system. But current worldwide convention places Canada and the United States toward the same end of a regime spectrum, the end labeled "democracy." On the other end of the spectrum is "autocracy" or "authoritarianism." Countries such as China, Russia, Iran, and Venezuela are closer to the autocratic end of the spectrum, even though their regimes are also diverse. In Chapter 1 we noted that modern democracy is a marriage of majority rule and individual rights, achieved through a set of institutions that include the separation of powers and regular competitive elections. An autocracy is a regime that to a significant degree lacks these institutions. Autocracies often claim to feature popular sovereignty and to uphold various individual rights, but they lack the mechanisms of divided powers and accountability that democracies have—the guarantee of regular competitive elections—to provide confidence that their citizens will actually enjoy those things.

Most countries' regimes are stable most of the time. But as we saw in Chapter 1, countries do move in either direction along the democracy–autocracy spectrum, sometimes rapidly and sometimes slowly. In recent years more have moved toward autocracy than toward democracy, including the United States. From the mid-1970s through the 1990s, the opposite movement—toward the democratic end—was much more common. Chapter 5 discusses how China's ruling Communist Party fears international pressure to end its monopoly on power— which, party leaders believe, would cripple their country.

Figure 2.1 depicts how one prominent research team, the Varieties of Democracy (V-Dem) group at the University of Gothenburg, Sweden, tracks movement along a democracy–autocracy spectrum. V-Dem uses a large set of indicators to measure liberal democracy; one may challenge some of its conclusions, but the V-Dem group is transparent about its criteria and measurements.[20] Note the movement of countries between 2010 and 2020: V-Dem claims that the United States and India,

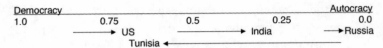

Figure 2.1. V-Dem's democracy–autocracy spectrum.
(Source: Varieties of Democracy [V-Dem], University of Gothenburg, "Country
Graphs," https://www.v-dem.net/data_analysis/CountryGraph/, retrieved on April
16, 2021.) Between 2010 and 2020, the United States moved from 0.85 to 0.73; India
from 0.57 to 0.34; Russia from 0.14 to 0.1; Tunisia from 0.1 to 0.64.

both democracies, moved in an authoritarian direction; Russia
and China, already authoritarian, autocratized further. Tunisia, on the other hand, jumped from autocracy to democracy
following the Arab Uprising. Overall, whereas 48 percent of
the world's population lived in autocracies in 2010, the figure
had risen to 68 percent by 2020.[21]

What causes states to move along this regime spectrum
in either direction? Democratization, as in Tunisia, has long
been one of the largest topics in political science. One recent
book argues that democratization sometimes happens when
an autocracy abruptly experiences a marked worsening in economic inequality. That generates sustained public anger and
raises the possibility of revolution. Revolution being dangerous, rulers and other elites respond with democratic reforms.[22]
Another recent book is skeptical that economic inequality
plays a large role, and finds more idiosyncratic political causes
within each democratizing country.[23] Another argues that states
democratize when elites fear that their unaccountable authoritarian government might seize their assets or remove their
privileges at any time. These elites design democracy so as to
safeguard their assets and privileges.[24] Still other scholars argue
that democracy diffuses from state to state. Elites in an autocracy worry about their country's weakness and instability; they
observe how democracies are stable and prosperous; they em-

ulate the prestigious countries that have democracy, or simply find that they need to democratize to remain internationally competitive.[25] In Chapters 5 and 6, I examine the worries that rulers in China and Russia have about democratization.

Political scientists have become interested in the opposite movement—autocratization—more recently, thanks to the lamentable overall global trend in that direction. Sometimes the motion is abrupt, a lurch in the form of a coup d'état led or aided by military officers. Coups were once the most common method of autocratization, and the early 2020s saw an epidemic of them in some poorer countries.[26] In recent years, however, more gradual and subtle autocratization has been more typical, as would-be dictators have adjusted their strategies and tactics to an age when democracy is globally regarded as the only legitimate system of government. Since 1946 more than one-quarter of dictatorships have been imposed by a democratically elected government that "authoritarianized."[27] In our time democracies tend to die slowly, not suddenly, as elites gradually weaken norms and institutions by pushing them beyond what has been acceptable—for example, when they compromise the independence of courts by packing them with pliant judges, who then allow them to weaken democracy in other ways, or when they fragment opposition parties by co-opting some of their members.[28] The result is *competitive authoritarianism,* a regime in which opposition parties compete in elections but inevitably lose.[29] Intense partisan polarization can lead to that kind of gradual autocratization by making politics into a zero-sum game, in which the consequences of losing an election become unacceptable. Compromise or even discussion across political divides becomes nearly impossible, and populist leaders who despise constitutional constraints and promise to vanquish political opponents gather strength.[30]

For all of the complexity and scholarly disagreement about regime transitions in both directions, a common basic change is at work when a state moves in either direction on the spectrum: *support for the status quo regime among elites, ordinary people, or both, drops.* When that happens, all else being equal, the regime is endangered and other processes may kick in to erode or overturn it.

How the International Environment Affects Democracy

Various changes *outside* a state can end up reducing support *within* that state for its regime, pressing its government to adapt and make trade-offs that it would rather avoid. Figure 2.2 depicts these ecological pressures.

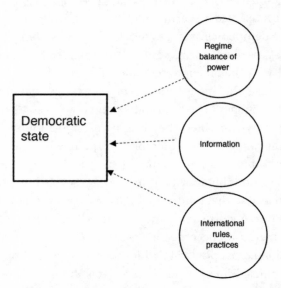

Figure 2.2. Elements of a state's environment
that affect its domestic regime.

BALANCE OF POWER AMONG REGIMES

International relations scholars have long known that the balance of power among states is a central variable. When it comes to the health of a country's democracy, the international balance of power among *regime types* is central. That balance, in turn, is a function of two things: how many states have which type of domestic regime, and the relative power of those states. The greater the power base of democracies, the easier it will be for countries to become and remain democratic.

Particularly important are great powers or hegemons. Between 1800 and 2000, during periods when a democracy was the world's most dominant power, the number of democracies expanded. As a rule, when one great power emerges from a hot or cold war as supreme—a "hegemonic shock"—elites in other states want to emulate the new hegemon.[31] When a great power exemplifying one regime type manifestly proves superior to its rivals, smaller states tend to conform to the ideology of that winning great power.[32] Especially prone to change are states whose domestic regimes are already wobbly.[33]

Location matters as well. Recent studies show that support within a country for democracy can decline among elites and the public when its neighborhood is dominated by autocracies. Conversely, support for democracy within a country can grow as it has more democratic neighbors. Social scientists call the process "cross-border diffusion."[34] Since 1815 the probability of a randomly chosen country being a democracy is 75 percent if more than half of its neighbors are democracies, but only 10 percent if more than half are autocracies.[35] Autocracy, too, can diffuse.[36] Domestic regimes diffuse because neighboring countries tend to interact more, and interaction can make the other's system of government seem normal and even desirable.[37] All else being equal, countries tend to trade more with their neighbors and with larger countries (which have larger economies).[38] The same goes for societal exchanges—educational, scientific, sports, cultural, and tourism. Buying another country's goods, benefiting from its investment, studying in its universities, even discovering the charms of its culture—these things can lead to emulation. Scholars have found emulation or socialization based on interaction to be a prominent mechanism in the international diffusion or spread of democracy.

INTERNATIONAL RULES, INSTITUTIONS, AND PRACTICES

Political scientists have studied international rules and institutions extensively. Scholars have focused mainly on how those things affect states' behavior—for example, how belonging to the same international organization can make it easier for countries to cooperate.[39] But international institutions can also help change or preserve a state's domestic regime. One way is by favoring the policies that are more consistent with one regime type than with alternatives.

For example, international human rights norms can damage the reputations of authoritarian states and expose them to economic sanctions.[40] A military alliance such as NATO, or a free-trade zone such as the European Union, may be open only to democracies. Or, a free-trade zone may be open to all kinds of states, but have rules that give states incentives to liberalize by making it easier to punish those with large state-owned sectors than those with free-market economies. That was the Obama administration's aim with the ill-fated Trans-Pacific Partnership, discussed in Chapter 5. In a similar way, international financial institutions can require a borrowing country to reduce the state's role in its national economy; under the influence of the U.S. Treasury and other entities, that has been the strategy of the International Monetary Fund since the 1980s.

These sorts of international institutions give free-market democracies an advantage over autocracies by helping assure the democracies of ongoing economic openness and military security, things that their governments rely on for continuing success.[41] At the same time, liberal international institutions press a regime-power dilemma on autocracies: remaining competitive means conforming to the rules and moving in a democratic direction. Refusing can cause performance to suffer and domestic support for the regime to weaken.

INFORMATION ABOUT REGIME TYPES

By "information" I do not mean unmediated truth, but rather putative facts about events and trends that are spun and received in various ways. Recent scholarship has turned up evidence that elites in government, business, academia, the law, and the military monitor the policies and regime types of other countries to see what works for the country as a whole and what will help or hurt their interests.[42] Samuel Huntington argues that when democracies are more successful than autocracies, democracy becomes the "prevailing nostrum"—the perceived best remedy for all problems—making it more likely that democracy will spread.[43] In the modern world, the kind of success that inspires imitation includes economic growth, political stability, and national sovereignty or independence. Michael Miller finds that when democracies experience high economic growth, the number of democracies increases.[44]

This kind of learning is particularly likely in a country undergoing a crisis that its current government seems unable to solve. An economic depression can alienate business elites. A lost war can turn military officers against their government. Corruption can cause elites who are excluded to turn against the regime. Or chronic or acute failures—high food prices or taxes, or blatant and persistent corruption—can generate unrest among the mass public, which can in turn lead some elites to oppose their leaders. If at the same time a democratic great power is enjoying sustained national success, these disaffected elites may conclude that the problem is their authoritarian regime itself; they may then begin to bargain with democratic leaders for reforms or regime change. That same democratic great power's virtuous example can reinforce democracy in states that already have it by making authoritarianism implausible to most elites; whatever problems their country has, they conclude, cannot be due to democracy.

Even if neighboring states do not become democracies, they can be more or less sympathetic to democracies and more or less supportive of their policies. That, in turn, can affect a democracy's fortunes and ultimately the credibility of its domestic regime. Democracies can enjoy what Joseph Nye calls "soft power," a form of power that can lead another country to want what you want.[45] Soft power also can lead that country's elites or public to want their country to be more like yours. Scholars have called this "promoting ideas through providing an authoritative model."[46]

The same logic applies to autocracies: when an autocratic great power is enjoying sustained success, elites in other countries will tend to draw the lesson that autocracy is the better route to national success. That was the story for democracy in Europe in the 1930s, when fascist states pulled their countries out of the Depression more quickly than the democracies did (see Chapter 3). The Soviet Union had a great deal of soft power across dozens of countries through the early 1980s.

INTERACTIONS

The three elements of a state's environment are not sealed off from one another; each can strengthen the effects of the others. Democracies, for example, have some distinctive practices. They tend to avoid wars with one another; some scholars claim that there never has been a war between two liberal democracies—the democratic or liberal peace.[47] Assured peace can mean more trade and investment across democracies, as merchants and investors prefer to do business where war is unlikely to disrupt. Some studies show that democracies are unusually likely to belong to international institutions, to remain in them, and to comply with their rules.[48] One influential study has shown that international institutions dominated by democracies can spread democracy. Membership in an international organization that prohibits government seizures of private property or defunding the military can reassure wealthy people and military officers that democracy would not hurt them. It can also socialize them into democratic values so that they accept a more equitable distribution of resources.[49] All of these virtuous effects can alter the information environment for states by enhancing the reputation of democracy as a regime type.

But the effects of international institutions on domestic regimes can be complicated. A multilateral trade organization that includes both rich and poor countries can potentially undermine democracy in the rich members. In rich countries, labor tends to be scarce and capital plentiful, while in poor countries the opposite is the case. Opening up trade will lower wages and increase returns to capital in rich countries, while it will raise wages and lower the returns to capital in poor countries.[50] In the rich country, a sharp rise in inequality can cause the losers to question their domestic regime. The design of the rules, in other words, can influence an institution's effects on domestic regimes. In Chapter 4 we look at how in recent years international openness has actually undermined the popularity of democracy in some of the liberal democracies themselves, including the United States.

The most important way in which the elements of the international environment affect each other is when regime type and influence get entangled. Political scientists often argue about whether power or ideas matter more. When Russia invaded Ukraine in February 2022, was it because Putin feared the eastward spread of American power (via NATO)? Or was it the eastward spread of democracy that triggered his invasion? The answer is "both." A stable democratic Ukraine would threaten Putin's regime. It also almost certainly would be aligned with the West and not with Russia. Mark Haas has studied how and why states with similar ideologies are more likely to be allies.[51] Regime type and power are often entwined.

The entanglement comes because people who favor a regime type tend to want their country to have good relations with countries that exemplify that regime type—especially big, powerful exemplars. And this tendency makes sense once we grasp the way the international environment can select for one or another regime type. People need not use evolutionary jargon to grasp intuitively domino or snowball effects: they sense that the more interactions their country has with democracies, the better are the prospects for democracy in their own country; they know that the same goes for autocracy. This means that democratic politicians should tend to favor and want good relations with foreign democracies, especially powerful ones. In like fashion, authoritarians tend to want good relations with foreign autocracies. Those tendencies, in turn, mean that powerful democracies such as the United States tend to have more influence among democratic politicians, parties, and regimes in other countries, while authoritarian powers such as China and Russia enjoy the same among authoritarians. I call this the ideas-power nexus.[52]

Protecting Democracy via Reform

Suppose that various types of environmental pressure are weakening support for democracy among the elites or public in a democracy. Its government can respond in various ways. If the country's leaders actually want to become despots—more likely, indeed, when the environment mitigates against democracy—they can simply exploit the situation and proceed, selecting any number of tools from the aspiring autocrat's toolbox: decry journalists as enemies of the people, weaken judicial independence by packing the courts, scapegoat one or more minority group, deploy government cameras in every public space, stage a crisis and declare a state of emergency. A government desiring to weaken democracy will welcome an antidemocratic environment.

For the typical democratic government, however, even in times of great stress the preservation of democracy is a top priority. The government's most obvious option is to enact policies that it thinks will boost support for democracy among elites or the general public. If economic inequality looms large, the government can redistribute wealth, provide job training for the unemployed, or restrict imports to increase high-wage employment. If authoritarian countries in the region or around the world appear to be outperforming democracies, the democratic government can try to boost economic growth through fiscal or monetary policy or take steps to degrade the performance of neighboring autocracies. If powerful authoritarian neighbors are networking among its country's elites, the government can increase surveillance and spread propaganda about fifth columnists. (An obvious problem with these latter steps is that they can move the country in an autocratic direction to avoid autocracy—that is, they can be self-defeating.)[53]

Should the crisis worsen, a savvy and capable government can respond in a more fundamental way, with *reform*. By "reform" I mean extensive legal and policy changes that set the country on a different political, economic, and social path. Reform of this deep sort not only addresses the current challenge but attempts to prevent future such challenges from arising. It is surgery, not a mere bandage. The goal of reform is not regime change, but regime preservation. The government must take care to frame the reform as not only consistent with the regime's original principles but also necessary to carry on those principles under fundamentally changed conditions. In that sense, reform is conservative, designed to preserve democracy under a new situation that older generations could not have anticipated. When such reform is implemented and gains broad support from elites and the public, it becomes entrenched and the new centrism. Most elites and many ordinary citizens invest in the reform, making them more likely to defend it as time goes on. Reform comes to be identified with the regime itself—an outer layer of protection essential to its preservation. The ideology justifying the regime itself incorporates the reform. Supporting the regime means supporting the reform; questioning the reform amounts to questioning the regime itself.

The New Deal in the United States, discussed in Chapter 3, was a fundamental reform of this type. The Great Depression began in the United States but became an international phenomenon that actually fed back into America and worsened the situation. The successes of fascism overseas made matters worse. The New Deal was an effort to preserve liberal democracy with new and different methods. Its enemies accused it of gutting individual liberty. Welfare liberalism, however, reconceived what individual liberty required in a modern industrial economy and enacted a significant reorientation of how the state and market related to one another. A few decades later, following the very different cultural and economic crises of the late 1960s and early 1970s, leaders in the United States and other mature democracies concluded that preserving democracy required yet another basic reform, which I call "open liberalism." This reform recast liberal democracy as a project to remove economic and social barriers to personal emancipation. Open liberalism is the predominant liberalism of our own time.

From the Outside: Engineering the Ecosystem

But in a world where the health of states' domestic regimes is affected by the international environment, domestic reform may not be enough to save the regime. Protecting democracy may require manipulating elements of the international environment. As historian John Lewis Gaddis has written, "Definitions of national interest in international affairs all seem to boil down . . . to the need to create an international environment conducive to the survival and prospering of a nation's domestic institutions."[54]

Consider the kind of environment-shaping that occurs in the natural world. Species mold their surroundings to their advantage: birds build nests and plants extend roots into the soil. In recent years, scientists have become increasingly interested in a more consequential kind of environment-shaping that entails the redirection of evolution itself. In so-called "niche construction," an animal or plant species alters its environment in such a way that the reshaped environment actually selects for different traits in the species than it would have if the species had not built the niche.[55] It takes long-toothed, sociable beavers to build dams. The dams trap the plants that beavers eat and give those beavers a reproductive advantage over short-toothed and antisocial beavers who cannot build dams. Over time, long-toothed, sociable beavers come to predominate, but that would not have happened had these beavers not built dams. Beavers actually (and unintentionally) participate in their own evolution.

In what is sometimes called *ecosystem engineering*, organisms can also (unintentionally) steer the evolution of other species as well.[56] Beaver dams not only make the environment select for long-toothed beavers, but also for plant life that thrives in pooled rather than running water. Biologists call a species that is the most influential in its habitat a "keystone species."[57] When these dynamics are present, organisms and environment *coevolve*.[58]

A democratic great power threatened by authoritarianism can engineer its ecosystem as well by pressing its domestic reform outward so as to redirect the very international pressure that is undermining its regime. An entire body of international relations scholarship, hegemonic stability theory, is devoted to the outsized influence that great powers have on the international system.[59] As discussed in Chapter 3, the United States at the end of World War II was by far the world's most powerful country, but the international appeal and strength of fascism and communism had its leaders worried about the future of democracy. They used American power to alter the international environment, extending the New Deal outside of its own borders. America went beyond simply shaping its surroundings to its advantage as a great power. It had to be a *democratic* great power, and changed its environment so as to allow it to be one—to thrive without moving in an authoritarian direction.

It is not only democratic great powers that go out and mold their international environments. As James Monroe noted in 1823, the powerful absolute monarchies of Europe had built the Holy Alliance to safeguard their domestic regimes from unrest and revolution by coordinating interventions to suppress liberalism in smaller states. After World War II, Stalin's Soviet Union did something similar when it forged the Iron Curtain—the rule of communist parties along a chain of states on the Soviet Union's western border—in order to safeguard Soviet communism from an anticommunist international environment. In fact, any international environment bears the imprint of one or more great powers. The environment is not "natural," but consists of states and things that they produce and reproduce—institutions, rules, and information—even as those things shape the behavior and traits of those same states.[60] The ability to mold the environment is part of what we mean when we say a state is powerful.

States, then, can engineer their ecosystem to protect their domestic regimes. Some such engineering by states is unintentional, and some produces unintended consequences. But great powers can and do try to mold their environments to their advantage, and sometimes they infuse it with a bias that favors their own regime type.

Figure 2.3 depicts coevolution between a democratic great power and its environment. Note that elements of the environment interact as well, sometimes reinforcing one another. For example, when a democratic state infuses a liberal bias into international rules, it can improve the performance of that state and change the information in the environment about the success of democracy.

Recent scholarship and historic statecraft reveal a number of tools available to the government of a powerful state wishing to engineer the ecosystem to protect its domestic regime.

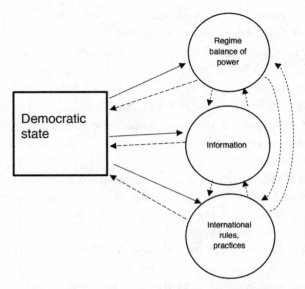

Figure 2.3. A democratic state shapes the environment
that affects its own domestic regime.

Because the elements of the environment can interact and feed
off of each other, the tools can have multiple direct and indirect effects.

BALANCE OF POWER AMONG REGIMES

Above we noted studies showing that when there is a democratic hegemon, democracy tends to spread. A democratic great
power can engineer its ecosystem by promoting democracy or
rolling back autocracy in other countries. An important recent
study argues that Western leverage and "linkage" have been
important factors in whether authoritarian states democratize.
A democratic great power has leverage over a target state to
the extent that the target's economy is dependent on the great

power relative to autocratic powers. Linkage consists of the "density of ties" and "cross-border flows" of money and goods, people and groups (particularly elites in and outside of government), information, and more.[61]

A powerful democracy can propagandize in other countries to try to increase elite and public support for democracy and turn people against autocracy. It can cultivate and fund democratic groups and infiltrate and undermine authoritarian ones.[62] It can help democrats gain positions of influence in government, the military and state security, business, and the professions.[63] It can engage in covert action to weaken or overthrow an autocratic regime.[64] At a maximum, it can use its military to impose democracy. The United States engaged in most of these policies at the end of World War II in Japan and West Germany, and in some of them in Italy and France to keep the communists out of power.[65] From the 1950s through the early 1970s, it acted covertly in a number of Third World countries to contain and roll back communism.[66]

A democratic great power can act in less direct ways toward the same ends. Greater economic openness—more movements of goods, services, and capital—can enrich and empower actors in the other state who want democracy and free markets.[67] The Marshall Plan was designed to undermine communism in recipient countries by tying the Western European and Japanese economies to that of the United States— that is, so that financial and commercial relationships would be forged and economies become complementary. (Thus the Americans also offered Marshall aid to the new communist bloc countries, and thus the Soviets forced them to decline.)[68] As the Cold War matured, U.S. economic ties with Third World countries often stymied democratic development, but in the long run most U.S. partners democratized.[69]

The democratic great power can increase its social and

cultural interaction with other states, using its soft power to socialize their elites and public to think of democracy as normal and desirable. Scientific and academic exchanges, business contacts, sports, tourism, cultural exports, and charitable and other nongovernmental organizations can all carry with them the habits and values of liberal democracy. Music, movies, art, and literature can make both the exporting country and its values more attractive. So can the material culture of the great power. During the Cold War, the United States promoted its values through the public diplomacy of the U.S. Information Agency, which put American art, literature, and other cultural products before foreign audiences in hopes that their creativity and innovation would outshine that of Soviet culture.[70]

Exporting certain technologies and techniques may make it easier for importing states to move in a democratic direction. The great power can bring foreign students to its universities to show them how openness to empirical correction and relative independence from state censorship aid research and education. The social sciences and humanities are particularly important in this regard, as autocracies are especially prone to censor them. Professionals trained in law and business are necessary for a modern liberal democracy. The training and technology required for holding free and fair elections are also important.[71] Since World War II, the United States has engaged in all of these activities and more, opening its universities to students and faculty from other countries and facilitating educational and scientific exchanges.

Autocratic great powers can use some of these same tools to undermine democracy or promote autocracy in other countries.[72] During the Cold War, the Americans and Soviets made much of the world a field of competition in regime promotion.[73] As we shall see in later chapters, Russia in recent years has been especially focused on keeping liberal democracy out of most of the neighborhood to its immediate west. It is important to note, too, that democracies do not always promote democracy in other countries. Various foreign policies, including foreign aid and peacekeeping, can have the unintended effect of enabling autocrats to stay in power. Democracies even can be intentional about authoritarianism. During the Cold War, the United States often found that, in the "developing" or "Third" world, whatever interest it had in more democracies was overridden by its fears that communists or socialists would win elections and align with the Soviet Union; better, its presidents concluded, to go with a friendly despot than assume the risks that free elections brought. Those fears only subsided in the late 1980s, when democratic capitalism started routing its ideological foes in most of the world.[74] Today, worries that democracy will usher in Islamist radicalism and anti-Americanism keep the United States from promoting democracy in the Muslim Middle East.[75]

INTERNATIONAL INSTITUTIONS AND RULES

A democratic great power can construct and maintain international institutions and rules that favor liberal democracy in general. Beth Simmons has shown how states that ratify human rights treaties really do come to respect human rights more.[76] Great powers are the states best able to make and sustain institutions and rules. Their outsized wealth and power equip them to provide public goods, or benefits that all states share equally and from which none can be excluded, such as freedom of navigation on the high seas or a stable and convertible currency.[77] Great powers are also best able to coerce compliance, even among allies, by threatening punishment or the withdrawal of protection.[78] John Ikenberry has shown how great powers often engineer their ecosystems after winning a big war, when

they enjoy the most leverage vis-à-vis other states.[79] Kyle Lascurettes has further shown how they build orders to exclude
threatening countries or movements by, among other things,
propagating ideas and rules that delegitimize them.[80]

Indeed, liberal multilateral institutions can spread and
consolidate democracy across states. By entering a formal military alliance or informal security partnership with another
democracy, the great power helps protect it from intimidation
by autocracies. Sometimes having a democratic military patron also can lead military officers in the recipient state to
value civilian dominance, the rule of law, and electoral democracy. If the other state is already democratic, the alliance protects it from intimidation by other countries and can make the
regime more stable and popular. U.S. military ties in the Cold
War often enabled authoritarianism in the Third World, and
critics have accused the U.S. military of training Latin American soldiers to violate human rights.[81] In the long run, again,
U.S. allies tended to democratize.[82]

Building international institutions can help safeguard a
great power's own democratic regime by solidifying the kinds
of economic, military, and political relations with other states
on which its good performance depends. As discussed in Chapter 3, this is what U.S. leaders had in mind in the aftermath of
World War II, when they did the heavy work in founding the
World Bank, International Monetary Fund, and General Agreement on Tariffs and Trade. Each of these allowed democracies
to enjoy the benefits of openness while retaining a measure
of control over their economies. Washington also pressed the
Western European states to form the European Economic Community. The U.S.-centered network of military alliances protected democracies from intimidation by the looming threat
of Soviet communism. Protecting the other industrial democ-

racies through multilateralism indirectly protected American democracy itself by giving it stable economic and political partners.

Authoritarian governments can play the same game. As political scientist Daniëlle Flonk writes, "Illiberal international norms counter the diffusion of democracy. Notions of sovereignty and non-interference protect autocracies from unwanted interference in their regimes and prevent sanctions and demands for reform. [And] shared international norms can increase the legitimacy of authoritarian practices."[83]

INFORMATION

Finally, a great power can add information about democratic success and admirability to the international environment. This works through a back-and-forth dynamic. The great power's economic, military, and political successes raise the credibility of democracy and help push more states toward the democratic end of the spectrum.[84] In turn, the expansion of democracy abroad confirms the domestic credibility of the great power's own regime and boosts morale among elites and the public. The great power can augment this virtuous cycle with propaganda or what is more agreeably called "public diplomacy."[85] Journalists and academics, too, can be counted on to propel the narrative of success. The process feeds on itself, as a confident liberal democracy makes the regime still more attractive to much of the rest of the world.

An authoritarian challenger can try to turn the environment in its favor by putting some information of its own into it. Political scientist Daniel Drezner argues that a smart challenger to an existing hegemon will try to alter the information environment before attempting any material changes to the international order; changes to information are least likely to provoke the current hegemon to retaliate.[86] In later chapters, we will see how China and Russia are doing just that.

INTERACTION AND VIRTUOUS CYCLES

A democratic great power can engineer an ecosystem whose elements all reinforce one another in a grand, virtuous cycle. Promoting democracy abroad, building economic ties, and training and education in liberal democracy and market economics involve social interaction, which can produce emulation, which in turn can lead to more invitations to intervene, aid, and train. A democratic great power that can carry off all of these policies will tend to be more successful. It will have more foreign influence, allies, trading partners, debtors, and beneficiaries, and everyone concerned will have confidence that these beneficial relationships will endure.[87] These other countries will tend to return the favors, adding to the great power's success and hence to the overall impressiveness of democracy. Finally, to the extent that the great power actually succeeds in increasing the number of democracies, it intensifies these mechanisms even more and sets off a kind of snowball effect, in which more democracies lead to still more, particularly in the same region.[88] All of this puts new information into the international environment concerning the benefits of democracy. Table 2.1 summarizes how a democracy can engineer its ecosystem.

This kind of virtuous cycle took hold in the late 1980s with the liberalizing reforms in the Soviet Union, the fall of communism in Eastern Europe, and the U.S. victory in the Cold War. The conviction that there was no alternative to democratic capitalism not only pressured autocracies to join the club but boosted democracy's popularity in the United States. Long

Table 2.1. How to engineer a democratic ecosystem.

Element of environment	Tool	Means	Result
Balance of power among regimes	Promote, protect democracy	Coercion, economic relations, military protection, social interaction, cultural exports, technical assistance	National success, empowering liberals, morale boost
International rules, practices	Liberal content (trade, finance, human rights, communication)	Diplomacy, leverage	National success, norms
Information	National success, propaganda	(see other tools)	Morale boost, learning

gone were the 1930s, when the sustained Great Depression caused many Americans to lurch toward the extreme Right or Left. Gone too were the late 1960s and 1970s, when so many Americans were beset with deep doubt about the basic goodness of their country and its political and economic system. The United States, in that rare moment, ran the table.

When Ecosystem Engineering Backfires: Reform and Reengineering

So far, the story is a happy one for the democratic great power and for democracy in general. A savvy government has enormous agency not only in looking after its country's interests but in setting conditions in the outside world to perpetuate its domestic regime and handicap alternative regimes. It can fix the international environment to select for democracy, fending off challenger ideologies by making them choose between becoming more democratic or underperforming.

But this is not a teleological story of inevitable progress. Richard Lewontin's caution about progress in biological evolution applies in international politics too: "Evolution is not an unfolding but an historically contingent wandering pathway through the space of possibilities."[89] World politics is too complex for any permanent transformation of the international ecosystem.

First, no government, no matter its access to information and soundness of analysis and judgment, can anticipate all events. The further into the future it peers, the more any government's foresight of the consequences of its own policies deteriorates. At some point, the democratic great power will find that the engineering that worked in the past works no longer. Events will overtake it; its standard manipulations of the international environment that once brought success can prove ill-suited to new developments and end up undermining liberal democracy in some of the states, including itself. The costs and benefits of maintaining the ecosystem may not be fairly distributed across the great power's own domestic society. Free trade and foreign investment can especially damage the working class in a mature democracy. Wars to promote or defend democracy draw predominantly upon the working classes, unless the great power has military conscription. The economic openness that modern free-market economies rely upon can shift resources from the working classes of the wealthy democracies to the working classes of poorer countries. Related, cultural divides can emerge within the great power. All of this can lead to disillusionment among large segments of the great power's citizenry, making them think that liberal democracy is a bad bargain.[90]

Second, as already noted, reform and ecosystem engineering are not limited to democracies. Authoritarian great powers can adapt to new circumstances by reorienting their policies so as to safeguard their domestic regime. They may also engineer an ecosystem of their own, feeding a bias into the international environment that favors autocracy and handicaps democracy. They may intervene directly in other countries on behalf of autocracy; form international organizations that have more authoritarians; export training and technology that enables authoritarianism; increase social interaction and use soft power to make authoritarianism more attractive; and build and sustain international institutions that they, the authoritarians, dominate.[91] They may thrive in their ecosystem and set an example of authoritarian success. All of this may have an effect, putting pressure on democracies to adapt or suffer, and enabling authoritarian states to flourish. In Chapters 5, 6, and 7, we look at how China and Russia today are gradually engineering an authoritarian ecosystem to privilege their authoritarian-capitalist regime.

When these two problems combine—another great power with a different regime doing some ecosystem engineering of its own, and unanticipated developments degrading the ecosystem—evolutionary selection effectively shifts. The democratic great power will be compelled to undertake some re-engineering of the ecosystem. Earlier in this chapter I discussed how deep reform takes place when a government recognizes that if its domestic regime is to be preserved, it must surround it with a new protective belt of policies and find a different language for its guiding ideology. That is what FDR did with the New Deal in the 1930s. But Roosevelt and Harry Truman, his successor, found that domestic reform was inadequate. At the end of World War II, with fascism still present and communism on the rise, the United States needed to reengineer its international ecosystem. Jimmy Carter and Ronald Reagan, for all of their disagreements, found the country in a similar situation in the late 1970s.

Today, a similar pressure is at work and has become nearly unbearable in America and some other mature democracies. The basic policy orientation of the United States that once protected liberal democracy is now undermining it; at the same time, authoritarian China is engineering an international ecosystem that encroaches on that of the United States and the West. The remainder of this book probes how we got to this situation, in which the international environment increasingly selects for authoritarianism over democracy. I begin with an exploration of liberalism's evolution from the late eighteenth century to the present day, with particular attention to Great Britain, the United States, and their serial efforts to engineer an international ecosystem to perpetuate liberal democracy.

3
Liberalism
Classical to Welfare to Open

He who does anything because it is the custom, makes no choice.

—*John Stuart Mill, 1859*

Individual freedom cannot exist without economic security and independence.

—*Franklin Delano Roosevelt, 1944*

The 1940s: A New Liberalism, a New Internationalism

In 1940 the international environment presented America with a terrible dilemma: *either become more authoritarian or accept national decline.* Nazi Germany and militarist Japan were on the move. They had answered the global Great Depression by centralizing political and economic power in the state and seeking autarchy—economic self-sufficiency—to free them from the vicissitudes of global markets and Anglo-American hegemony. The Axis powers were rolling over neighboring countries and building formal empires. Germany had conquered most of Northern and Western Europe, with only Great Britain holding out. Japan ruled northeastern China and looked poised to move into Southeast Asia.

At the time, it was commonly accepted among the industrial democracies that constitutional democracy was in danger, and that they had to enact significant changes in domestic policy to save it. In the 1930s the Great Depression had wiped out immense amounts of wealth and thrown millions of factory and farm workers out of work. Confidence in free-market economies and multiparty democracy was at a low. The administration of Franklin D. Roosevelt had tried out an experimental set of policies—expanding the federal government's role in the economy and overall power—to restore faith in democracy. But Roosevelt saw that changes within the United States were not enough. Fascism was sealing off much of the world from the U.S. economy and attracting followers in the democracies themselves. The international environment had become hostile to democracy in America and the world over.

FDR's administration began to push back by becoming the "Arsenal of Democracy," supporting Britain with war matériel and trying to coerce Japan into halting its imperial project. In December 1941 Japan attacked Pearl Harbor, and the United States finally joined the war. The Allied victory in 1945, with the indispensable contributions and sacrifices of the communist Soviet Union, was total; fascism and militarism were crushed in Germany, Italy, and Japan. But FDR and other democratic leaders had not forgotten about the 1930s and the crisis that nearly ended democracy and pulled the world into its most catastrophic war ever. The leaders of the industrial democracies were determined to have a postwar international environment that would support, not undermine, democracy.

The planning began while the war was still on. In July 1944

a United Nations conference in Bretton Woods, New Hampshire, established international institutions designed to keep economies stable and radicalism at bay. The International Monetary Fund (IMF) and World Bank aimed to help countries with balance-of-payments problems. Currencies would be pegged to the U.S. dollar, which was convertible to gold at the fixed price of $35 per ounce. Three years later, the Truman administration helped inaugurate the General Agreement on Tariffs and Trade (GATT) to coordinate the reopening of international trade. These economic institutions aimed to help governments escape the zero-sum aspects of international relations that had been so destructive in the 1930s. The Truman administration also engineered the international ecosystem by promoting or imposing democracy on West Germany, Japan, and Italy, and by entering military alliances with Western Europe and Canada (the North Atlantic Treaty Organization, or NATO) and Japan.

Any of these multilateral moves alone would have been unprecedented for the United States. Together, they were a fundamental shift in how the country related to the outside world. The country had long-standing traditions of bilateral economic arrangements, trade protectionism, and no permanent military alliances. Why did protecting democracy from the outside require this web of international commitments? It had not needed such elaborate architecture in the past. Why in the late 1940s?

The New Deal gives a clue: it was because liberal democracy itself had changed in the 1930s. More precisely, liberalism, the doctrine that upholds individual freedom, had been reconceived and reformed through a new array of laws and policies. The Austro-Hungarian polymath Karl Polanyi had laid out the story in his 1944 book *The Great Transformation.*[1] While Germany, Japan, and Italy responded to the Depression with fascism and empire, the United States and other market democracies experimented with various new kinds of state intervention in their economies—deficit spending, devaluing the currency, taxing imports, redistributing wealth, expanding the state's share of the economy. That set of remedies, however, created new problems at the international level. The economies of these countries were linked to one another. If they did not coordinate these interventions, they would just make matters worse. If one country devalued its currency to raise its exports, the others would do the same, and all would be poorer— and that would place their democratic institutions in danger. The survival of democracy, then, required that governments figure out how to square the circle, to keep their economies open yet give each government leeway to intervene in its own economy.[2]

The IMF, World Bank, and GATT helped them square the circle. In what political scientist John Gerard Ruggie calls "embedded liberalism," these multilateral institutions both encouraged openness and allowed government intervention when really needed.[3] Borrowing governments could control capital flows into and out of their borders to keep their economies stable. The GATT winked at governments that violated its trade rules if they did so in order to maintain full employment.[4] A compromise between national sovereignty and openness was found.[5]

The Great Transformation points to a crucial fact, one that is essential if we are to understand how international order and American democracy affect one another: liberalism has changed over time. The changes can be seen as evolutionary. A set of challenges arises that the old liberalism cannot remedy, and so a new, reconstituted liberalism is called forth.

Liberalism is a complex thing, a mixture of continuity and change. It has a fixed, abstract commitment to individual liberty. But it has filled in that commitment with different content over time. From the late eighteenth century through the early twentieth, most European and North American liberals conceived of personal freedom in terms of *classical liberalism.* They favored a minimal state to protect property rights and contracts. In Britain and the United States, where classical liberalism was most consequential, the result began to generate discontent in the late nineteenth century with the rise of the working class, and a long contest ensued with what is sometimes called *welfare liberalism,* a liberalism that deployed the state to ensure liberty for working men. In the 1930s international and domestic pressure led to the triumph of welfare liberalism. It was upon welfare liberalism, with its imperative of an active state to assure individual freedom, that FDR, Truman, and their counterparts in other democracies built the liberal international order.

Discontent with welfare liberalism began already in the 1960s with the counterculture on the Left and free-marketeers on the Right. In the 1970s welfare liberalism showed itself inadequate to the cultural and economic challenges of the time and began to give way to what we can call *open liberalism,* a fusion of these two discontents that produced another fundamental policy reorientation. The United States reshaped its international environment accordingly, exporting open liberalism into global order.

In two historical moments, liberals have reinterpreted what individual freedom means and reoriented law and policy to protect that reinterpretation. These refoundings responded to evident failings in the way liberalism was working—to sustained periods in which liberalism was not fulfilling its own promises to democratic citizens. Liberalism, in other words, has done some evolving of its own, with international consequences. All three of these liberalisms—classical, welfare, and open—purport to uphold individual freedom, but each gives a different account of what that means in theory and in practice. Understanding the differences, and how liberalism has evolved, is essential to understanding liberal internationalism and democracy's predicament today.

On Liberalism

As noted in Chapter 1, by "democracy" I mean the mixed regime that political theorists call *liberal democracy*. The "liberal" modifier has to do with individual rights. But the ways liberals think about rights has changed several times. Where more rigid and hierarchical ideologies, such as communism, are brittle and snap when placed under pressure from new situations, liberalism's abstractness and minimalism render it flexible enough to respond to new pressure by reorganizing itself.[6] When liberals find themselves confronting problems that their political program cannot solve, and face growing radical, anti-liberal movements in their own societies and abroad, they locate features of the radical movements that they believe can be peeled away and grafted onto a reformulated vision for individual liberty. Liberalism rolls on across the decades precisely because it adapts and evolves.

WHAT IS LIBERALISM?

But what is liberalism's fixed, unchanging core? In the United States, liberalism is commonly associated with the Democratic Party, praised as "caring government" by its friends and derided as "big government" by its foes. In Europe, liberalism traditionally connotes small government and free markets— nearly the opposite of what it means in America. Political theorists define liberalism so that it comprises both of these senses. Following them, I define liberalism here as *a political ideology that takes individual freedom as the highest political good.* Liberalism contrasts with "-isms" that uphold other things as the highest political good: obedience to God, the sovereignty of the legitimate monarch, the dictatorship of the proletariat, unity of the state, or something else. Liberalism asserts that these other ideologies are wrong—that the individual person's right to freedom comes first. Some liberals dissent from that definition, but it is the best guide to help us understand this complicated and shape-shifting thing called "liberal internationalism."[7]

What do liberals mean by "freedom," then? A number of definitions and groundings for "freedom" are available, including in the natural-law tradition that religions such as Christianity offer.[8] Here I use the common notion of *autonomy,* from the Greek for "self-legislating."[9] The ancient Greeks applied the word "autonomy" to city-states, not to individuals; an autonomous city was one that made its own laws.[10] It was the Enlightenment philosopher Immanuel Kant who first applied autonomy to individuals. Kant's autonomous person lived only by rules or maxims that he accepted for himself, of his own free will. A self-legislating individual did not follow rules that were imposed on her or that she accepted solely on the authority of others. Kant did not mean that free individuals simply made up their own rules. Rather, what made them free was their voluntary assent to objective rules or maxims that were already "out there." Freedom meant agreeing to follow the moral law for no other reason than that one's own reason said to do so.[11]

The importance of the principle of individual, rational consent emerged well before Kant wrote his treatises. The Protestant Reformation that began in 1517 introduced a new religious pluralism into Christian Europe. After decades of futile and destructive civil and international wars, a new norm took hold in which the individual could choose freely his religious beliefs and affiliation so long as he was loyal to his monarch or

republic. A few pockets and short periods of religious toleration developed in the sixteenth century, notably in the Polish-
Lithuanian Commonwealth, but the norm took hold permanently in the Netherlands in the seventeenth century and then
spread to England and elsewhere.[12]

Still, individual autonomy is an abstract notion. Who
counts as an individual? What does it mean to choose freely?
How do we know freedom when we see it? Over what areas of
life does autonomy apply? What are the limits to the beliefs and
norms that people can legitimately choose for themselves? The
answers to these questions have changed over the centuries,
even over the past half-century. This means that, in important
ways, liberalism itself has changed.

Liberalism has gone through three historical stages, each
with a distinctive story about what autonomy means and what
the chief threats to it are. All three versions of liberalism have
been present from the start, but in Europe and North America,
each has predominated in a particular period. From the late
eighteenth century through the early twentieth century, *classical liberalism* was king. This first-stage liberalism left little
international imprint, apart from a commitment to relative
economic openness. It was replaced in the 1930s by *welfare liberalism,* which was dominant until the late twentieth century.
This second-stage liberalism produced a robust form of liberal
internationalism after World War II designed to protect democracy in the industrial countries. In the 1970s and 1980s, welfare liberalism gave way to third-stage, *open liberalism,* which
transformed internationalism into the form we have today. Each
transition was caused by pressure from the domestic and international environment. Conditions had arisen that rendered
the old liberalism unable to defend the overall regime of liberal
democracy. The new liberalism took hold because consensus
formed that it could save constitutional self-government.

Political scientist Mark Blyth has studied transitions in the economic program of liberalism—"classical" to "embedded" to "neoliberal" are his terms—and argued that this movement in history is not only a story of clashing material interests, with the strong winning and the weak losing. They are struggles among ideas about what people's interests really are.[13] That is the view I adopt here. Indeed, each form of liberalism has offered a justifying narrative that gives an account of what individual liberty is, what its enemies are, and how it is best secured. Each narrative has brought with it a culture, a set of practices built around a predominant notion of what freedom looks like. Liberals have a bedrock commitment to the liberty of the individual; the story of changes in liberal internationalism is partly a story of change in what they believe that means and the kind of life it entails.

The remainder of this chapter looks back in history at the emergence of classical liberalism, and then the transitions to welfare and later to open liberalism. It pays particular attention to Great Britain and then the United States. The narratives that follow may seem to imply that Britain and America were thoroughly liberal countries all through these centuries, roiled only by the question of which brand of liberalism should predominate. In fact, all through the decades surveyed below, both countries have had their share of illiberal and anti-liberal movements—grounded in traditionalism, bigotry, or hypernationalism—and sometimes these movements have enjoyed large followings and significant political influence. Most obviously, by the 1840s the determination of many American southerners to retain the institution of chattel slavery had curdled into an embrace of the "peculiar institution" as a positive good; gone were Thomas Jefferson's regrets and fears about slavery. Following the Civil War and emancipation, from the 1870s through mid-1960s, white supremacy was institutionalized in law and practice in many places, excluding millions of black Americans from enjoying the liberties promised by liberalism. I pay little attention in this chapter to these illiberal and anti-liberal movements and institutions in these countries, except as they became so powerful as to help force one of the transitions.

The First Stage: Classical Liberalism

At its origin in the eighteenth century, liberalism was a theory and program to protect individual freedom from what liberals called the "old regime." The old regime was the alliance of throne and altar—monarchs, who claimed to rule by divine right, and their aristocratic enablers in partnership with the institutional church and its prelates. This cluster of institutions aimed to inculcate piety and good order, but it was a regime of hierarchy and privilege that severely circumscribed ordinary people's chances in life. The son of a peasant would almost certainly die a peasant. The eldest son of a noble would inherit his father's title, land, tenants, and income. All, regardless of rank, lived and moved in a society that reinforced this hierarchy. Even in lands with religious toleration, dissenters were second-class subjects; in relatively easygoing England, Baptists, Catholics, and Jews could not attend university or sit in Parliament. The crown had an outsized role in the economy, granting monopolies based on the king's favor and imposing taxes without giving the taxed much, if any, say.[14] Most kings could declare war against one another without legislative constraint, imposing still more taxes, impoverishment, and death on their subjects.[15]

It did not have to be this way, said classical liberals. Men's true interests were naturally in harmony; it was the coercive state that distorted their interests into dissonance. Wrote Thomas Paine in *The Rights of Man* (1795), "Common interest regulates [men's] concerns, and forms their law; and the laws which common usage ordains, have a greater influence than the laws of government."[16] An artificial imposition on natural society, the old regime of throne and altar used coercion to thwart the good of the whole in favor of the good of a privileged few. Enlightened government, said classical liberals, would be smaller and far less coercive. It would involve a smaller state whose main duties were to safeguard property rights, enforce contracts, and defend the territory. Each man—and early classical liberalism attended only to adult men, as heads of households—would then get to enjoy the fruits of his own labor.

The old regime closed off avenues to its own reform by suppressing criticism of monarchs and ministers and inhibiting any mobilization of opposition. Breaking out of this pathological system required a new kind of state, one built to uphold individual autonomy by either restraining or replacing the old throne-altar alliance. For classical liberalism, government should be constrained by laws made by legislators elected at regular intervals, laws interpreted by judges who are not lackeys of the monarch: a legitimate government ruled not by divine right, but by an implicit social contract between rulers and ruled. The social contract obligated the rulers to defend the rights of their citizens, and the ruled to obey the rulers so long as they did so. Most influential was the account of English philosopher John Locke, who argued that men had natural rights to life, liberty, and property, and that they agreed to set up government because these things were not secure in the "state of nature."[17] Other seminal liberal thinkers include France's Voltaire and the Marquis de Condorcet, Scotland's Adam Smith, England's Paine, the United States' Thomas Jefferson and James Madison, Prussia's Kant, and Switzerland's Benjamin Constant. The classical-liberal state limited government by dispersing power within it, typically by separating the legislative and judicial from the executive functions. It upheld individual rights over against the state, including the freedom of speech, assembly, the press, and religion, as well as rights to a fair trial and against most state seizures of property. It limited rulers' control over commerce and lending. Early designs include the U.S. Constitution (1787) and the constitutions of the American states, various constitutions of the French Revolution (1791, 1793, 1795), and the Spanish constitution of 1812. Some of these documents influenced others and were imitated widely at the time.

Classical liberalism did not require democracy in the mature sense of today.[18] For much of classical liberalism's heyday, women could not vote anywhere; in many countries, only whites could vote; and in some, for much of the period, only white men who owned property could do so. Free individuals were those who were independent economically. Those who relied on others for their living were vulnerable and would vote, it was thought, in service of their employer's or patron's interest. Also common was the prejudice that only adult males who owned property had the capacity to vote rationally and responsibly. In the young United States, this strict principle began to relax in the early nineteenth century, and by the 1820s most U.S. states had granted universal white male suffrage. But in Britain, as late as the 1860s even "radicals" such as John Stuart Mill favored denying the vote to men who paid no tax and were on public assistance; Mill also favored weighted voting for those of "superior knowledge and cultivation."[19] Typical was the liberal politician Henry Grey, 3rd Earl Grey, who wrote in 1858 that "men enjoy [under the U.S. Constitution] far less real liberty than they do with us, because the tyrannical pressure of the majority cramps the freedom of thought and action of individuals."[20] For original classical liberals, equality before the law actually precluded equal political power.

Yet, over time, classical liberalism proved to be a force for democracy as it adapted itself to conditions that it helped create. One of those conditions was universal education of children. A productive society was a literate one, said liberals, and so they pressed for general education; as more and more of the population became literate, arguments against universal suffrage fell away. The most striking hypocrisy during the predominance of classical liberalism was chattel slavery in the United States. Early liberals such as Thomas Jefferson and James Madison wrote affectingly of the rights of man while owning slaves and failing to press for abolition. That they were hypocritical, however, suggests that classical liberalism did not sit well with slavery. Concerning the potential spread of slavery into the new state of Missouri, Jefferson wrote, "We have a wolf by the ear, and we can neither hold him, nor safely let him go. Justice is in one scale, and self-preservation in the other."[21]

Historian Eric Foner argues that the Free Soil movement—which developed into the Republican Party—feared that the spread of slavery would take land in new states away from independent farmers and hand it to the "Slave Power," the idle aristocracy that held millions in bondage and destroyed republican government. The goal of the Free Soilers was straight from classical liberalism: to expand the strength of "free labor" so as to raise prosperity and support self-government.[22] Abraham Lincoln, a leading Free Soiler, argued that Jefferson's own words that "all men are created equal" were put in the Declaration of Independence to help kill off slavery.[23] To be sure, many who sought slavery's end were Evangelicals and Quakers motivated by religious humanitarianism rather than liberal individualism. And, as Foner writes, the failure of the U.S. government to compensate freed blacks with land of their own held them back from the independence central to classical liberalism; thus they, along with women, continued to be denied the full benefits of citizenship.[24] But classical liberalism's internal tension over slavery was ultimately resolved in its abolition.

Reforming to Save Democracy:
Welfare Liberalism

Classical liberalism is still alive in the mature liberal democracies. Since the 1980s it has enjoyed influence in conservative parties in Anglophone countries, including the British and Canadian Conservatives, Australian Liberals, and the U.S. Republican Party. Most European democracies have small-government liberal parties, such as Germany's Free Democrats and Sweden's Liberals, and some of the larger center-Right European parties have classical liberal factions as well; the Mont Pelerin Society is a center of gravity for European classical liberalism.[25]

But among political and business elites in these countries, classical liberalism's attachment to the nation and the national economy has attenuated. As explained later in this chapter, what appears to be first-stage liberalism is often third-stage or open liberalism, which is more cosmopolitan and socially liberal. First-stage liberalism was toppled from its high perch long ago. In evolutionary language, it was "selected out" by the international environment when its laissez-faire internationalism proved unable to meet the dire challenges that economics and politics were throwing at the democracies. The crisis of classical liberalism became fatal in the 1930s, when it became evident in country after country that liberal democracy itself was in jeopardy. Saving that cherished domestic regime, democratic governments came to believe, required experimentation with a different kind of liberalism that had already had some influence in parties and policy: welfare liberalism.

Like their classical predecessors, welfare liberals were concerned with safeguarding individual freedom. Welfare liberals, however, conceived of this bedrock principle in a new way. They saw the primary threat to liberty not as the long-vanquished old regime but as unfettered capital. Classical liberalism had reduced and tamed the state, but that small state was now part of the problem. For welfare liberals, the state should no longer get out of the way of individual freedom but instead get in the way of the rich and powerful corporations that were binding the individual. Only state intervention that could restore liberal democracy's legitimacy and hence ensure the survival of liberalism itself. As British politician William Beveridge put the matter in 1944, the moment of welfare liberalism's triumph, "We can and should use the organized power of the community to increase the rights of individuals."[26]

The deep cause of the ecological pressure that shifted the democracies from classical to welfare liberalism was the industrial revolution that spread across Europe and North America over the course of the nineteenth century. The industrial economy generated stupendous wealth and technological innovation. The wealth was distributed less evenly than classical liberalism had promised, however, and discontent among workers and intellectuals congealed in various ways. In the late nineteenth and early twentieth centuries, classical and welfare liberalism were essentially stalemated. It was the trauma of the Great Depression, which made clear that the working class bore too much of the risk in industrial economies, that allowed welfare liberalism to rout its classical ancestor.

THE "SOCIAL QUESTION"

Over the nineteenth century, improvements in manufacturing, mining, energy, and transportation technology created the working class consisting of factory workers, miners, and others who fed the industrial economy. Vast numbers of men, women, and children whose ancestors from time immemorial had farmed the land now assumed very different jobs and ways of life, with high hopes of material prosperity for their families. They found themselves working long hours for low wages in miserable settings, however, and without a path to improvement. Classical liberalism considered them free individuals offering their labor to the highest bidder, hence in no need of help. But often there was only one bidder for their labor, and many such employers—"monopsonists," economists call them—took full advantage of their position.

The plight of labor was called the "social question," and a few liberals had raised it early in the industrial revolution. In 1819 Jean Charles Léonard de Sismondi of France published his *New Principles of Political Economy*, calling for a larger role for the state to protect already growing numbers of factory workers from exploitation by owners. In the waves of unrest and revolution that broke out periodically in France and other parts of Europe—in 1830, 1848, and 1871—left-liberal hopes of gaining political power rose and then fell again. In each wave, the determination of classical liberals, who feared the abolition of private property, helped thwart welfare liberalism.

Classical liberalism's unresponsiveness to the social question swelled the ranks of radical socialists and anarchists who did indeed aim to end private property.[27] In 1864 Karl Marx helped organize the International Workingmen's Association, later called the First International, with an inaugural gathering of labor leaders and activists in London. The growing power of radical labor at the time is seen in the concessions that illiberal authoritarian or "Cæsarist" governments made to the working class. Napoleon III, who ruled France from 1852 to 1870, offered "soup kitchens, price controls on bread, insurance schemes, retirement plans," and assorted other government benefits. Otto von Bismarck, Germany's authoritarian chancellor (in office 1871–90), implemented the world's first welfare state, including socialized medicine.[28]

The popularity of these defensive measures by authoritarian regimes led some liberal thinkers to conclude that a reconceiving of liberalism was in order. British writers T. H. Green and L. T. Hobhouse tried to put liberalism on a new footing that would allow more state intervention in the economy. Locke and the classical liberals were wrong, they argued: individual rights were not natural after all. Society invented rights, and so society could withhold rights from wealthy owners who refused to serve the common good.[29] "The function of State coercion is to overcome individual coercion, and, of course, coercion exercised by any association of individuals within the State," wrote Hobhouse in 1911.[30] Classical liberal heavyweights such as Herbert Spencer and William Graham Sumner mightily resisted these new ideas.[31]

In the early twentieth-century United States, journalists such as Herbert Croly and Walter Weyl, founders of the *New Republic* magazine, laid out the case for welfare liberalism.[32] Progressive politicians increased the power of government over commerce as they implemented new policies. As president (1901–9), Theodore Roosevelt asserted great executive power through antitrust law and enforcement. In his unsuccessful 1912 third-party campaign, Roosevelt impugned rival Woodrow Wilson for being unwilling to use government to defend the weak against the strong.[33] But Wilson, as president himself (1913–21), moved left, increasing federal regulation of the economy in areas such as workers' compensation and child labor.[34] In Britain, the sacrifices that working men and their families made in the Great War (1914–18) provoked some democratic governments to promise more governmental help after the war. David Lloyd George's government promised veterans "homes fit for heroes." Yet, after peace was restored most industrial democracies shifted back toward classical liberalism.[35] In the United States, too, the Republican Harding, Coolidge, and

Hoover administrations moved the country back to classical liberalism.

Welfare liberals did not give up. Some abandoned liberalism altogether by conceding that government action to restrict the operation of the market did in fact spell an end to individual liberty. Others stood with liberalism. A central figure who made the new liberalism more *liberal*—focused on individual rights—and hence more acceptable to Americans, was the pragmatist philosopher John Dewey. In "Individualism: Old and New," a six-part series published in 1929–30 in the *New Republic,* Dewey gave no ground on the fundamental importance of the freedom of the individual. But he argued that in twentieth-century industrial society the state needed to shape society so as to create the conditions under which citizens could enjoy their liberties.[36] Dewey's ideas took hold among many liberals.

DEPRESSION AND WAR

The Great Depression, triggered by the stock market crash of October 1929, quickly destroyed vast wealth and threw millions of Americans out of work. It spread to other countries and did the same there. That the wealthiest countries—the liberal democracies—seemed incapable of relieving the deep and wide distress of their own people handed opportunities to authoritarians. Democracy was exposed as weak, liberals were demoralized, and fascism—already in place in Italy since 1922— rose in parts of Europe and Latin America. The fascist states, particularly Nazi Germany, outperformed the democracies economically and impressed and intimidated foreigners with their societal discipline and sense of purpose.[37] The communist Soviet Union, which maintained full employment and was industrializing rapidly, attracted interest and devotion from others in the West.

By the end of 1932, the U.S. unemployment rate exceeded 23 percent. The hapless Hoover administration, unable to halt the slide, was roiled by a wave of labor unrest and homelessness. Ramshackle tent cities called "Hoovervilles" sprouted around the country. In the summer of 1932, a ten-thousand-strong "Bonus Army" of World War I veterans camped in Washington's Anacostia Flats and marched on the Capitol to demand an early payment of a promised military bonus. Hoover ordered their dispersal, and General Douglas MacArthur scattered the men with tear gas and—exceeding his command from Hoover—pursued them to Anacostia, burning their Hooverville to the ground.[38]

The debacle of the Bonus Army helped Franklin Roosevelt defeat Hoover in the presidential campaign that November. As president, FDR set out not to jettison the country's traditions of democracy and individual liberty, but to place them on a different footing, one more suited to a modern industrial economy. As he had said in an address in the 1932 campaign, "Under the [Declaration of Independence] rulers were accorded power, and the people consented to that power on consideration that they be accorded certain rights. The task of statesmanship has always been the redefinition of these rights in terms of a changing and growing social order. New Conditions impose new requirements upon government and those who conduct government." The 1936 Democratic Party platform mimicked the Declaration to make the point: "We hold this truth to be self-evident—that government in a modern civilization has certain inescapable obligations to its citizens."[39]

In order to show that democratic capitalism still worked, extensive reform was required—a reorientation of law and policy consistent with the founding principles of the country. Scholars disagree on how premeditated the New Deal was. Some see it as a set of experiments by a pragmatic president; others, as a deliberate plan for a new "economic constitutional order."[40] In any case, Roosevelt increased state intervention in the national economy to increase employment and restore public confidence in liberal democracy. Robust theoretical support came in 1936 with the publication of British economist John Maynard Keynes's *General Theory of Employment, Interest, and Money*. Keynes, too, did not want to abandon liberal democracy or capitalism, but to build a new hedge around them.[41]

The New Deal was far from a complete success. In the middle of the 1930s, continuing distress and fear pulled many elites and ordinary citizens toward political extremes. On the Left, communism rose in popularity as Stalin had declared a "popular front strategy" of working with socialists and backing the New Deal. On the Right, authoritarian politicians and movements gained support under the example of fascist success in Europe. A collection of populist personalities and politicians called, in effect, for a weakening of the country's constitutional regime. Each week thirty million radio listeners heard Father Charles Coughlin broadcast his anti-Semitic theories and statist proposals. The moment of greatest danger for the regime may have been when Huey Long, governor and then senator from Louisiana, prepared to challenge Roosevelt for the Democratic nomination for president in 1936. Something close to an autocrat in his home state, committed to radical redistribution of wealth, Long, "the Kingfish," was named by Roosevelt as "one of the two most dangerous men in America" (the other being MacArthur). A lone gunman assassinated Long in September 1935, assuring FDR's renomination.[42] Roosevelt handily defeated his Republican opponent, Alf Landon, in November 1936.

In trying to save liberal democracy, Roosevelt himself pushed too hard at times against its boundaries. After the Supreme Court blocked several New Deal initiatives, in 1937 he introduced bills in Congress to authorize up to six additional justices and to expand the administrative powers of the presidency. Both bills were defeated. Stung, FDR set about purging anti–New Dealers from the Democratic Party, and in 1939 a compromise bill, the Executive Reorganization Act, was passed. As Sidney Milkis writes, the Act marks the foundation of the modern presidency.[43] In 1940 Roosevelt sought and gained a third term, breaking the 150-year tradition begun by George Washington limiting presidents to two terms. Still, excesses notwithstanding, Roosevelt's reorientation of the country lent new legitimacy to its domestic regime.

Aided and reinforced by the liberal internationalism that we examine in Chapter 4, welfare liberalism was adopted by virtually all industrial democracies after World War II. It worked as advertised for several decades.[44] Economic and political stability became the normal state of affairs. From the late 1940s through the early 1970s, the industrial democracies maintained low unemployment yet high economic growth and low inflation. Annual economic growth averaged 4 percent in the 1950s and 5 percent in the 1960s.[45] It was the Golden Age of Capitalism: decades of stable high growth and optimism in the United States and Canada, the years of West Germany's *Wirtschaftswunder* and France's *Trente Glorieuses,* matched by economic booms in Japan, Britain, Italy, and smaller countries. There were periodic recessions, but nothing nearly so deep as the Depression of the 1930s.[46]

In these countries, the leading parties were center-Right

and center-Left. These competed for power, sometimes fiercely. The center-Left wanted to deepen the welfare state, while the center-Right wanted to maintain the status quo. But neither side feared that the other would try to overturn or erode the democratic regime itself. Extremists either were too shriveled to affect elections or were shut out of power. Fascism all but disappeared, and socialists and social democrats broke with communist parties, which found themselves having to defend Soviet invasions of East Germany in 1953, Hungary in 1956, and Czechoslovakia in 1968. Fears that the working class in the industrial democracies would fall for communism receded.[47] The late 1960s did bring social and political turmoil. Some of the strife followed efforts to make practices conform to liberal principles.[48] Historian Mary Dudziak argues that more just treatment of America's black citizens was partly driven by Cold War competition—namely the country's need to appear consistently liberal.[49]

Reforming Again to Save Democracy:
Open Liberalism

Yet, within half a century, welfare liberalism had been retired and the factories it had kept open were starting to be shuttered. In the late 1970s, liberalism entered its third stage. *Open liberalism* was another reorientation of law and policy designed to sustain democracy through a new legitimacy crisis. The societies that welfare liberalism had shaped, for all of their economic and social successes, were strikingly conformist and generated a rebellious counterculture. As the conformity demanded support for a questionable war in Vietnam, the counterculture spread rapidly among young Americans and other westerners. The counterculture, in turn, alienated vast numbers of middle- and working-class citizens who liked welfare liberalism. Democratic societies polarized. On top of these troubles, in the early 1970s an economic stagnation set in that welfare liberalism seemed unable to cure. The United States and Western democracy settled into an unwanted stalemate with Soviet communism, with no apparent way out.

Open liberalism, or what Philip Zelikow and Condoleezza Rice call the "rights revolution," was a hybrid response.[50] This reconstitution of liberalism proved a potent solution to the mid–Cold War torpor of welfare liberalism. It restored economic confidence in the mature democracies. It pushed the new values of expressive individualism into established institutions. It pushed democracy outward into new places, pushing the Soviet empire and communism over a cliff in the process. It helped power hyper-globalization, the opening of state boundaries to an unprecedented volume and velocity of economic and social interaction. By raising production efficiency to new levels, hyper-globalization has helped increase global wealth and lifted hundreds of millions of people out of poverty.

Welfare liberalism as an ideology is still very much with us, in leftist political parties and movements, labor unions, academic research, educational curricula, art and literature, and the political opinions and preferences of millions of democratic citizens. To be sure, the welfare states that it built in the democracies did not disappear; government spending as a percentage of GDP shrank little if at all.[51] But in the halls of power, it was elbowed aside decades ago by open liberalism. The liberalism of today prioritizes jobs less than individual self-development; it prizes national prosperity less than overall global growth. It is a liberalism of both robust antidiscrimination laws and regulations and of free international movements of goods, services, money, and, increasingly, people. Open liberalism's success is also its paradox: it brings together two things that originally seemed at odds. The first is social liberalism, growing out of the 1960s counterculture. In the U.S. case, social liberalism began to take over the Democratic Party after the debacle of the 1968 convention in Chicago. The second is "neoliberalism," a descendant of classical liberalism that is nearly indifferent to national sovereignty and democracy. The fused ideology is both pro-market and pro-liberation—a remorseless drive toward a society that efficiently delivers choice and change to individuals in most areas of life.[52]

Like its predecessors, open liberalism upholds individual liberty as the highest political good. But it conceives of liberty differently because it locates a different threat: not the despotic state, not unfettered capital, but traditional norms and institutions. For open liberalism, unchosen customs, roles, and notions of work, religion, family, identity, and the good life are what hold people back from true emancipation. It is shaped by what Charles Taylor calls an "ethic of authenticity": "the understanding of life . . . that each one of us has his/her own way of realizing our humanity, and that it is important to find and live out one's own, as against surrendering to conformity with a model imposed on us from outside, by society, or by the previous generation, or religious or political authority."[53] Robert Bellah's term is "expressive individualism."[54] Robert Inglehart refers to "post-materialist values"—an attachment not to survival and hard work but "self-expression," including "gender equality, environmental protection, tolerance, interpersonal trust, and free choice."[55]

Open liberalism is not simply an updated version of classical liberalism, as some of its critics charge. James Traub notes that for the classical liberal James Madison, an individual was "a citizen, a member of a blessed community," not "a private, autonomous being." Such citizens "must be counted on to curb their wishes—their interests—for the good of the republic."[56] In some ways, open liberalism is more purely market-oriented than its ancestor. Adam Smith, a founding father of classical liberalism, titled his famous 1776 work *An Inquiry into the Nature and Causes of the Wealth of Nations,* not *Wealth of Individuals* (or *Wealth of the World*). As Stephen Brooks writes, Smith understood that states face trade-offs between sovereignty and wealth.[57] "We do not love our country merely as part of the great society of mankind—we love it for its own sake, and independently of any such consideration," Smith wrote in his *Theory of Moral Sentiments.*[58] Even Richard Cobden, leader of the laissez-faire Manchester school in Victorian Britain, valued free trade for its contribution to the good of the nation. Today's open liberalism, by contrast, does not particularly value nations or their sovereignty, for they are depreciating assets.[59] It prizes markets and private enterprise for the power that they bring the individual, regardless of where she lives. It tells people that they are primarily consumers of the goods of capitalism rather than producers of them.[60] It seeks complete openness, a world without "legacy" boundaries to human interaction and fulfillment. John Mearsheimer calls it "unbounded liberalism."[61]

Nor is open liberalism simply a more developed and inclusive version of welfare liberalism.[62] It is true that third-stage liberalism seeks to extend personal freedom to people who were formally ignored by older liberalisms, people it categorizes by race, ethnicity, sexual orientation, gender, and so on. But open liberalism insists on a kind of fluidity of identity that was foreign to welfare liberalism. Second-stage liberalism was predicated on more or less fixed roles inherited from tradition. It aimed primarily to keep adult men employed and thereby to protect their wives and children from economic distress.[63] Open liberalism, by contrast, embraces a multiculturalism for which the good life is one of moving into and out of groups at will. George Crowder articulates this multiculturalism when he argues for a society of autonomous individuals able to judge for themselves the variety of ways of life on offer.[64] The byword of welfare liberalism was "security"; that of open liberalism is "change."

Third-stage liberalism is embodied in law and administration in most mature democracies and in the European Union that overarches dozens of them. For welfare liberalism, the champion of liberty was the interventionist state; for open liberalism, it is an alliance of the state and various non-state institutions, including large corporations, schools and universities, philanthropic foundations, international and nongovernmental organizations, the entertainment and news media, and the digital realm.

In open liberalism, the social Left and the economic Right have made peace. Individual emancipation and market efficiency, it turns out, go together.[65] Alan Greenspan, former chairman of the Federal Reserve, said in 2007 that "it hardly makes any difference who will be the next president. The world is governed by market forces."[66] Mark Lilla concludes: "The cultural and Reagan revolutions have proved to be complementary, not contradictory, events."[67]

HOW WE GOT TO OPEN LIBERALISM

Ecological pressure vaulted open liberalism to predominance, just as it had welfare liberalism decades earlier. The emergence of new technologies, new ideas, and a new class rendered the status quo unable to handle the problems of the day. Politicians, academics, cultural entrepreneurs, and businesspeople coalesced around a different notion of freedom that seemed better able to make sense of the contemporary world, to address the crises of the day, and to chart a path forward.

The seed was present at the origin of liberalism. It can be

discerned in 1784, in Kant's motto for the Enlightenment, "*Sapere aude!*," or "Have the courage to use your own understanding!"; that is, do not rely on the authority of other people, institutions, or traditions.[68] Kant's fellow Prussian Wilhelm von Humboldt wrote in 1792 that the goal of freedom was "individuality of power and development."[69] These Enlightenment liberals were already displaying the sensibility of the coming Romantic era, which valorized the individual who struggled for independence from stifling society. The Romantic ethos was everywhere in nineteenth-century culture, from the poetry of Byron and Whitman to the operas of Wagner and the dramas of Ibsen.[70] In Europe and North America, groups of freethinkers carried out what John Stuart Mill called "experiments in living," forming communes and households without marriage, producing transgressive art, and dispensing openly with Christianity.

Mill complained that in England, "few people . . . even comprehend" Humboldt's doctrine; dead custom suffocates spontaneity.[71] And indeed, in the nineteenth century, that kind of bohemian nonconformity was not intended for the masses. It required money—either one's own, or that of a patron—and its political program was to build and sustain a society that allowed the talented few to think for themselves. Romantic individualism, in other words, was antidemocratic. Alexis de Tocqueville, Mill, and other liberals were wary of universal suffrage partly because they believed that the masses' conservatism disposed them to use what political power they were granted to constrain the freedom of the enlightened few whom they envied. (Anti-liberals such as Friedrich Nietzsche shared this conviction that democracy led to conformity.)[72]

Democracy had its revenge, however: the prosperity of welfare liberalism democratized bohemianism. In 1962, the middle of the Golden Age of Capitalism—welfare liberalism's

highest achievement—the Students for a Democratic Society
(U.S.) released a condemnation of American conformity that
echoed across the world. The Port Huron Statement decried
American complacency about racial inequality and the threat
of nuclear war, but grounded its protest in a faith that "men
have unrealized potential for self-cultivation, self-direction,
self-understanding, and creativity," and that "the goal of man
and society should be human independence: a concern not
with image of popularity but with finding a meaning in life that
is personally authentic."[73]

The New Left that took shape over the next few years
across Western societies combined a drive to take power from
established institutions with a high value on personal expression. As Todd Gitlin—both participant in and analyst of the
movement—writes, the movement was very much about the
individual putting himself forward to disrupt the normal way
of doing business. The world saw the clash between the new
and old values at the Democratic Party's 1968 convention in
Chicago. Mayor Richard J. Daley, his ward bosses, and his
police represented the old welfare liberal homogeneity. Abbie
Hoffman, Jerry Rubin, and the Youth International Party (Yippies) exemplified the new openness. It was not mere whimsy
that led the Yippies to propose hijinks such as "floating nude
. . . in Lake Michigan" and "releasing greased pigs" among the
convention delegates. The goal was "not only to win demands,
but to *feel good*."[74] The New Left inherited a primary aim of the
nineteenth-century French bohemians: "*épater les bourgeoisie*"—
to shock the middle class. And it was an international movement in 1968, summed up by the Parisian slogan "*Il est interdit
d'interdire!,*" or "It is forbidden to forbid!" Whereas liberal autonomy had always meant freely consenting to objective rules,
it now meant freely making up one's own rules.

Indeed, the New Left was relatively uninterested in the

working class, who were said to be co-opted and without revolutionary potential. The German-American philosopher Herbert Marcuse was probably the first to write in this vein, calling in 1965 for a coalition of "the outcasts and outsiders, the
exploited of other races and other colors, the unemployed and
unemployable."[75] Marcuse's ideas were absorbed by student
activists, who designated themselves the vanguard of this in-
cipient coalition against the Old Left's working class. As one
Progressive Labor campus group representative put it, "We saw
the main problem, really, as: THE PEOPLE. . . . As 'middle-
class' students we learned that this was the working class—the
'racist, insensitive people.'"[76]

Even as expressive individualism attacked the stale con-
ventionality of Western society, welfare liberalism began to fail
to deliver on its economic promises. Keynesian economics had
promised growth and full employment at low levels of inflation and without the boom-and-bust cycles that had seemed
endemic to mature capitalism. In the late 1960s, however, wages
began to outpace productivity growth. Chronic inflation set
in, and many in the working class found that their rising income no longer brought a rising standard of living. Millions of
families began to feel they were running in place. Economic
historians differ on why productivity growth slowed but wage
growth did not. Some blame an exhaustion of technological
innovation. Others cite a slowing of the supply of workers to
train in efficient manufacturing methods. Stephen Marglin argues that it was the sustained low unemployment: if workers
lost their jobs at General Motors, they could easily get jobs at
Ford; the unions thus could credibly demand higher wages of
GM and Ford without raising worker productivity.[77]

Whatever caused the unexpected economic stagnation,
inflation in seven major Organization for Economic Co-Operation and Development (OECD) countries between 1965 and

1973 had averaged 4.5 percent; but from 1974–82 it jumped to 9.5 percent. From 1962–73 growth of real GDP in the OECD countries averaged 5 percent, while unemployment averaged 3 percent; between 1974 and 1981, average growth fell to 2.4 percent and unemployment rose to 5.3 percent.[78] In April 1973 the Oxford economist John Hicks, himself a Keynesian, lectured on "The Crisis in Keynesian Economics." Now, "instead of producing *real* economic progress, or growth, as they had for so long appeared to do, [Keynesian policies] were just producing inflation. Something, it was clear, had gone wrong."[79]

"Stagflation," the miserable combination of low growth and high inflation, was a problem not only because of discontented middle classes but because the Soviet Union and its model of state socialism seemed to go from strength to strength. (It was encountering chronic stagnation of its own, but the Soviet communist party kept its true statistics well-hidden until the mid-1980s.) These were the years of book titles in the West such as *Social Limits to Growth* and *Legitimation Crisis.*[80]

By the 1970s, then, the democracies had reached a new crisis of legitimacy. The middle-class values of welfare liberalism— values that policy-makers had moved heaven and earth to defend decades earlier—only alienated millions of younger people. The promise of a perpetually improving material life was broken. The United States and other Western countries responded to this pressure as they had done to similar pressure in the 1930s: with fundamental reforms designed to preserve liberal democracy by setting it onto a different path, a path both more consistent with the countercultural values of the 1960s and more likely to restore economic growth.

In the economic realm, open liberalism meant shifting to an alternative economic paradigm that had been waiting in the wings. *Monetarism* drew upon neoclassical economic theory. Friedrich Hayek, Milton Friedman, and others had long argued that states' attempts to regulate demand by increasing governmental spending and manipulating the money supply were bound to fail. Increasing the amount of money in circulation to prime the economy was bound to increase inflation.[81] Their prophecies having come true, monetarists won the day in the OECD countries. Industrial nations, it seemed, could no longer afford welfare liberalism.

Thus came the era of powerful independent central banks, deregulation of finance and the corporate sector, lower taxes, restrictions on redistribution, and privatization—the mix of policies that critics came to call "neoliberalism." It took more than a decade after the first hints of crisis for OECD governments to shift fully to this general strategy. U.S. President Jimmy Carter, who took office in 1977, pioneered deregulation of oil prices and of the airline industry. The election in Britain of Margaret Thatcher's Conservative Party in 1979 signaled a decided move toward free-market economics in a country that had built a strong welfare state since the war. In 1982–83, France's Socialist President François Mitterrand soon found that he had to follow suit, selling off state-owned companies and imposing austerity to reduce inflation.[82] In country after country the story was similar: social democrats either lost power to neoliberals on the Right or converted to neoliberalism themselves. Small democracies with leftist governments embraced the new political economy.[83] The United States had always had one of the weaker welfare states in the OECD countries, and it began to move more decisively in a free-market direction with the economic deregulation begun by the Carter administration (1977–81) and furthered by the Reagan administration (1981–89).

These economic changes entailed the emergence in the wealthy democracies of what analysts call the "knowledge economy," in which the highest value goes to technical and design innovation and the management of these things. In the knowledge economy, disruption is common, and adaptability rather than loyalty is rewarded.[84] The knowledge economy naturally brought with it a new kind of worker, called the "symbolic analyst" by Robert Reich and the "managerial elite" by Michael Lind.[85] These are well-educated engineers, lawyers, consultants, designers, brokers, and others who produce value not by using their hands but by manipulating symbols. Reich's 1992 prophecy proved correct, as symbolic analysts have come to earn most of the money in the knowledge economy.

Which leads us to the culture of open liberalism. The values of the New Left proved a good fit with this new class of symbolic analysts, as the drive toward individual expression worked its way into law, policy, and social practice. One of the sources of liberal democracy's longevity is its flexibility, its ability to absorb transgressive movements and people and render them supportive while allowing them to continue to pose as transgressive. Capitalism quickly co-opted the counterculture's music—it did not take long for rock and roll to become big business—fashion, art, and patois to construct what David Brooks calls "bourgeois bohemian," or "bobo," culture.[86]

Educational and parenting theories, once fortresses of parental authority, began to urge the cultivation of each child's individuality. A comparison of the conformity on display in a typical American high school yearbook of 1955 with the desperate attempts to look distinctive in a yearbook of 1970 (or any year since) makes the point clear: nonconformity became the new conformity. Expressive individualism soon transcended its New Left origins and became the doctrine of everyone. Even the U.S. Army fell into line: its recruitment slogan during the 1980s was "Be all that you can be"—far from the patriotic appeal of past generations. An exemplary statement of the new liberal ethos at the highest level of law is from the U.S. Supreme Court's decision in the 1992 abortion-rights case *Planned Par-*

enthood v. Casey: "At the heart of liberty is the right to define one's own concept of existence, of meaning, of the universe, and of the mystery of human life."[87] Penned by Republican appointees to the court, that assertion would have surprised classical and welfare liberals, who would consider the right to free association or to earn a fair return on one's labor as being at the heart of liberty.

Open liberalism's two faces—social liberalism and neoliberalism—came from different places. Yet they were joined together in a sometimes contentious but fruitful and long marriage. The consummation came in the "Third Way" of the 1990s, under the political patronage of U.S. President Bill Clinton, British Prime Minister Tony Blair, German Chancellor Gerhard Schröder, Canadian Prime Minister Jean Chrétien, and other OECD politicians. Midwifed by intellectuals such as the social theorist Anthony Giddens, Third Way politics explicitly relegated to the past heavy state regulation, strong labor unions, robust safety nets, and interest-group politics. The imperative of rapid technological change meant that a liberal society had to be more fluid. No longer could roles be fixed and secure. Instead, the norm became perpetual movement from job to retraining to new job. But open liberalism promised that the system would be fair because it would reward merit. Old privileges of race, ethnicity, gender, age, religion, or other markers would fall away; those with talent, diligence, and flexibility would be rewarded.[88]

It has become customary to refer to the Third Way in the past tense, but its central premises are still widely held by elites on the center-Right as well as the center-Left. Those on the Right favor a less regulatory state, and are less socially liberal, than those on the Left. More important than these differences, however, are the similarities: a faith in social mobility, meritocracy, technology, credentials, and creativity.[89]

Who exactly are the open liberals? It is those who have benefited from the meritocratic system and those who believe they will do so. These are credentialed people in government, business, law, the media and entertainment, the nonprofit sector, the bureaucracies of international non-governmental organizations (INGOs), and the academy. Centuries ago, Europe under the old regime had a layer of aristocrats at the top who identified more with each other than with the lands they inhabited. Just so, today's elite meritocracy is transnational. Early in the twenty-first century, James Davison Hunter and Joshua Yates interviewed a set of "globalizers," elites in international commerce, finance, and humanitarian and religious INGOs. These were people with advanced degrees who traveled to many countries each year, staying in nice, predictable hotels and interacting mainly with other globalizers.

Notwithstanding these people's different, sometimes competing goals, Hunter and Yates found a remarkable consistency in how the globalizers presented and justified what they did. Capitalists and humanitarians alike spoke in the *"language of universal individual human rights and needs."* Corporate executives and NGO workers alike saw themselves as upholding the autonomy of the individual, empowering people in various countries to make choices. And all agreed that "the nation-state is weakening" and "national borders are increasingly transparent, porous, and meaningless." All were working to further these trends that they hailed.[90]

Table 3.1 summarizes and contrasts the three stages of liberalism.

Like all versions of liberalism, open liberalism is not just a modifier of democracy in the United States and other countries. It is an international ideology with international ramifications. In the 1980s the United States in particular began to press it into the international environment. Welfare liberal

Table 3.1. Three liberalisms compared.

Type of liberalism	Classical (L1)	Welfare (L2)	Open (L3)
Obstacle to liberty?	Throne and altar	Unfettered capital	Traditional institutions
Period of dominance	1770–1920	1930–1976	1977–today
Shifts power to . . .	Propertied (white) men	Labor and allies, the state	Symbolic analysts
Precipitant	War taxes from monarchs	Great Depression	Welfare state failure and 1960s counterculture
Program	Constitutional democracy, laissez-faire	Social democracy/welfare state	Expressive individualism, hyper-globalization
Agents	Civil society (lawyers, religious dissenters)	Labor unions, intellectuals, the state	Big capital, foundations, universities, lawyers
Intellectual sources	John Locke, Adam Smith, James Madison, Marquis de Condorcet	T. H. Green, John Dewey, John Maynard Keynes	John Stuart Mill, Herbert Marcuse, Milton Friedman
Political leaders	Thomas Jefferson, Richard Cobden, William Gladstone	Theodore Roosevelt, Franklin Roosevelt, Clement Atlee	Margaret Thatcher, Ronald Reagan, Bill Clinton, Tony Blair
Tensions with L1		Redistribution, regulation	Traditional institutions, norms
Tensions with L2	Redistribution, regulation		Working class vs. women and minorities
Tensions with L3	Traditional institutions, norms	Working class vs. women and minorities	

internationalism was transformed into open liberal internationalism; what had been a club of countries became a society open, in principle, to all individuals.[91] It was open liberalism that brought down the Soviet Union, spread democracy to new regions, and propelled the countries of the world to new levels of economic openness in what Marc Levinson calls the "Third Globalization."[92] But it is open liberalism that is now polarizing mature democracies, enabling populism and illiberalism, and making democracy itself look less viable for the twenty-first century. Its disdain for legacy borders is skewing the distribution of wealth and culturally alienating millions. Chapter 4 tells that story.

4
Liberal Internationalism, Then and Now

The problem of establishing a perfect civic constitution is dependent upon the problem of a lawful external relation among states and cannot be solved without a solution of the latter problem.

—Immanuel Kant, 1784

Liberalism is not only a set of ideas about life within countries. It is equally concerned with relations among those countries, because the two levels are related. In the late eighteenth century, the German philosopher Immanuel Kant was thinking through the conditions for human freedom. Kant wrote that republican government was necessary for freedom, but that a peaceful, rational international environment was necessary to sustain republics. The rule of law *among* states was necessary for the rule of law *within* states.[1] He went on to argue that republics can in fact achieve the rule of law among themselves by setting up a league of peace.[2] In so many words, he was writing about coevolution.[3]

   Over the centuries democratic governments have tried to

shape international order so that they can be secure and prosperous while protecting their own domestic regimes. They have
infused their international ecosystem with liberalism as far as
they could. But as I argued in Chapter 3, liberalism itself has
evolved over the centuries. That means that liberal internationalism has evolved along with it. Governments shape domestic
and international order according to the predominant ideas of
the day—ideas about what liberty is, what its obstacles are, and
how those obstacles are best overcome.

At two moments in the twentieth century—the 1940s
and late 1970s—leaders of the mature democracies found that
they had to reengineer their ecosystem. Classical liberalism
was unequal to the challenges of the 1930s not only within democracies but among them; its international institutions were
thin and were crushed beneath the weight of the Great Depression. Likewise the welfare liberal internationalism of the
1970s: inadequate to the time, it gave way to the open liberal
internationalism of today. Now the latter's turn in the dock has
come.

LIBERAL INTERNATIONALISM,
CLASSICAL EDITION

From the emergence of classical liberalism in the late eighteenth century, its theorists and practitioners were fully aware
that most countries, including many of the most powerful ones,
were not liberal. They understood that this was a problem,
partly because the rulers of these non-liberal countries often
believed liberalism was a threat to their own power and influence. Led by their wealthiest and most powerful exemplar,
Great Britain, liberal states responded to this hostile international environment by engineering a rudimentary liberal
international ecosystem within the broader global order.

Few if any classical liberals had it in mind to spread freedom to the entire world, except perhaps indirectly and over an
indefinite period. Many liberal states engaged in imperialism,
subjugating peoples in Asia and Africa and justifying their empires as grand, long-term educational projects in rationality
and civilization; the same double standard that permitted slavery and limited suffrage enabled liberal imperialism.[4] Classical
liberals were, however, networking across states and trying to
implement on the international level what they were implementing within their own countries.[5] They were trying to shape
the international environment to make it favor liberal states.
What they constructed was often unilateral, sometimes bilateral, and always fragile.

One mode of liberal ecosystem engineering was the attempt to keep absolute monarchy, the greatest threat to their
own regime, from spreading. America's Monroe Doctrine of
1823, sketched at the beginning of Chapter 2, is the most famous instance. For seven decades, the United States was too
weak to enforce the doctrine. The Monroe Doctrine was effectively enforced by liberal Great Britain, which also opposed
the attempts of the European great powers to spread absolute
monarchy.[6]

John Ikenberry recounts classical liberals' attempts at ecosystem engineering in other areas such as trade, international
law, peace, labor rights, and technical cooperation (such as uniform measures and postal service).[7] Concerning trade, most
classical liberals wanted to it to be as free and nondiscrimi-
natory as possible. Free trade was, in a sense, a scaling up of
classical economics to the international realm, getting the
state out of the way of private commerce among, as well as
within, nations. The resulting prosperity, so went the theory,
would reinforce political liberty and peace. Tom Paine had said
as much in 1795: "If commerce were permitted to act to the

universal extent it is capable of, it would extirpate the system of war."[8]

Such ideas gathered momentum in the second quarter of the nineteenth century in Britain under the rhetorical skill of the Manchester school of Richard Cobden and John Bright. The British eliminated agricultural tariffs unilaterally in 1846, providing cheaper food for their factory workers and exposing their wheat farmers to foreign competition. Liberals agitated in other countries too. In France, Frédéric Bastiat and Michel Chevalier did as Cobden and Bright did in Britain, and in 1860 came the Cobden-Chevalier Treaty, an Anglo-French free-trade agreement. There followed a flurry of trade agreements among European states that were both experimenting with liberal political reform.[9] These late nineteenth-century agreements were all bilateral; there were no multilateral trade institutions such as today's World Trade Organization (WTO).

But trade liberalization in the nineteenth century proved unsustainable. It was halted in the 1870s, as the Long Depression that began in 1873 made tariffs irresistible again. Economist Dani Rodrik notes that the globalization of the nineteenth century, such as it was, "rested on awkward and fragile institutional pillars."[10] Indeed, until the late 1940s, international trade was hostage to the booms and busts of free-market capitalism. The last spasm of protectionism came during the Great Depression of the 1930s—an event that was to trigger changes not only in international trade, but in liberalism itself.

All the while, the classical-liberal United States was not a free trader (although southern slaveholders, with their comparative advantage in cotton production, wanted it to be one). Alexander Hamilton's *Report on the Subject of Manufactures* (1791) had argued that a great country must have manufacturing, and that building American manufacturing would require protection from foreign competition.[11] For many decades Hamilton's arguments were common wisdom, and the United States heavily taxed imports of textiles and other industrial products. Liberal internationalism instead showed up in America's preference for nondiscrimination in trade, that is, the principle that all countries should have the same tariffs with all other countries. Thus the United States pressed for an "open door" in China, with no country enjoying special privileges. Classical liberal internationalism also showed up in the informal imperialism of Theodore Roosevelt's "Corollary" of 1904, which updated the Monroe Doctrine by claiming for the United States the right to intervene in Latin America to restore order and efficiency.[12]

Classical liberal internationalism succeeded in its modest core aim of helping the United States and Great Britain thrive internationally while remaining liberal states. During certain periods, this first-stage liberal internationalism also indirectly spread liberal government by enabling reform in more authoritarian states. After the 1848 revolutions in Europe, the British model of reforming liberalism gained luster because Britain had dodged the upheaval that hit its rivals. "Conservative liberalism" became the order of the day in France, Germany, Austria, Italy, and elsewhere.[13] The victory of the liberal democracies in World War I produced a period of democratization all over Europe in the 1920s.[14]

As recounted in Chapter 3, however, the Great Depression and rise of fascism in the 1930s overwhelmed classical liberal internationalism. The "Polanyi problem"—that if interdependent states were going to interfere heavily in their own economies, they had better coordinate—was part of what we mean by the inadequacy of classical liberalism and a chief reason why it ceded the ground to welfare liberal internationalism.

Welfare Liberal Internationalism: 1946–75

The much more elaborate liberal internationalism that began in the mid-1940s, featuring formal alliances and economic institutions and active American democracy promotion, was of a piece with the domestic welfare liberalism that generated it. In fact, it had been previewed after World War I by Woodrow Wilson, a progressive who late in his presidency embraced the welfare liberal, state-directed governance of his old rival Theodore Roosevelt. At the end of the war, Wilson attempted to move the United States and the world toward a more institutionalized liberal internationalism, with the League of Nations at the center. Wilson's attempt to, as he put it, "[make] the world . . . safe for democracy" failed, both because he could not persuade his own country to join the league and because in the 1930s fascist states aggressively shaped the international environment to favor their regime type.

Sustainable welfare liberal internationalism had to await the entrenchment of the welfare state in the United States and other industrial democracies and their victory in World War II. The result was something more active, coordinated, regulatory, and intentional than classical liberal internationalism. As welfare liberalism at home required more centralization of power, welfare liberal internationalism required a concentration of power in a hegemonic state, and that state was, by general agreement, the United States. John Ikenberry has argued that America practiced "self-binding" with its fellow democracies, guaranteeing that it would abide by rules it was setting for others, which allowed its allies to trust it.[15] Having a United States with such outsized power was not the best of all possible worlds for these other democracies, but having a liberal hegemon in a dangerous world was good enough.

The international environment did throw crises at the mature democracies during the years of welfare liberal internationalism, some of which they badly mishandled. Decolonization—a kind of international reckoning against Western imperialism—thrashed the politics of those democracies that had formal empires, particularly France. The Third World became an arena of superpower competition, and the United States was pulled in most deeply in Indochina. The Vietnam War was a lengthy and failed U.S. attempt to shape the international environment in Southeast Asia, one that boomeranged and put American democracy in its most fraught situation during the Cold War. Indeed, outside the club of industrial democracies, the U.S.-dominated order was much more coercive, and Washington did not promote constitutional self-government. It trusted autocracies to be more reliably anticommunist and actively helped keep them in power, even against democratic parties and movements.[16]

Then, too, the Soviets had some good years, enjoying about the same rate of economic growth per capita as the United States from the end of World War II until the mid-1960s. As they engineered their own ecosystem to favor communism, Soviet leaders seized the opportunity presented by decolonization. In 1961 Premier Nikita Khrushchev announced that the Soviets would back "wars of national liberation" in hopes of luring new Third World states into their own sphere and away from the United States.[17] The Soviets also increased trade with and military aid to many governments.[18] Khrushchev predicted publicly that within twenty years the Soviet economy would overtake the American in material consumption. To many at the time, the prophecy did not seem fanciful.[19] Then the late 1960s brought legitimacy crises in several industrial democracies. In France, democracy wobbled in 1968 as students and workers went on strike and the government of Charles de Gaulle fell. The American model continued to fray in the 1970s

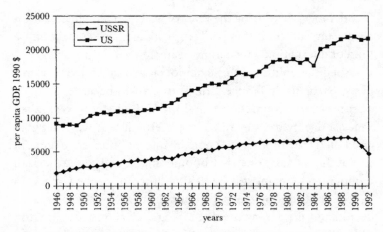

Figure 4.1. GDP growth in the superpowers, 1946–1992.
(Source: Philip Hanson, *The Rise and Fall of the Soviet Economy: An Economic History of the USSR from 1945* [New York: Routledge, 2003], 244.)

as the loss in Vietnam, the Watergate scandal, Richard Nixon's resignation, two energy crises, and the hostage crisis in Iran piled up. Economic growth in all the democracies slowed.

Yet, in the end, the American and Western system of liberal democracy proved superior. Soviet growth permanently stalled in the 1970s and early 1980s. Figure 4.1, depicting GDP growth rates for the two superpowers from 1946 to 1992, shows how the Soviet and American curves have roughly the same slope until the mid-1960s, when the U.S. curve steepens slightly. The trends began to work against the Soviet model, and any chance of catching up to the United States faded.[20] The Soviets falsified their own economic data, but the top leadership knew the truth: as of the 1970s the Americans were increasing their lead, and the Soviets were unable to reverse the trend. The consequences for world communism provide the strongest evidence available that the ecosystem the United States had engineered had worked. The industrial democracies got what they wanted: they remained democratic, got richer, and were secure.

Open Liberal Internationalism: 1976–Today

Welfare liberal internationalism pressed hard against the Soviet system, but open liberal internationalism delivered the coup de grâce. It also propelled the third wave of global democratization and razed more and more national barriers to the movement of goods, services, capital, and labor.

Liberalism by definition is internationalist, in the sense that it sees all persons as fundamentally the same regardless of nationality, religion, culture, and so on. But open liberalism goes beyond internationalism to embrace globalism or cosmopolitanism. Under its logic, nation-states are barriers to the two related goods of efficiency and individual emancipation. All boundaries of politics, culture, and tradition are artificial and should be perpetually open to crossing, revision, even erasure. Under open liberal internationalism, what had been the defense of democracy in industrial countries became the active promotion of liberal self-government nearly everywhere. NATO, originally a military alliance against Soviet power, became an expanded club of democracies that enforced human rights on its periphery. The multilateral institutions of welfare liberalism, designed to allow each government to respond to the needs of its people, adopted the new mission of prying government hands off national economies. The European Economic Community became the European Union (EU), a new kind of entity with sovereignty over many areas of its members' economies, laws, regulations, and immigration.

To its great credit, open liberal internationalism does not regard democracy as something only for wealthy industrial countries. Self-government is for everyone. But the form of democracy on offer is now tethered tightly to open liberalism's notion of liberty as expressive individualism and consumption. In the end, democracy comes to mean the maximization of the efficient delivery of perpetual personal choice—over not only which smartphone to buy, but what kind of person to be—to all individuals everywhere. Liberty becomes a dream of the unencumbered movement of ideas, goods, services, capital, and people across all physical and symbolic boundaries.

It is an alluring dream for many around the world, and at the close of the twentieth century its fulfillment seemed within sight. Open liberalism was so successful that democracy no longer seemed to need defending. Ancient problems of politics had become problems of global governance, to be addressed by technical expertise. Any difficulties that open liberalism encountered (or created), such as climate change or pandemics or job displacement, could be remedied by science and management.

Open liberal internationalism proudly compromises states' sovereignty.[21] Countries give up some control over their domestic affairs in exchange for more prosperity and opportunity for their citizens. For many citizens, this trade-off has gone sour. Benefits are not distributed widely or fairly within the United States and other wealthy democracies. Free elections—democracy's ultimate mechanism for course correction—are not doing the job. In election cycle after cycle, the open liberalism that America pushes into its environment pushes back into America, widening gaps in income, wealth, and culture, to the point that a severe "two nations" problem has become entrenched. America no longer has the inevitable and healthy cross-cutting divisions of a free society. It has instead a binary division, one that is self-reinforcing, difficult to reverse, and potentially fatal. Open liberalism, it turns out, does not work for the majority, and too many are losing the norms of democratic life and confidence in democratic institutions. Power has migrated from publics to international bureaucracies and corporate heads.[22] Open liberalism is not making the world select for democracy. It is doing something like the opposite.

THE EARLY YEARS

Democracies adopted open liberal internationalism to remedy the stagnation that beset them in the 1970s. The crisis of welfare liberalism manifested at the international level in two ways: the brokenness of postwar multilateral economic institutions, and the stalemate in the Cold War struggle against Soviet communism. In the early 1970s, welfare liberal internationalism seemed nearly as weak as classical liberal internationalism had looked in the 1930s.

Stagnation in Western democracies was due partly to the breakdown of the international financial system. That welfare liberal system was designed to allow national governments to regulate their economies while staying open to trade and investment. The values of the British pound, Japanese yen, German mark, and other currencies were pegged to the U.S. dollar, which in turn had a fixed value in terms of gold. In 1971, determined to stop its democratic partners from selling off dollars and feeding inflation, Richard Nixon abruptly ended that system by ending the dollar's convertibility to gold. Currency exchange rates began to float. Governments lost their ability to control movements of capital in and out of their borders.[23] The wealthy economies of the West became more volatile, and voters began to lose confidence in their governments.

This new challenge to liberal internationalism was actually welcomed by many elites in the United States and Europe. These were economists, lawyers, and government officials belonging to an intellectual movement that had developed parallel to welfare liberalism in the 1920s and 1930s. Originating in Austria and Germany, including such thinkers as Friedrich Hayek, Ludwig von Mises, Wilhelm Röpke, and Gottfried Haberler, these "neoliberals" wanted goods, services, capital, and labor to move perfectly freely across national borders. As classical liberals, they had once believed that nation-states and free markets were compatible. From World War I and the Great Depression, however, they had concluded that the modern nation-state, with its tendencies toward economic protection, empire, and war, was an obstacle to their goal. Some overarching force was needed to keep democratic governments in check. The neoliberals wanted international rules and institutions, but not the same type that welfare liberals wanted. Welfare liberals wanted an internationalism that allowed democracies to run their economies without closing up. Neoliberals wanted an internationalism that protected markets from being hobbled by democratic nations.[24]

In the 1940s the neoliberals had lost out to the Keynesians. In the 1970s, when the failures of welfare liberal internationalism were manifest, the tables were turned. Neoliberals were waiting in the wings with a diagnosis and a remedy. It was intervention by governments, they argued, that had produced the perverse incentives that caused the stagnation. Forcing the state to lift its cold hand from markets would maximize growth.[25] The explicit goal was to serve not national democracy but the free choices of individuals everywhere.[26]

For the neoliberals, multilateral institutions were still necessary. In the language of coevolution, governments still had to alter the environment, but in a very different way from before. First came reform of the international financial architecture. In 1975 George Shultz, the U.S. treasury secretary, and his deputy, Paul Volcker, began to work with Helmut Schmidt, chancellor of West Germany, and Valéry Giscard d'Estaing, president of France, to coordinate tight, anti-inflationary monetary policy across their economies. This was the beginning of what became the Group of 7 (G7), the biggest economies among the liberal democracies. Jimmy Carter, the first Democrat to be elected president under the party's post-welfare orientation, continued with the reforms after assuming office in 1977. In Britain, Margaret Thatcher, who became prime minister in 1979, took them to a new level, as did Ronald Reagan in the United States during his presidency (1981–89).[27]

In the 1980s and 1990s "deregulation" and "privatization" became watchwords at the U.S. Treasury, the International Monetary Fund (IMF), and the World Bank. Under what economist John Williamson dubbed the "Washington Consensus," these institutions began to press borrowers to reduce the role of the state in their economies. Williamson implied that opponents to the Washington Consensus were corrupt: "Rules that make state help [to the economy] the exception rather than the rule, and require it to be transparent and based on agreed principles, will cramp the style of those politicians whose main objective is to feather their own nests rather than to further any concept of the public good."[28]

The promise of the Washington Consensus was that it would create more wealth by leading companies to invest more. And indeed, as less developed countries deregulated their economies, they attracted more investment from multinational corporations. Wages and benefits were already lower in the poorer countries; less government interference made the new converts to neoliberalism irresistible investment targets. Between 1983 and 1990, the value of world trade grew by 130 percent. And that was only the beginning, as container shipping developed in the 1970s and government subsidies dropped the cost of transportation dramatically, making the offshoring of production still more profitable.[29]

The spread of so-called "value chains"—where the design and physical components that go into a product are scattered across several countries—finally made good on capitalism's promise to bring manufacturing to less developed countries in Asia and Central Europe. An iPhone 5, released in 2012, contained components from the United States, China, Japan, South Korea, Taiwan, Germany, Italy, France, and the Netherlands.[30] Value chains gave firms and national economies a large stake in openness and made globalization more and more profitable for more and more people.[31]

In keeping with open liberalism's view that national borders clog up commerce, limit growth, and artificially shorten the menu of lifestyle choices for individuals, the wealthy democracies allowed more and more immigration as well. The United States had already increased migration from overseas greatly with the 1965 Immigration and Naturalization Act, and in the 1990s the rate increased still more (Figure 4.2). In the EU, the 1985 Schengen Agreement allowed citizens of member states to live, work, and study anywhere in the EU. Intra-Europe migration skyrocketed, as intended.

SELECTION PRESSURE AND COMMUNIST ADAPTATION

As the United States and its allies found new ways to use capitalism and democracy as weapons in the Cold War, open liberal internationalism also altered the realm of national security. Welfare liberalism had aimed to contain communism in hopes of outlasting it. It did not have a program for vanquishing the Soviets' system, and so it had little to offer when a Soviet-

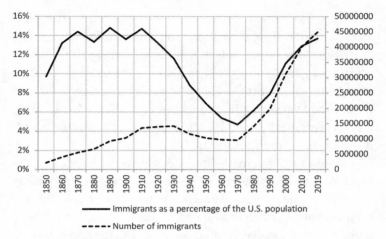

Figure 4.2. U.S. immigrant population
and share over time, 1850–2019.
(Source: Migration Policy Institute, "U.S. Immigration Trends,"
https://www.migrationpolicy.org/programs/data-hub/us
-immigration-trends#history, retrieved on March 22, 2021.)

American stalemate took hold around 1970. The United States
was stuck in Vietnam; its allies were losing confidence in its
leadership; its lead in nuclear weapons had vanished. The two
superpowers entered a decade of détente or relaxation, each
maintaining the ecosystem it had engineered to protect it domestic regime but agreeing to a set of ground rules for bilateral
competition. The Americans and Soviets began to trade and
engage in scientific cooperation.[32] Mainstream opinion in the
West accepted the bipolar stalemate as an equilibrium.

Jimmy Carter took office as a post–Cold Warrior, but reversed course in December 1979 after the Soviets abruptly invaded Afghanistan. Carter ordered a halt of grain sales to the
Soviet Union, the deployment of new nuclear missiles to Western Europe, the funding of anti-Soviet fighters in Afghanistan,
and a U.S. boycott of the Moscow Olympics in 1980. Ronald

Reagan took matters still further by not only restarting the arms race but infusing the international environment with still more open liberalism, effectively reengineering the international ecosystem. Henry Nau terms Reagan's strategy "conservative internationalism"—a grand strategy that asserted that if the United States were true to its principle that individual liberty and free markets were best for everyone around the world, it would show communism up as a failure.[33]

In 1982 Reagan made liberal democracy a weapon in the Cold War by announcing a policy of "foster[ing] the infrastructure of democracy, the system of a free press, unions, political parties, universities, which allows a people to choose their own way to develop their own culture, to reconcile their own differences through peaceful means"[34] U.S. support for anticommunist forces in Afghanistan and democratic movements in Poland pressed particularly hard on the Soviets. After a deep recession in 1982, the U.S. economy grew for the rest of the decade, reaching a staggering 7.2 percent in 1984.[35] Recovery in all of the mature democracies in the 1980s injected new information into the international environment: liberal democracy's ability to self-correct made it superior to communism.[36]

Reagan ensured that democracy's superiority was made clear around the world. Declaring the USSR the "evil empire," he propagandized more brazenly than any of his predecessors. In 1987, standing before the Berlin Wall, a symbol of the unjust Cold War stalemate, Reagan called on Mikhail Gorbachev, the Soviets' reformist president, to come to the divided city and "tear down this wall." The German correspondent of the *Financial Times* spoke for many world-weary westerners when he called the demand "impossible."[37] Yet, two and a half years later, Germans themselves tore the wall down as the East German government and Gorbachev stood by. Reagan even reversed the old American tradition of supporting friendly dictators, dropping Ferdinand Marcos of the Philippines in early 1986 and other autocrats later.[38]

The successes of early open liberal internationalism pressed hard on communist countries to move in a liberal direction or submit to long-term national decline. The first concrete sign came in China. Deng Xiaoping, who succeeded Mao Zedong in 1978 as China's leader, began experimenting piecemeal with market mechanisms and soon set the country firmly on a path of reform (see Chapter 5).

The Soviet Union followed a few years later, and went much further by adopting some democratic reforms as well as economic ones. It was desperation to reverse national decline that prodded the ruling party's central committee to select Gorbachev as its leader in March 1985. Known as a reformer, Gorbachev gave the party's leadership more than it asked for by implementing radical reforms. *Perestroika* (restructuring) involved lifting central planning and allowing markets to distribute resources. *Glasnost* (openness) involved allowing public criticism of officials, policies, and Soviet history. The international environment, reengineered by the United States and the West, made the regime-power dilemma acute for the ruling party: to stay in the game with America, the Soviet Union had to become more liberal and democratic.

But the Soviet Union proved unable to adapt. A broad and deep loss of confidence in the model set in among its own party and communist parties around the world. The story of the fall of communism in Eastern Europe in 1989 has been told often.[39] The Soviets' satellite states had long been plagued by dissenting groups. These dissenters knew something of life on the west side of the Iron Curtain, and they wanted it for their countries. Gorbachev granted the communist parties in Eastern Europe permission to enact liberal reforms. In the spring, Poland and Hungary held multiparty elections and seated non-communist governments. Czechoslovakia did the same later in the year. In the fall, mass demonstrations in East Germany pressed the government into opening the Berlin Wall, and talks commenced to reunite the two Germanys. The communist boss in Bulgaria resigned, and elections were scheduled for 1990. Only in Romania did the ruler, Nicolae Ceaușescu, refuse all reforms. Protesters tried and executed Ceaușescu and his wife on December 25.[40]

Perhaps even more surprising were the sea changes in political thinking and coalitions in the Third World. For most of the Cold War, democracy did not flourish in Latin America, Africa, and Asia. In part this was because, as noted in Chapter 3, the United States mostly undermined rather than supported liberal self-government for fear that democracy would usher in communist or at least pro-Soviet governments. When the Soviet Union itself began to abandon communism in 1985, socialism lost its luster in the Third World as well. Democrats in scores of countries came to believe that dealing with the West and adopting its ways provided the only reliable route to development. Washington, less worried about communism in the Third World, began dropping its old dictator friends and supporting free and fair elections in country after country, beginning with the Philippines in 1986.[41] State-driven industrialization was out; foreign investment and exporting were in, and the United States finally began promoting democracy in much of the less developed world.

Reagan's Cold War policies entailed serious risks. They increased U.S. debt and exposed developing economies to new hazards. They remain controversial today even among U.S. allies. Berlin has a John-F.-Kennedy-Platz, an expression of German gratitude for that president's support of democracy, but no Ronald-Reagan-Platz.[42] Yet, Henry Nau and Andrew Busch both present much evidence that Reagan's policies drove up the costs to the Soviets of waging the Cold War.[43] No doubt liberal democracy would eventually have proved superior to communism, even without Reagan's manipulations of the environment. But Reagan almost certainly hastened the process. Until the late 1980s, it was not at all clear to most westerners that democracy would prevail any time soon, if ever. In 1987 historian Paul Kennedy published his magisterial *Rise and Fall of the Great Powers,* which ended in a gloomy assessment of the United States as an overextended power that needed to reduce its foreign commitments.[44] The book was an award-winning bestseller, even as Reagan continued to intensify the Soviets' regime-power dilemma and Gorbachev continued to respond.

PEAK OPEN LIBERALISM: 1990–2007

Two years after Kennedy published his masterwork, a political scientist at the RAND Corporation, Francis Fukuyama, published an article titled "The End of History?"[45] Although he relied more on political philosophy than history, Fukuyama grasped more surely what was happening in the late twentieth century. Authoritarian dominoes were falling in many parts of the world. Political scientist Samuel Huntington called it the world's "third wave" of democratization. The third wave actually had begun fifteen years earlier, as open liberalism was first flexing its muscles, with the fall of autocracy in Portugal and Greece in 1974 and Spain the following year. The third wave spread to Latin America, Asia, Eastern Europe, and Africa.[46] The Soviet Union itself cracked into pieces in 1991, leaving a dozen independent states, many of which set off on a democratic path. One widely accepted democracy scale calculates the world's democracy score as 0.58 in 2015, double the 0.29 score of 1970. The steepest increase took place in the early 1990s (Figure 4.3). Reagan's successors continued to embrace open liberal-

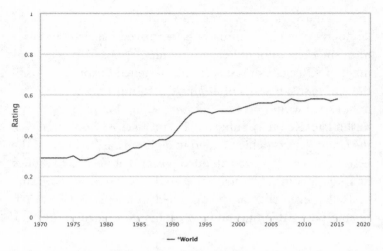

Figure 4.3. Democracy in the world, 1970–2015
(by number of countries).

(Source: Varieties of Democracy Project [V-Dem], University of
Gothenburg, https://www.v-dem.net/data_analysis/CountryGraph/,
generated on March 19, 2021. The graph uses the democracy scale of
Carles Boix, Michael Miller, and Sebastian Rosato: "Boix-Miller-Rosato
Dichotomous Coding of Democracy, 1800–2020 Dataverse," Harvard
Dataverse, https://dataverse.harvard.edu/dataverse/BMR.)

ism's principle that liberty was for all individuals everywhere in
the world, and in the present rather than at some unspecified
future time.[47] Political scientist Tony Smith argues that post-
Reagan presidents took the imperative to spread democracy
well beyond what liberal internationalism would authorize,
particularly through the use of force.[48] In 1989 George H. W.
Bush sent an invading force to Panama to oust dictator (and
former U.S. client) Manuel Noriega and restore civilian government. In 1994 Bill Clinton sent an invading force to Haiti
with a similar purpose and similar result. In 1995 and 1999, in
the face of atrocities committed in civil wars in the former Yu-
goslavia, NATO intervened with air power to bring the viola-

tors to heel. NATO countries also used diplomacy and economic sanctions to promote democracy in the Balkans.

Under George W. Bush, president from 2001 to 2009, the United States and some other wealthy democracies finally agreed to support democratization in the one region they had excluded from it: the Middle East. Their predecessors had supported authoritarian rulers for fear that radical Islamists would win in free elections. It was the jihadi terrorist attacks of September 11, 2001, that led to the final universalizing of open liberalism. Bush led military coalitions to topple the theocratic Taliban in Afghanistan and the authoritarian Baathist regime in Iraq and spent many years and much blood and treasure trying to install democratic governments in their place.[49] The initiatives were bipartisan, at least at first: Al Gore, John Kerry, Hillary Clinton, and other leading Democrats had called for the ouster of Saddam Hussein in the late 1990s, and 58 percent of Democratic Senators voted for the Iraq War Resolution in 2003.[50] Under Bush, open liberalism's imperative to spread democracy reached its zenith. "So it is the policy of the United States to seek and support the growth of democratic movements and institutions in every nation and culture, with the ultimate goal of ending tyranny in our world," he declared in January 2005.[51]

The United States and other mature democracies pushed the new norms into international institutions as well. In 1999 NATO adopted a Membership Action Plan stipulating that new members must be democracies.[52] NATO had already accepted Poland, Czechia, and Hungary as members, and in 2004 the alliance took in seven more Eastern European states. In 1992 the European Communities (EC) became the European Union (EU), a much more ambitious project of economic, legal, regulatory, governmental, and even cultural integration. Goods, services, capital, and people moved freely within the EU. Most member states adopted a common currency, the euro, regulated to keep inflation low. Although the EU explicitly valued the preservation of the national and regional cultures of Europe, the emphasis was on free individuals moving across, into, and out of member states as they saw fit—that is, on making traditional cultures less shapers of identity and more options for free individuals to sample, adopt, and abandon at will.[53] Like NATO, the EU expanded eastward, taking in most of the old Warsaw Pact states and evincing a willingness to take in some former Soviet republics, including Ukraine.

The wealthy democracies' project of opening all national borders to the free movement of goods, services, capital, and people rolled on. Neoliberal economists and lawyers such as Jan Tumlir and Ernst-Ulrich Petersmann had long sought to make the General Agreement on Tariffs and Trade (GATT), the postwar international trade institution, more potent.[54] Success came in 1995, when the GATT was reformed into the WTO. The WTO added rules limiting states' ability to regulate finance, tax systems, and industrial policies. It featured a dispute-resolution mechanism to adjudicate complaints about rule violations.[55] The average tariff was 11.1 percent in 1996, and 9 percent in 2019.[56] After 1995 global trade climbed even more steeply than before (Figure 4.4), with an interruption after the 9/11 terrorist attacks, until the 2008 financial crisis. In international financial policy, the Washington Consensus on market-based reforms continued to hold sway, in modified form, at the U.S. Treasury and IMF.[57]

OPEN LIBERALISM BEGINS TO TURN
ON DEMOCRACY: 2008 AND AFTER

In many respects, open liberal internationalism continues to move forward. Its core institutions—the IMF and World Bank,

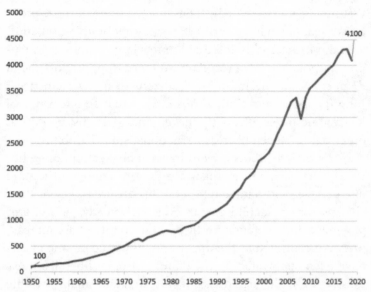

Figure 4.4. Volume of global trade, 1950–2020 (1950=100).

(Source: World Trade Organization, "Evolution of Trade under the WTO: Handy Statistics," https://www.wto.org/english/res_e/statis_e/trade_evolution_e/evolution _trade_wto_e.htm, retrieved on August 14, 2022.)

the WTO, NATO—do their work. The United States and Europe promote liberal democracy in various parts of the world through more subtle and perhaps more effective means: Western-based NGOs and public-private initiatives train civil society in Eastern Europe to combat corruption, fixed elections, and the like.[58] "Western linkage" has enabled democratization in a number of regions of the world.[59] If one talks only to the democracy promoters, one may conclude that all proceeds apace. Notwithstanding the inevitable struggles and setbacks, democracy marches on.

Yet it is not so. Like classical and welfare liberalism before it, open liberal internationalism has encountered problems that it is unable to remedy. It has created some of those problems itself. Open liberalism tells a story about universal, individual self-determination that attracts large numbers of people. Its policies, however, have softened support for liberal democracy among millions of citizens in many countries.[60] John Ikenberry and Daniel Nexon write that an international hegemonic order affects the hegemonic state just as it does other states.[61] Open liberal internationalism is Exhibit A.

As the court ideology of hyper-globalization, open liberalism has helped deindustrialize entire regions of mature democracies and rendered generations unsure if they or their children or grandchildren can ever have steady, gainful employment. Income and wealth in these countries are increasingly concentrated at the upper end. Those economic effects have been aggravated by the culture of open liberalism: expressive individualism does not suit rural and small-town life very well, and even among many urbanites and suburbanites, open liberalism has not delivered on its promise of the good life of personal emancipation.

In Chapter 1, I went over some dreary features of democracy's trials in the United States and the wider world, with special attention to the challenges of populism and polarization.[62] Populism tells discontented citizens that the nation—always defined as the *real* people—is being destroyed by a conspiracy of self-serving elites and minority and foreign groups.[63] Polarization is the separation of citizens into two mutually hostile groups for whom every social and personal question is political, and every political question is apocalyptic. Populism and polarization form a self-tightening knot. Elites and minority groups may draw closer together over opposition to populism, to the point where they mirror the populists, implying that they may not really belong to "our democracy." Populists take such elitism as evidence that they are correct about the conspiracy. So the knot constricts, and more and more people start to think that the other side is too dangerous for democracy.

ECONOMIC EFFECTS

Some analysts blame the populism-polarization dynamic on the economic effects of hyper-globalization. Others blame the cultural changes that were set in train in the 1960s. Both are correct. Open liberal internationalism, like any successful political reform, is a marriage of the economic and the cultural: it aims to get rid of old boundaries and traditions so as to bring about the efficiency needed for economic growth and the choice that will allow people everywhere to live lives of their own fashioning. In that sense, it does not matter a great deal whether culture or economics is more important. They are mutually supporting and difficult to disentangle.

In the realm of economics, the marked increase in countries' openness, seen in the growth in world trade (see Figure 4.4), did indeed accelerate global wealth creation. In the mature democracies that make up the Organization for Economic Co-Operation and Development (OECD), overall growth has continued at roughly the same rate as obtained up to 1970. But in those same countries, the rich have done far better than the working class and poor. Labor's share of national income has fallen since 1980 (Figure 4.5). Thomas Frank reports that, whereas between the 1930s and 1980s the lower 90 percent of the U.S. population pocketed 70 percent of the country's economic growth, since 1997 *all* economic growth has accrued to the top 10 percent.[64] The biggest manufacturing job losses tend to be in those cities that relied most on manufacturing before 1970. That is because job loss can be self-reproducing in a locality; for every manufacturing job lost since 1970 in the United States, 1.6 jobs of other types were lost in the same community.[65]

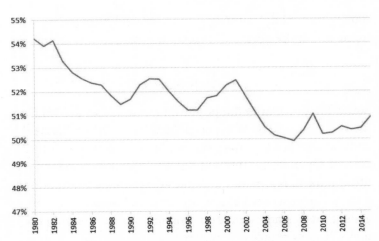

Figure 4.5. Wages as percentage of GDP in
selected wealthy democracies, 1980–2014.
(Source: Ana Maria Santacreu and Heting Zhu, "How Income Inequality
Is Affected by Labor Share," Federal Reserve Bank of St. Louis, July 31, 2017,
https://www.stlouisfed.org/on-the-economy/2017/july/income-inequality
-affected-labor-share, retrieved on August 17, 2022.)

Much of this stagnation in the working class comes from
the automation of production.[66] But much has also come from
open liberalism's remorseless razing of barriers to the movement of goods, services, capital, and labor. The benefits of openness accrue chiefly to highly talented people, unusually productive firms, and "heavily agglomerated cities."[67] This shift in
wealth produced a shift in political power from wage earners
to owners and financiers. It is important to recognize that this
is a story about communities, not only individuals or families.
That is, the people hurt by openness tend to live in the same
towns, cities, and regions, so that there are bad multiplier effects. "Jobs and income decline, property values fall, the local
tax base erodes, more educated residents leave, and local public
services deteriorate. After a couple of decades the city, town, or

neighborhood is reeling from waves of economic and social shocks, affecting everything from school quality to opioid addiction."[68] Much of the populist pushback has been against economic openness, and hence is a threat to the current version of liberal internationalism.[69]

The greatest flashpoint has been immigration, perhaps because it is more visible than capital movements or low tariffs. To some degree, the entry of low-skilled foreigners into a country is always polarizing for its effects on labor markets. Immigration typically enriches an economy overall by driving down wages; but the native-born are not grateful at having to compete with immigrants for jobs.[70] The EU's open-borders policy has brought laborers from Eastern and Southern Europe into Northern and Western Europe. In the United Kingdom between 1995 and 2015, immigrants from other EU countries tripled from nine hundred thousand to 3.3 million. There was no net loss in jobs for native-born Britons, but a study found that high-wage earners were made better off and low-wage earners worse off after the influx.[71] Those results are consistent with the findings of economist George Borjas concerning the United States. Census data show that between 1995 and 2015, immigration into the United States increased the low-skilled workforce by around 25 percent. During the same period, the income of native-born high school dropouts fell by between $800 and $1,500 each year.[72] In 2019, 14 percent of Americans were immigrants—close to the all-time high of 15 percent in 1910 (see Figure 4.2). As Figure 4.6 makes clear, populist parties and movements seize on anti-immigrant sentiment with great success.

Then there is trade. Economists have found that its acceleration since 2000 has shifted manufacturing jobs away from the wealthy democracies. Cheap imports mean jobs get exported.[73] The most dramatic effect has been that of Chinese

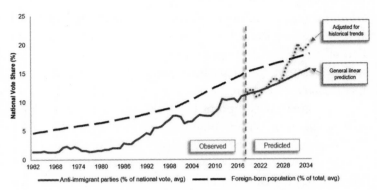

Figure 4.6. Immigration and anti-immigration
voting in Europe, 1962–2034.

(Source: Nate Breznau, "Europe's Ageing Populations Need Immigration—and That
Means Anti-Immigration Politics Is Here to Stay," *Social Europe,* February 2, 2018,
https://www.socialeurope.eu/europes-ageing-societies-need-immigration-means
-anti-immigration-politics-stay, retrieved on May 29, 2021.)

imports on manufacturing jobs in the United States. When
China joined the WTO in 2001—a massive change in the world
economy justified by the principles of open liberalism (discussed in the next chapter)—manufacturers in the United States
and elsewhere began to insist that suppliers buy from China
unless an alternative source could match the "China price." Beijing's export subsidies made that price low indeed.[74] Figure 4.7
shows an inverse relationship between Chinese imports and
U.S. manufacturing jobs. In this case, correlation points to
causation. Economist David Autor and his colleagues estimate
that between 1999 and 2011, the so-called "China Shock" brought
the loss of between 2 and 2.4 million such jobs.[75]

It is difficult to imagine the old welfare liberal internationalism, with its overriding concern for full employment in
industrial democracies, tolerating the sudden lowering of barriers against imports from a country with such a vast number
of skilled workers. Areas that lost jobs have been slower to re-

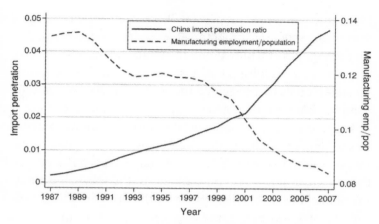

Figure 4.7. U.S. manufacturing employment
and Chinese imports, 1987–2007.

(Source: David H. Autor, David Dorn, and Gordon H. Hanson, "The China
Syndrome: Local Labor Market Effects of Import Competition in the United
States," *American Economic Review* 103, no. 6 (October 2013): 2122.
Copyright American Economic Association; reproduced with
permission of the American Economic Review.)

cover than experts predicted and are fertile ground for populist politicians.[76]

The political impact of the distress has been worse than most economists and political scientists had anticipated. Economist Dani Rodrik lists several leading colleagues who changed their minds about globalization; where they once taught that it would enrich everyone, at least indirectly, they now concede that it has increased and entrenched inequality in wealthy countries.[77]

These economic trends—higher volume and velocity of immigrants and imports—were building from the 1980s, the early years of open liberal internationalism. In 1992 Ross Perot's populist third-party presidential bid, built on opposition to free trade, earned just under 19 percent of the popular vote; his

1996 campaign earned 8.4 percent. It was another aspect of open liberalism's economic program—the "unleashing of finance"—that brought the turning point: the global financial meltdown of 2007–8 and resulting Great Recession. The U.S. subprime mortgage crisis that triggered the meltdown was exceedingly complex, but it would not have happened without the removal of safeguards in the U.S. financial industry and governments' loss of ability to control inflows and outflows of capital. Investors all over the world held U.S. debt that was much riskier than they thought and that exposed them to the inevitable bursting of the housing bubble.[78] The growth in power of the financial industry was both cause and consequence; in the United States, finance's share of domestic corporate profits from 1973 to 1985 was never above 16 percent, whereas in the early 2000s it reached 41 percent.[79]

The meltdown had consequences for everyone. In 2009 the U.S. economy shrank by 2.5 percent and global GDP fell by 2.9 percent, the first shrinkage since 1945.[80] The political centrists in power from both major U.S. political parties meted out punishment to the banks, fining them billions of dollars, but no major banking executive served time in prison.[81] Reaction from Left and Right at the lack of accountability was ferocious. Populism gained strength on the Left with the Occupy movement, which blamed Wall Street, and on the Right with movements that blamed the government and were to make their presence felt in the next decade.

SOCIAL EFFECTS

The cultural face of open liberal internationalism—expressive individualism—pervades the wealthy democracies and much of the rest of the world. A culture by and for symbolic analysts, it has been madly popular among city dwellers, suburbanites, professionals, and the young across dozens of countries, not all of them democracies. It is carried around the world by the movies, music, fashion, design, patois, and other cultural artifacts of today's liberal democracies. It is pervasive in the talk and action of corporate leaders, human resources departments, lawyers, educators, journalists, and foundations. The devices that convey this content are themselves part of the culture of open liberalism. Billions of people carry with them at all times smartphones, their own instruments of self-creation, products of the open liberal hothouse of Silicon Valley. Advertising for these devices encourages the "curation" of self-images, always instantly updatable and sharable with others who are doing the same. It is difficult to escape what sociologist Zygmunt Bauman called "liquid modernity."[82]

Expressive individualism has proved a poor fit, however, in working-class, small-town, and rural areas of democracies where more traditional labor is (or was) done. This incongruity has helped drive populism and polarization. Those tempted to reduce today's skepticism about liberalism to economics, who believe the answer is simply to redistribute wealth more widely, should note that the Right-populist Sweden Democrats are now the third-largest party in heavily redistributionist Sweden.[83] Clearly, culture is driving much of the reaction.

Political scientists Pippa Norris and Ronald Inglehart put the matter pejoratively: the problem is reactionary people and movements opposed to post-materialist values such as experimentation and autonomy. These people are "authoritarian-populist," a natural fit for the politics of "intolerance, racism, homophobia, misogyny, and xenophobia."[84] Social psychologist Jonathan Haidt has studied extensively how pejoratives of that sort do not go deep enough, and actually propel the polarization that is damaging democracy. Haidt articulates the problem more circumspectly and argues that those who resist open liberalism have more traditional, and broader, sets of moral foundations. Today's progressives have three moral foundations: care, sanctity (at least of the natural environment), and liberty. Those alienated from the new culture of open liberalism value three moral foundations in addition: loyalty, authority, and fairness (understood as getting only what you earn). They care about the sanctity of things other than the environment, such as the family and their country's symbols. They believe that disrespecting authority leads to disorder, that betraying friends and family is a terrible offense, and that receiving what you did not earn is an injustice. They find these values lacking in open liberalism.[85]

However we describe it, the uptake of open liberalism among rural, working-class, older, less educated, and more religious people is different from the uptake among urbanites, the young, and highly educated symbolic analysts. Open liberalism has filleted countless communities in wealthy democracies. Not only have jobs and wages shrunk, but so have the old institutions that open liberalism saw as barriers to self-realization—churches, labor unions, civic associations. What economists Angus Deaton and Anne Case call "deaths of despair"—from suicide, drug overdoses, and alcohol abuse—have risen sharply among white, middle-aged (aged forty-five to fifty-four) Americans without a college degree. In 1990 there were thirty such deaths per one hundred thousand people; by 2017 the figure had more than trebled to ninety-two per one hundred thousand people.[86]

Marriage, divorce, and childbirth—practices that affect the health of communities—are very different across classes as well. In the United States in 1970, the percentages of high school dropouts, high school graduates, and college graduates between the ages of twenty-five and fifty-five who were married were virtually the same—82 to 83 percent. By 2015 the figure for college graduates had fallen to 63 percent, but that for high school graduates had fallen much further, to 51 percent, and for high school dropouts even further, to 48 percent. Even more striking are the effects of class on births out of wedlock. In 1982, 33 percent of the least educated American women had had a child while not married; in 2006–8, 54 percent had done so. The comparable figures for the most educated women were 2 percent (1982) and 6 percent (2006–8).[87]

Cruelest of all, perhaps, is that the escape routes into the middle class are disappearing. The meritocracy promised by open liberalism has turned out to be a heritocracy. Open liberalism's erosion of traditional boundaries and norms was supposed to mean that, finally, any American child really could grow up to be the president or CEO of a large corporation. Talent, diligence, and flexibility were to be the tickets to success. Elite universities, the chief filters and developers of talent, strove for multiethnic, gender-balanced student bodies and faculties. Yet, perceptions of unfairness have risen, especially in the United States. In 2016 and 2020, 71 percent of Americans reported believing that "our economic system is rigged in favor of the wealthiest Americans"; those who strongly believed that rose from 31 to 40 percent.[88]

The suspicious are not imagining things. Social immobility has become severe. Figure 4.8 depicts the decline in the percentage of children who earn more than their parents at age thirty. After a slight increase in upward mobility for people born after 1964, a steady decline began for those born after 1970—that is, who reached age thirty on or after 2000. Part of the problem is education, but not simply in the purely academic sense. The elite university of today has its own codes, dialect, and tastes in clothes, food, decorating, and art; it has its own range of acceptable opinions and words about politics and religion. People from rural backgrounds or who are the

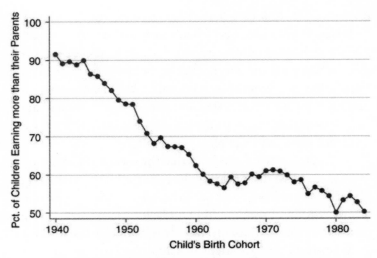

Figure 4.8. Social mobility in the United States over time.
(Source: Raj Chetty, David Grusky, Maximilien Hell, Nathaniel Hendren, Robert
Manduca, and Jimmy Narang, "The Fading American Dream: Trends in Absolute Income Mobility since 1940," *Science* 356, no. 6336 [April 28, 2017]: 398–406, https://
science.sciencemag.org/content/356/6336/398.full, retrieved on March 25, 2021.)

first in their family to attend an elite college report difficulty
fitting in.[89]

Philosopher Richard Reeves argues that the American
upper-middle class are "dream hoarders," placing a glass floor
beneath their children consisting of exclusive neighborhoods,
well-resourced private and public schools, tutoring for stan-
dardized tests, tax subsidies for college savings, legacy admis-
sions to colleges, and the ability to finance unpaid internships.[90]
Journalist David Brooks, who coined the "bobo" (bourgeois
bohemian) label for open liberals, now writes:

> I got a lot wrong about the bobos. I didn't anticipate
> how aggressively we would move to assert our cul-
> tural dominance, the way we would seek to impose

elite values through speech and thought codes. I underestimated the way the creative class would successfully raise barriers around itself to protect its
economic privilege—not just through schooling, but
through zoning regulations that keep home values
high, professional certification structures that keep
doctors' and lawyers' incomes high while blocking
competition from nurses and paralegals, and more.
And I underestimated our intolerance of ideological diversity. Over the past five decades, the number
of working-class and conservative voices in universities, the mainstream media, and other institutions
of elite culture has shrunk to a sprinkling.[91]

Adding insult to injury, from the standpoint of many in
the white working class, are the cultural changes that rapid
immigration has brought to their communities. As William
Galston writes, "This ongoing demographic shift [resulting
from accelerated immigration] has triggered palpable anxiety
among native-born Americans, especially those outside the
metropolitan areas that have always served as immigration
gateways. These Americans have a sense, understandable in
light of their experience, that they are the rightful owners of
the country and that new entrants threaten their control."[92]
Elites often reduce these convictions to simple bigotry, and no
doubt bigotry is at work. But research shows that lower levels
of social capital—trust among neighbors—are also responsible. In upper-middle-class urban and suburban areas, social
capital tends to be high enough that natives can absorb new-
comers from foreign lands. In poorer communities, low social
capital makes it more difficult to accept new neighbors with a
different language, dress, food, religion, and so on.[93]
    Nor has open liberalism favored black or Latino Ameri-

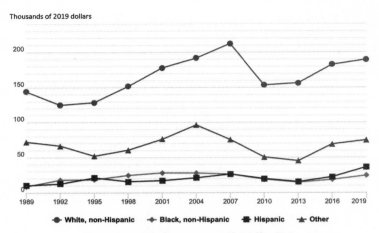

Figure 4.9. Median net worth in the U.S.
by race/ethnicity, 1989–2019.

(Source: U.S. Federal Reserve, "Survey of Consumer Finances visualization tool,"
https://www.federalreserve.gov/econres/scf/dataviz/scf/chart/#series:Net_Worth
;demographic:racecl4;population:all;units:median, generated on August 25, 2022.)

cans in the aggregate. Legal segregation and disenfranchisement
were ended in the mid-1960s under late-stage welfare liberalism. But while open liberalism has to its credit America's first
black president, on the whole it has done little better than its
predecessors at extending opportunities to all, regardless of
race or ethnicity. In the United States, the median net worth of
blacks and Latinos in 2016, taking inflation into account, was
roughly the same as it was in 1992—$20,000—while for whites
it grew from just below $110,000 to $170,000 (Figure 4.9), even
after the stumble of 2008–10. That is, the average white person
went from having 5.5 times the wealth of the average black
person in 1992 to having 8.5 times the wealth in 2016.

Even open liberalism's winners, the meritocrats themselves, are not always happy with the result. Diagnoses of anxiety and depression have increased sharply in recent years on

U.S. college campuses. A 2018 survey found that 63 percent of U.S. college students had felt "overwhelming anxiety" over the preceding year, and 23 percent reported being diagnosed with anxiety disorders.[94] A 2020 survey reported 26 percent of students said they had taken prescribed medication for mental health. Eleven percent reported having made a suicide attempt.[95] The stressors on these students are many and intense. Sociologist Joseph Davis has interviewed hundreds of students and reports that they often feel anxious or depressed because they hold themselves to an impossibly high standard of "standing out from the crowd," a norm that the meritocracy has pressed onto them.[96]

With a little imagination, one can always find danger signs for American democracy. Countries always have challenges and are never without social divides. But deindustrialization, an increasingly skewed distribution of wealth and opportunity, despairing communities, and institutions that trap people in one of two dominant groups, each regarding the other with contempt, have combined to make the situation dire. The center has been depopulated; more and more people cannot accept as good fellow democratic citizens those with whom they disagree even on trivial issues. Traumas and searing injustices that in less polarized times might have reduced the divide—video of the police suffocation-murder of George Floyd, a once-in-a-century pandemic—only widened it.

Polarization is milder in most European democracies, but similar patterns are evident. In the June 2016 Brexit vote, older, less educated, and rural voters tended to vote "leave," while younger, more educated, and urban voters chose "remain."[97] In Germany's 2018 parliamentary elections, the Right-populist Alternative for Germany (AfD) party did best among rural and older voters.[98] Polarization, in other words, is the handmaid of populism. But populism only aggravates the problem that produces it. Surveys in the United States in 2020 showed no depolarization from four years earlier. Donald Trump came to personify the divide, which only deepened each side's contempt for the other.[99]

Polarization implies symmetry, and it is important to recognize that only one side, the Right, has stormed the U.S. Capitol to try to overturn the duly administered election of a president. January 6, 2021, was a singularly dangerous moment for American democracy and a frightening one for democrats around the world. The danger did not end with the sunset that day. Behind the asymmetry of threat to democracy, however, lies an asymmetry of perceived power trends; many on the Right believe that time is not on their side, and that most authoritative institutions of society and government are hostile to them. But the embrace by many individuals and institutions on the Left of what author Wesley Yang has dubbed "the successor ideology"—which holds that every word and action by every individual and institution either supports or dismantles the hegemony of white, heterosexual, cis-male supremacy—has not helped matters.[100] Neither has the constant shifting of the boundary between acceptable and unacceptable speech. One symmetry between the poles is striking: the only major threat that the two tribes perceive in common is polarization itself.[101]

Not all of democracy's endangerment can be laid at the feet of open liberal internationalism. In the crucial American case, extreme polarization may be due in part to the two-party system, which gives everyone incentives to crush the opposition; democracies with proportional representation are less polarized.[102] All over the mature democracies, technological change is driving much of the problem, from automation to container ships to smartphones and social media.[103]

Technology and open liberalism, however, are mutually

supportive and reinforcing. The lurch away from liberalism that is pulling American democracy apart is to a significant extent powered by the content that America itself has been infusing into the environment for several decades. Open liberal internationalism did good work in the late twentieth century, but in its maturity it has become a project for the few. It has left millions behind in the wealthy democracies. It holds working-class and rural citizens in contempt when it notices them at all. It tells black, Latino, and young citizens that it is handing the future to them, but statistics tell a different story.

As in the 1930s and 1970s, the remedy for democracies is not to throw out liberalism. It is to rethink and reform it. Such is the case now, and I return to it in this book's final chapter. But the task is complicated by the second large challenge to democracy from the international environment. Ironically, the challenge is one of open liberalism's greatest achievements: the vanquishing of communism in the Soviet Union and, effectively, in China. China and Russia have both benefited from open liberal internationalism in many ways, but the leaders of both are keenly aware of how it handicaps them and favors the West. They now seek to reshape the international environment, to reengineer the ecosystem so as to suit their domestic regimes. We begin with China.

5
China
From Adaptation to Ecosystem Engineering

Deng Xiaoping Threads the Needle

It was May 18, 1989, and Deng Xiaoping, China's top leader, had decided to clear Tiananmen Square. For several weeks that spring, thousands of university students had encamped in Beijing's immense central plaza, flanked by the Forbidden City, the Great Hall of the People, and the mausoleum of Chairman Mao. The students had gathered initially to mourn Hu Yaobang, a beloved liberalizing reformer who had died of a heart attack the previous month. They stayed in the square, and thousands of ordinary citizens joined them. As the gathering grew, its theme shifted from mourning Hu to protesting China's lack of personal freedom and democracy.[1] The protests spread to 132 Chinese cities; every province had at least one.[2] When Mikhail Gorbachev, the Soviet reformist leader, arrived in Beijing on May 15 on a long-planned visit to herald improved Sino-Soviet relations, the protestors' numbers swelled to 1.2 million.

The crowd in Tiananmen Square was encouraged by news of democratic stirrings in Eastern Europe and Gorbachev's toleration of them. Zhao Ziyang, Hu's successor as the party's general secretary, recommended accommodating the students with more reform. Li Peng, China's premier, pressed a hard line. In the end, Deng sided with Li and fired Zhao.[3] Deng's attitude toward open challenges to Communist Party rule was very different from that of Zhao or Gorbachev. He was repulsed by chaos.[4] Order was what China needed to advance, and order meant tight control over society by the party. At a meeting with advisors, Deng pointed out that when party leaders in Hungary had made concessions to protestors, the protestors had only raised their demands.[5] It was Deng who had sacked the late Hu—then his right-hand man—three years earlier for failing to quash student demonstrations. Now there were ominous signs that the workers and growing middle class in China's cities supported the students.

Humiliated at having to relocate the welcoming ceremonies for Gorbachev from Tiananmen, and alarmed at the determination of the protestors and the evident sympathy for them in the upper reaches of the party itself, Deng declared martial law and prepared to call in People's Liberation Army (PLA) units. The troops and tanks did their work on June 3 and 4. Estimates of the number killed in the massacre vary wildly. China's official figure is two hundred. The British ambassador reported that his contacts in the upper reaches of the party put the figure at ten thousand.[6] Regardless of the true figure, Deng ended the immediate crisis but spawned others. The wealthy democracies of North America, Europe, and Japan quickly imposed severe economic sanctions. Within China, the party's public reputation hit the lowest point in several years. Some party leaders continued to fear for the future of the regime.

Deng understood that the Tiananmen Square crisis was partly of his own making, and that the party now had a fundamental decision to make. In 1978 he had defeated his rivals to succeed Mao Zedong and begun to experiment with market mechanisms in rural areas. With the wounds of Mao's Great Proletarian Cultural Revolution still fresh, Deng and his circle did in China in the 1980s what Franklin Roosevelt had done in America in the 1930s: they turned the country in a different direction so as to help it thrive without altering its domestic regime. They reoriented policy in a fundamental way to avoid regime change. No longer would China seek autarchy (self-sufficiency) through the destruction of traditional society and private property, as it had done under Mao. Events elsewhere in the world, including in China's own neighborhood of East Asia, showed Deng and his fellow reformers that becoming wealthy required "reform and opening up" (*gaige kaifang*). China had to start selling things to the capitalist countries and importing their technology. The party remained committed to socialism, true to the founding principles of the People's Republic, but would take a different route to it. It would have "socialism with Chinese characteristics."[7]

But Tiananmen Square made it clear that opening up China brought high risk to the rule of the party. Far from strengthening China's domestic regime, Deng's 1980s strategy nearly brought it down. Indeed, over in the Soviet bloc, the same strategy was toppling the rule of communist parties. The handwriting was on the wall. If ever there was a moment for a strategic reversal, a return to the Chinese Communist Party's old ways of isolation from the West, this was it.

Yet, following Tiananmen, Deng doubled down on reform and openness. He was convinced that there was no turning back. The survival of party rule, and hence China's prospects for greatness, still lay in the accelerated economic growth and acquisition of technology that could only come from more foreign trade and investment. "What should we do from now on?" Deng asked a group of PLA generals five days after the massacre. "In my opinion, we should continue to follow un-swervingly the basic line, principles, and policy we have formu-lated." His message to party leaders on June 16 was the same. The goal remained a quadrupling of the size of the economy from 1980 to 2000 and a "moderately developed country" by 2050. The damaging economic sanctions from the capitalist democracies would not last long. "Westerners would forget," Deng assured party officials.[8]

By the end of 1989 Deng had retired from party leader-ship. But he remained the power behind the throne, and at the Fourth Plenum of the Thirteenth Party Congress, held later that same month, his successor, Jiang Zemin, and other new lead-ers hewed closely to Deng's "reform and open up" strategy.[9]

Two and a half years later, in late 1991, westerners still had not forgotten about Tiananmen Square. China remained ostracized at the United Nations and in human rights fora. Most sanctions remained in place. The flow of foreign invest-ment essential to Deng's strategy for China had not resumed. The wealthy democratic world was not going to allow China to become a rich and powerful country unless it made changes that the party simply could not accept. The United States and other Western democracies clearly wanted the country to do as the Soviet Union and Eastern Europe had done and tran-sition to multiparty democracy. If it did that, the taps would reopen, and China would be welcomed into the liberal inter-national order.

But for the Communist Party's leadership, that price would be far too high. In the autumn of 1991 the Soviet Union was collapsing as its ruling communist party disintegrated. That was where liberal-democratic reform led; that, it seemed, was what the West wanted to happen to China. On his own view—shared by most of the party's leadership—Deng had acted in Tiananmen Square in June 1989 to save China from chaos and collapse. The wealthy democracies of North America and Europe were persecuting China for this act of self-preservation. The entire international order was biased against China.

In November 1991 China's propaganda ministry circulated a "White Paper" among the country's diplomats on how to defend the country against foreign charges that it violated human rights. Written by propagandist Zhu Muzhi, the paper opened with a reminder of how in the past Western imperialists were among the worst violators of human rights in China.[10] From there, it argued that state sovereignty—which the party had labored to build for China—is an essential condition for human rights, and that human rights were an internal affair for each country. In pressing China to democratize, the Western powers were violating its sovereignty. They were doing to China what they had done in the nineteenth century, only through different means. The party knew that the "right to subsistence" was the paramount human right, and that anyone who evaluated a country's practices must take its specific situation into account.

Zhu's White Paper has guided Chinese officials in human rights fora and discussions ever since.[11] For many years, the 1991 guidelines were followed in a quiet way, as Beijing followed Deng's "hide and bide" strategy of inconspicuousness and patience. Deng gambled that China could remain open, and hence continue to grow and develop its economy and society, while remaining a political anomaly in the liberal international order, a one-party state. The gamble paid off handsomely, as over the course of the 1990s China began to grow again. In real terms, its gross domestic product grew by more than a factor of six between 1980 and 2000.[12] In 2001 it officially joined the World Trade Organization (WTO), and its exports and foreign investment accelerated still more. By one standard measure, China's GDP surpassed that of the United States in 2016; by another, many (but not all) economists say it is on track to do so by 2030.[13]

But the risks remain. As Susan Shirk has written, "China's leaders face a troubling paradox. The more developed and prosperous the country becomes, the more insecure and threatened they feel."[14] Xi Jinping was elected party leader and national president in 2012. Under his leadership, the ruling party has decided to eliminate the paradox by abandoning "hide and bide." China was going to start to try, directly and openly, to reengineer the international ecosystem.

The International Environment versus Authoritarian China

For many years, analysts of global order predicted that, with Western cooperation, China would become a "responsible stakeholder" in the liberal international order. It would not try to wreck or even substantially change the order. Participation in the liberal international order had propelled China to its current wealth and power. Why would it change a system that has brought it so far—that has put it in a position to become a superpower?[15]

But China's leaders are discontented with the liberal bias built into their country's international environment. In the twenty-first century, the party has begun to assert both that the West, especially the United States, is a human rights hypocrite, and that China has its own conception of human rights that it follows consistently.[16] Xi Jinping has proclaimed that developing nations would do well to imitate China's emphases on development and on "economic and social rights."[17] The principles of Zhu Muzhi's 1991 White Paper are now asserted aggressively at human rights fora and in statements to the press.

The party's complaints about international order extend

beyond human rights. On a number of issues, from trade and finance to the cyber realm, party officials believe that this order is biased against China.[18] Analysts observe that in international finance China wants to be a "rule-maker" not a "rule-taker."[19] Nadège Rolland notes that official discourse about international order frequently uses the phrase "unfair and unreasonable" (*bu gongzheng, bu heli*). Chinese officials distinguish "international order" from "world order." *International* order is the legal system that recognizes the sovereign equality of all states, and China accepts it as legitimate. *World* order, however, is unfair and unreasonable because it is really a Pax Americana that seeks to maintain the dominance of the West and to keep China and other less developed countries in their places. World order imposes Western values and institutions on countries to which they are ill suited. At a meeting with Joe Biden, then the U.S. vice president, in 2011, Xi was reportedly obsessed with the Arab Uprising, which he saw as a case of liberalism and democratization pressing chaos and instability onto orderly societies.[20]

When party officials say that world order is biased against China, they mean, of course, *their* China, the one that they have built: authoritarian-capitalist, socialist with Chinese characteristics, ruled by a party determined to hold on to its monopoly on power. Americans and other liberal democrats insist that they would welcome a different China, with the same people, culture, and enterprise, but under a liberal-democratic regime. Xi and the leadership are determined not to have that China. Not only would it end the party's monopoly on power, it also would divide, weaken, and perhaps destroy their country. Indeed, they suspect that is precisely what the Americans want. To be powerful, China must be ruled by the party, the only entity equipped with the wisdom to unify and guide the nation toward a glorious future.

Democrats may instinctively believe that China's leaders are cynical or self-deceiving—that they really care only about their own power, and that they cloak that power in palpably false rhetoric about Chinese greatness, socialism, and a "shared future for mankind." But evidence suggest that party leaders actually believe their own propaganda. They have reason to do so. The party has closely studied Soviet reform and collapse in the late 1980s and early 1990s. Back in 1989 Deng reportedly called Gorbachev an "idiot" for giving political liberalization priority over economic reform.[21] A cold-blooded reading of history would suggest that Deng was right.

Then there is China's own history of domestic disorder and violence and of foreign domination. The People's Republic, founded in 1949, has been marked by two periods of severe disorder. The Great Leap Forward of 1958–62, in which Mao Zedong and the party tried to force the rapid collectivization of farming, starved as many as thirty million to death.[22] The Cultural Revolution of 1966–76, in which Mao and the party tried to destroy the remnants of China's traditional feudal culture, killed as many as 1.6 million people (excluding battle deaths).[23]

Those post-1949 periods of chaos and mass death were imposed from the top, but one need look only a few years earlier to see bottom-up unrest and destruction. The twenty-three-year civil war between the Communist Party and the Nationalist or Kuomintang Party of Chiang Kai-Shek killed between six million and ten million people.[24] China had experienced an earlier revolution in 1911, replacing the ancient monarchy with a republic. Prior to that, the Boxer Rebellion against imperialists and Christians (1899–1901) killed an estimated one hundred thousand. The Taiping Rebellion (1850–64), in which a Christian-syncretist group fought against the Qing Dynasty, was probably the most lethal civil war in history, with an estimated death toll of twenty million.[25]

Over the past two generations, China has adapted extensively to outside pressure by reforming its economy. But its ruling party will never adapt to the point of risking regime change. The preservation of the country's authoritarian-capitalist domestic regime is not up for negotiation. In 1989 the party sacrificed some economic growth in the medium term, enduring harsh economic sanctions, for the long-term preservation of its monopoly on power. It is willing to do so again if need be.

In being bound and determined to thrive while maintaining its domestic regime, China is no different from the United States. Neither country wants to adapt to its environment to the point of jeopardizing its domestic order. In 2001 political scientist Rosemary Foot noted that China faced a dilemma: whether to fully invest in the norms of the liberal international order, or to build coalitions with states that, like China, had objections to aspects of that order.[26] Under Xi, China has begun to do the latter—to do something like the United States did at the end of World War II. China is attempting to alter the bias in its international environment so that it will select for its own regime type rather than a hated alternative. Deng Xiaoping always intended for the "hide and bide" strategy to be temporary. Under Xi, China has abandoned it in favor of "going out."

China and the United States are not doomed to spiral into a dangerous cold war, much less a hot one. Nor must East and West fall into a civilizational struggle. But there is a real and serious conflict of interest between the two giants: Will the international ecosystem select for democracy or authoritarianism? Who will engineer it? Understanding China's position and goals requires understanding the complex domestic regime it is trying to protect.

Protecting China's Domestic Regime

Article I of China's 1982 constitution declares that China is a "socialist state under the people's democratic dictatorship led by the working class and based on the alliance of workers and peasants." Article III refers to its "democratic centralism." Western scholars characterize China's regime in various ways. Political theorist Daniel Bell calls it "democratic-meritocratic." It is meritocratic, Bell argues, because officials rise in the ruling party through talent, and democratic because the party serves the interests of the people by fostering conditions for prosperity and stability.[27] Azar Gat represents many in labeling China's regime "authoritarian capitalist."[28] Stefan Halper refers to it as "market authoritarian."[29] Kenneth Lieberthal calls it "fragmented authoritarian."[30] Nicholas Kristof's clever phrase is "Market-Leninist."[31]

Each of these labels captures something important about the regime. The party monopolizes political power and ruthlessly deals with any potential challengers. It also has been fragmented rather than rigorously centralized. More than 60 percent of China's economy is privately owned.[32] The educational system and the party itself reward performance, making China a kind of meritocracy. We might add that it is not a dictatorship; the upper echelons of the party elect its top leaders (although that process is sealed from view and Chinese who have tried to lift the lid have been imprisoned), and yet Xi is the strongest leader since Mao Zedong.[33]

Any domestic regime has a number of facets. The important question for us is: Which of these facets does the party's leadership believe is most threatened by the international environment? When Chinese complain about a biased international order, against what do they believe that order is biased?

One potential threat to the regime comes from the far

Left, from the Maoism that China has never completely gotten over. In recent years, neo-Maoists have called for redistribution of wealth and a revival of old-style propaganda. As Xi
Jinping was consolidating power in the Chinese Communist
Party in early 2012, he purged Bo Xilai, a prominent rival who
was mayor of the inland megacity of Chongqing. Bo had developed a leftist critique of the country's status quo and had
begun to revive Maoist language.[34] Convicted for corruption,
Bo today sits in prison. Yet, Maoism is not a dire threat and
certainly does not press on China from the outside. Rump
Maoist groups still exist in India, the Philippines, Peru, and
Berkeley, California, but these are not exporting revolution to
China. There would be little sense in Xi meeting the Maoist
threat by reshaping the international order.

THE CHIEF THREAT: CONSTITUTIONAL DEMOCRACY

The party has made clear what it regards as its chief ideological
threat: "Western constitutional democracy." In 2013, shortly
after Xi's elevation to party head, a memorandum called "Document No. 9" circulated among the party's upper echelons. The
memorandum's main heading is "Noteworthy Problems Related to the Current State of the Ideological Sphere," and it
focuses entirely on Western constitutional democracy. Among
the central aims of this alien ideology, says Document No. 9,
are "separation of powers, the multi-party system, general elections, independent judiciaries, nationalized armies, and other
characteristics. These are the capitalist class's concepts of a nation, political model, and system design." The ideology is explicitly called "Western" and the document repudiates its claim
to be universal and to transcend cultures.

This alien set of doctrines, says the document, brings all

sorts of destructive forces in its train, including the notion of "civil society"; the primacy of individual rights over the state; "neoliberalism," or the "market omnipotence" that has wreaked havoc in so many countries; "freedom of the press" from "party discipline"; "historical nihilism," that is, denigration of the history of the People's Republic and the Communist Party; and complaints that reform has not gone far enough in China. Especially worrisome, says the document, is that Western constitutional democracy has infiltrated China and attracted support among many Chinese citizens. These people openly criticize the party by saying that China "has a constitution but no constitutional government" and "should catch up with the rest of the world's trend toward constitutional government." Foreigners and Chinese dissidents, Document No. 9 claims, are collaborating to disseminate non-Chinese ideas about human rights. The document makes clear the need for vigilance against this ideology and outlines steps that the party must take to defeat it.[35] Although it is unclear who authored Document No. 9, it clearly was approved by Xi.[36]

With respect to China's international environment, then, the party is trying to protect particular components of its own domestic power that are exposed to liberal democracy—its control over the making, interpretation, and execution of the law and its ability to fend off all competitors for that control. But we cannot stop there. Since Deng led China in the 1980s, the party has believed that maintaining its power entails a certain orientation of policy—one quite different from the orientation under Mao, and also one not well understood outside of China.

SOCIALISM WITH CHINESE CHARACTERISTICS

The party believes that its monopoly on political power goes hand-in-glove with its goal to "rejuvenate" the Chinese nation, to leave behind forever its "century of humiliation" from the 1840s through the 1940s, when it was picked apart by foreign powers. It has elaborate plans and guidelines to continue China along the path to rejuvenation while maintaining its grip. Those guidelines were mostly set by Deng Xiaoping and his inner circle in the late 1970s and early 1980s. To this day, party leadership is adamant that adherence to the guidelines is necessary to the entwined goals of making China great again and maintaining the party's grip on power. Just as many Americans identify open liberalism with American democracy itself, the Chinese Communist Party considers "socialism with Chinese characteristics" integral to its domestic regime.

"Socialism with Chinese characteristics": the clumsy phrase is still deployed relentlessly in party descriptions of China's regime. To foreigners it may seem a sentimental or cynical attempt to salvage the label "socialist" for what is clearly a mostly capitalist economy. We can argue that the party's meticulous theorizing about its brand of socialism tortures logic, distorts history, and engages in heroic rationalization. But the theorizing is not a game. Theorists in the party continue to work out what the phrase means, how to use it to make sense of China's history and current situation, and how it can chart the country's future path. A careful reading of party officials' words and policies suggest that "socialism with Chinese characteristics" is a deadly serious label.

Deng, who coined the phrase, never abandoned Marxism. But he was convinced by the catastrophes of the Maoist years that for China to become socialist, and therefore a great power, it needed to change course, to "seek truth from facts" and "liberate the forces of production."[37] Doing so meant experimenting with market mechanisms in some areas of the economy, but not betraying socialism for capitalism. For Deng, markets alone did not make a country capitalist. Capitalism and socialism are overarching systems; a capitalist country may have some public ownership, and a socialist country may include some private ownership.[38]

The difference between socialism and capitalism lies in the overall purpose of each. For capitalism, that purpose was profit. For socialism, it was "social benefit and meeting the needs of all people" (*gongtongti fuwu*). Deng called for the Four Modernizations—agriculture, industry, defense, and science and technology—to achieve a "moderately well-off country" (*xiaokang de guijia*). That is a phrase that all subsequent Chinese leaders, including Xi Jinping, have continued to use. The marks of a moderately well-off country are "managing profound risks . . . poverty alleviation, and environmental health."[39] Ensuring progress toward these goals requires "socialist democracy," with seven components: "electoral democracy" (a complex system, uncompetitive except at the local level); "consultative democracy" (consulting the other eight political parties, all of which are small and not remotely competitive with the party); "grassroots democracy" (local involvement in governance); "minority nationalities policy" (meeting the interests of non-Han citizens); "rule of law" and "leadership of the Communist Party" (understood in tandem as prohibiting the rule of one person and serving the goal of socialism); and "human rights" (chief of which is the right to "socio-economic well-being").[40]

The prose is tiresome, but it makes clear that China's rulers continue to believe that the country needs a great deal of private enterprise in order to liberate (*jiefang*) and advance (*fazhan*) its "productive forces." But Xi, in particular, has renewed emphasis on the predominance of the publicly owned sector: "the dominant role of public ownership and the leading role of the state sector must not change."[41] Even privately owned companies must be subordinate to the party. The party must have ultimate control over the economy so as to make sure it serves socialist, not capitalist, goals—that is, "common prosperity [*gongtong fuyu*] for the whole people" and harmony with the natural environment.[42]

THE PARTY'S GROWING CONTROL

Long gone are the days when the Chinese Communist Party owned all of the means of production. Yet, it is at pains to make sure that state-owned enterprises (SOEs) remain pillars of the economy. As of 2017, roughly 150,000 SOEs existed, with more than $21 million in assets and forty million employees.[43] The most important of these are the centrally controlled SOEs, including three oil companies.[44] The China Development Bank and Export-Import Bank of China, which finance most projects in the Belt and Road Initiative, are owned by the state. SOEs tend to have close ties to high party officials.[45] These firms' inefficiencies impose high opportunity costs on China's economy, suggesting that the party must have in mind for them political and social purposes not captured in standard economic analysis.

National champions such as the Alibaba Group (which owns Alibaba and Alipay), Tencent (owner of WeChat), and Huawei are privately owned. But "private" does not mean what it once meant. The party has planted members in companies and pushed management to shed debt and pursue "socialist" goals. SOEs have been swallowing up private firms as well. Clearly a major concern of Xi is that, without government control, private companies will take on excessive risk.[46] More fundamentally, the dilution of private ownership shows that Xi is serious that the public must dominate the private economy. An official document from September 2020 lays out how the party is recruiting and placing "united front work" cadres among shareholders and managers of companies, as well as in chambers of commerce and industry associations. A crucial goal is "to guide private economy practitioners to continuously increase their political, ideological, and emotional identification with the CCP and socialism with Chinese characteristics" and who are "reliable and useful at critical moments."[47]

In other areas of society, too, the party has tightened its control. The story is not a simple one of growing brute authoritarianism. In fact, the party has made its governance more transparent and open to citizen input even as it has increased control. In a set of ingenious moves, it has found ways to use digital technology to transcend the old trade-off between a government's power and its accountability.

During the early twenty-first century, when Hu Jintao and Wen Jiabao were China's main leaders, local governments in megacities such as Guangzhou and Shanghai began to experiment with Open Government Information Regulations. These required the local party to disclose to citizens information on budgets and other matters. In 2008 the national Communist Party adopted these regulations. The party also came increasingly to encourage public participation in policy formation and change through online comments on proposed national legislation. Public perceptions of government performance improved.[48]

At the same time, the party began to harness social media to uncover dissent, identify problems, shape public discourse, and mobilize opinion.[49] The party extended its power by exploiting the digital revolution to surround itself with vast amounts of information about what citizens want and how they feel and act.[50] Democratic theory assumes that when we say that a government is accountable, we mean that if it does not perform adequately, the voters will throw it out of office. But China's rulers purport to have learned how to satisfy their people while bypassing the mechanisms of democratic theory. This is not an old-style Communist Party that crushes all dissent, but a twenty-first-century party that monitors discontent and appeases it before it can grow.

Thus power has become more and more concentrated in the national party. Rivals to Xi Jinping have been purged; censorship increased; in some parts of the country a "social credit" system monitors all sorts of individual action and punishes "antisocial" behavior; limits to the president's term in office have ended; "Xi Jinping Thought" has become part of the country's constitution. State control over religious practice has increased, and hence so has persecution of Christians, Muslims, and others who practice outside of officially sanctioned bodies. The "one country, two systems" model that tolerated constitutional democracy in Hong Kong has all but disappeared.[51] Most notoriously, the party has set about to crush dissent in the majority-Muslim province of Xinjiang by forcing an estimated million Uighurs into residential "Vocational Educational and Training Centers."[52]

Xi and China's other leaders are adamant that permanent party rule is essential to making China great again. They know that they need to deliver economic growth to ensure party rule. Instrumental to those goals, and entangled with them, is the general strategy that China has followed for two generations. China must remain economically open to the outside world. It must retain a large private sector. But the party must dominate the economy to choke off other potential power centers and to minimize the risks of disruption, liberal-democratic ideology, and heavy inequality.

BUT IS THE PARTY WORRIED?

But is the party really bothered by outside forces? Does it need to manipulate the international environment to keep itself in

Table 5.1. Chinese public overall satisfaction with central government, 2003–16.

	2003	2004	2005	2007	2009	2011	2015	2016
1	1.3	1.8	1.4	0.6	0.3	1.2	0.4	0.3
2	7.6	9.5	7.6	5.2	2.9	5.0	6.3	4.0
3	60.7	59.2	59.8	54.1	50.9	54.5	55.2	61.5
4	25.4	22.9	20.7	38.2	45.0	37.3	37.6	31.6
Average	3.16	3.11	3.11	3.32	3.41	3.3	3.31	3.3
% dissatisfied	8.9	11.3	9.0	5.8	3.2	6.2	6.7	4.3
% satisfied	86.1	82.1	80.5	92.3	95.9	91.8	92.8	93.1

Source: Edward Cunningham, Tony Saich, and Jessie Turiel, *Understanding CCP Resilience: Surveying Chinese Public Opinion through Time* (Cambridge, Mass.: Ash Center for Democratic Governance and Innovation, 2020), 3, https://ash.harvard.edu/files/ash/files/final_policy _brief_7.6.2020.pdf.

power? A number of surveys have indicated a Chinese public broadly satisfied with the way they are governed. The Ash Center at the Harvard Kennedy School reports high and growing contentment with the central government.[53] Note in Table 5.1 that average satisfaction with China's central government on a 1 to 4 scale was already 3.16 in 2003, and that by 2016 it had risen to 3.3. (Satisfaction with local government started out much lower and rose dramatically during the same period.) China's is not a regime in immediate danger of collapse.

Of course, the problem of surveys in authoritarian countries applies here: no doubt some Chinese citizens are afraid to admit to any dissatisfaction with their government, particularly to a stranger asking them questions on behalf of a foreign entity. Yet, the survey does contain some variation and hence some information about citizen sentiment; Row 4 ("highly satisfied") does not register one hundred across the board.

Scholars attribute this relative satisfaction to the established fact that Chinese people, on the whole, tend to judge a

Table 5.2. Chinese opinion on what
makes a country democratic.

Feature of Government	Percentage Saying Essential to Democracy
Freedom to organize into political groups	5.3
Freedom to demonstrate in public	6.1
Media free to criticize government	12.3
Multiple parties compete freely	13.8
Legislative oversight	18.2
No corruption	33.9
Quality public services	33.9
Law and order	36.4
Basic necessities (food, shelter) for all	42.6

Source: "Asian Barometer Survey (2011)," QQ 86–88, Hu Fu Center for East Asian Democratic Studies, National Taiwan University, http://www.asianbarometer.org.

government not by the rightness of its principles or institutions but rather by its performance—how well it provides what they think a government should provide. A 2011 Asian Barometer Survey asked Chinese citizens which qualities were most essential to a democracy. The results are in Table 5.2.

Note that Chinese are relatively uninterested in the first five features, which are formal rights and mechanisms that adherents of constitutional democracy generally consider essential. The last four, which are substantive goods, are relatively more important to the Chinese.[54]

Lee Kuan Yew, the founder of the modern state of Singapore, would recognize these results. It was Lee who became famous in the 1990s for his "Asian Values" thesis, a justification for the authoritarian-capitalist regime he established in his city-state. "What Asians value may not necessarily be what Americans or Europeans value. Westerners value the freedoms and liberties of the individual," said Lee in a typical statement. "As an Asian of Chinese cultural background, my values are for a government which is honest, effective, and efficient."[55] In fact, plenty of Asians, including Chinese, value civil liberties highly; certainly millions of Hong Kongers and Taiwanese do. Some of the attachment to performance over institutions may result from effective propaganda and socialization by the party. Notwithstanding, the fact is that the Chinese public on the whole cares more about performance.

On the other hand, a 2019 study by the Eurasia Group Foundation found that nearly 54 percent of Chinese surveyed said they would like for their system of government over the next two decades to become more like the U.S. system. Twentynine percent were neutral on the question, and just over 17 percent did not want China's regime to become more like America's. Nearly 44 percent reported very favorable or somewhat favorable attitudes toward U.S. democracy.[56] The Chinese public may admire their government's performance, but many still would like more civil rights and political competition. Widespread protests in November 2022 over serial COVID-19 lockdowns show that the party is flirting with the limits of the public's patience.[57]

More important, it is hard to conclude that a ruling party so coercive of its own citizenry feels secure. The government's deepening digital system of monitoring, rewarding, and punishing citizens suggests that its leaders do worry about the regime's legitimacy. The persecution of Muslims in Xinjiang has damaged China's global reputation. The brutal ending of self-government in Hong Kong has ruined China's chances of reincorporating Taiwan peacefully. Since the 1990s Beijing had dangled the Hong Kong "one country, two systems" model before the Taiwanese to entice them into rejoining the mainland.

Xi and colleagues obviously concluded that the democratic threat in Hong Kong was serious enough to justify increasing the cost of reunification with Taiwan.[58]

Xi has not acted like a man untroubled. As he rose in the party in the early years of this century, he worried that China faced an emerging set of challenges that the party was not meeting. Corruption was rampant. The party lacked a clear governing ideology. Environmental protection and health care were inadequate for large numbers of people. Two hundred million migrant workers "could not legally live, receive medical care, or educate their children in the cities in which they worked." The year 2010 saw more than 180,000 popular protests in the country. Economic growth relied too heavily on investment, leading to alarming levels of public and private debt. Although a manufacturing juggernaut, China was not moving into the ranks of advanced economies by innovating in the service sector or industrial design. The years of Hu Jintao's leadership (2002–12) were to become known as the "lost decade." It was worries about a failing system that led Xi to centralize power.[59]

Like his predecessors, Xi is haunted by the Soviet collapse of 1991. He knows that economic development is no guarantee against secessionist movements in restive provinces such as Tibet and Xinjiang.[60] In speeches he has noted that the first republics to secede from the Soviet Union were the Baltic states, the wealthiest of all (in per capita terms). Xi also has argued that the Soviets' root problem was that their "ideals and beliefs were shaken"—that is, that Soviets lost confidence in communism. The turn back toward Maoist techniques of thought control, in the form of Xi's personality cult; the revival of more traditional propaganda and prohibition of "thought heresy" and "historical nihilism"; the mandatory presence of party officials in the management of both public and private companies; the banning of criticism of the party, including the catastrophes it visited upon China in the Great Leap Forward and Cultural Revolution: these are not the actions of a regime at ease.[61]

Adaptation and Defiance

China under party rule has entrapped itself. It has deeply enmeshed itself with the United States and other constitutional democracies in the international order that they built and maintain. That order, as we saw in Chapter 3, was designed to perpetuate liberal democracy in the original industrial countries of North America, Western Europe, and Japan. The Chinese Communist Party well knows that the same openness that exposes it to the liberal-democratic threat has also made it the economic juggernaut that it is today. Closing back up would be disastrous for the country's global position and ultimately for the regime.

Deng Xiaoping and his successors have been well aware of this contradiction and the risks it brings to party rule and their grand strategy to rejuvenate China. In May 1989 Deng determined that the country would stay the course he had begun to set eleven years earlier, at the Third Plenum of the Eleventh Party Congress. He declared that the country nevertheless would not turn back toward closedness and full party-state control of the economy. It would continue to grow in wealth by becoming an exporter of manufactures and moving up the global production hierarchy. But it would not allow openness to endanger the party's monopoly on power. Socialism with Chinese characteristics would continue to be the grand strategy. China would remain open for business but not for democracy.

How the party managed to do that makes for a complicated story. The tug-of-war between China and the United States over international trading rules and institutions is instructive. U.S. administrations have wanted trading rules that favor U.S.-style liberal democracy, including the open liberalism that has infused it for several decades. Chinese leaders have wanted rules that favor socialism with Chinese characteristics.

CHINA JOINS THE WTO

Successor to the General Agreement on Tariffs and Trade (GATT) that was inaugurated in 1947, the Geneva-based WTO is a pillar of the liberal international order. It encourages growth in international trade, and hence in overall global wealth, by sponsoring negotiations among countries to lower trade barriers, monitoring compliance, and ruling on trade disputes. In joining the WTO, a country commits to following its rules about openness; in return, all other members agree not to discriminate against that country's exports. WTO members give up some control over their economies in return for economic efficiency and greater overall growth. Like many other components of the liberal international order, the WTO is biased in favor of free-market economies. "Non-market economies" may be punished with severe punitive tariffs if the WTO finds that they have violated certain rules. In evolutionary language, the WTO selects for market economics by punishing or excluding countries that do not privatize.

As far back as 1986, in the early years of China's reforms, Deng Xiaoping sought Chinese membership in the GATT. Fallout from the Tiananmen Square massacre of 1989 froze that effort. Undaunted, Deng put the talented and determined Zhu Rongji in charge of carrying forward more economic reform so as to position China for membership later. Zhu believed that the country needed to turn over still more production to its private sector. In the 1990s the party-state sold off its small SOEs. It "corporatized" its large ones, selling shares to private investors while making sure the party retained majority interests.[62]

As Zhu was fitting China's economy for the GATT, the GATT itself was becoming more intrusive under the transforming hand of open liberal internationalism (see Chapter 4). In 1994 member states agreed to give the institution teeth by constructing a procedure for settling trade disputes among members. What had been a framework for negotiations became the WTO, a more comprehensive institution that made it harder for members to protect their domestic producers from foreign competition. Membership in the club became more lucrative than ever, and China redoubled its efforts to join, even though the WTO would put even more pressure on China to privatize its economy.

Early in his presidency (1993–2001), Bill Clinton was skeptical of allowing the "butchers of Beijing"—a reference to the Tiananmen Square massacre of 1989—into the GATT. Organized labor and advocates for human rights and the environment—all important in Democratic Party politics—opposed Chinese accession as well. But in the mid-1990s Clinton had a change of heart. The best way to induce China to democratize, Clinton decided, was to encourage it to open its economy still more. "By joining the WTO," the U.S. president said, "China is not simply agreeing to import more of our products; it is agreeing to import one of democracy's most cherished values: economic freedom. . . . We know how much the Internet has changed America, and we are already an open society. Imagine how much it could change China. . . . WTO membership is not in and of itself a human-rights policy. But still, it is likely to have a profound impact on human rights and political liberty."[63] Clinton was stating a bipartisan thesis; in 1994 the right-of-center Heritage Foundation had averred that "by increasing prosperity in China through greater trade, the U.S. can help to create the economic freedoms that are the foundation upon which political freedom will someday emerge."[64]

Zhu and Jiang Zemin, who succeeded Deng as China's president and the party's general secretary, were confident that China could defy the Americans' bipartisan liberal theory and join the WTO without dooming the rule of the Communist Party. China would need to adapt, to be sure, but the party could maintain its monopoly on power. Beijing and Washington both drove a hard bargain, and negotiations nearly broke down several times. Washington insisted that China be classified as a "non-market economy" for fifteen years, which would allow other countries to slap severe punitive tariffs on it if it were ruled guilty of "dumping," or exporting goods at below-market prices. Each side played brinkmanship, each side gave a bit, and on November 15, 2000, a deal was struck.[65] Just over a year later—on December 11, 2001—China officially joined the WTO.

Membership did indeed drive further privatization of China's economy. Beijing agreed to allow foreign firms to do retail business in China without Chinese intermediaries; to allow foreign banks to do business with Chinese counterparts; to subject SOEs to WTO rules about government procurement; to import fifty foreign films each year; and to abide by rules on intellectual property. But China found workarounds to maintain and even increase state control of the economy in other areas. Hu and Wen even turned the tables on the liberal West by subtly reshaping the international economic order to favor China's model.

First, Beijing insisted on being categorized as a "developing country," meaning that the WTO granted it extra time to liberalize its economy.[66] As of 2022 China retained developing-country status even though its economy was the world's second largest. In holding on to this designation, China weakened the WTO's norm of distinguishing developing from developed economies.

Second, the Hu-Wen government blocked a proposed rule that would have handicapped China's ability to regulate the value of its currency, the renminbi. After joining the WTO, China's central bank kept the value of the renminbi artificially low in order to keep Chinese exports artificially high. Because doing so did not violate WTO rules, the George W. Bush administration applied to another institution in the liberal order, the International Monetary Fund (IMF), for a remedy. In 2007 Henry Paulson, the U.S. Treasury secretary, prevailed upon the IMF to promulgate a new rule against "misaligned currencies," a net that would have ensnared China. But as the case against China gathered momentum, the 2007–8 financial crisis hit the United States and then much of the world. Paulson suddenly found that he needed China to help keep the global economy afloat and dropped the idea of calling China out on currency manipulation. With America's blessing, the IMF rescinded its "misaligned currencies" rule in 2009.[67]

Third, the party brought China's larger SOEs under stricter control. The State-Owned Assets and Administration Commission gave the central government control over 196 large SOEs. Government-set interest rates meant that banks could lend to the favored SOEs with little or no risk.[68] Fourth, the government established a National Development and Reform Commission to administer the next Five-Year Plan. The commission set prices of major commodities such as "electricity, oil, gasoline, natural gas, and water." Fifth, the Hu-Wen government set up a formal plan to develop science and technology for the years 2006 to 2020 to help China catch up to and surpass the mature democracies in those areas.

Finally, and most notoriously, China continued to require

foreign investors to share technology with Chinese partners. Indeed, after the 2008 recession, Beijing stepped up its efforts to increase the profit to China from China's exports—meaning, to produce more of the high-value components and the intellectual property.[69] Engaging in what Western companies regarded as intellectual property theft, Chinese companies moved rapidly up in the world. By 2015 its adoptions and modifications of foreign technology had enabled China to develop the world's fastest trains.[70] As a WTO member, China illustrates political scientist Sonal Pandya's finding that countries that restrict foreign direct investment tend to be autocracies that favor certain domestic producers and help them acquire foreign technology.[71]

These end runs allowed China to remain competitive while also protecting "socialism with Chinese characteristics." They thereby did something more fundamental and far-reaching. They showed the world that it was possible to thrive inside the liberal international ecosystem yet resist pressure from that ecosystem to move to a more market-based economy and democratic polity. In finding loopholes in WTO and IMF rules, the party fed new information into the international environment. China's government was not intentionally putting direct pressure on other countries to adopt its domestic system. It was simply rendering the liberal bias of the international economic order less potent by demonstrating to other governments that there were ways around it.

This is not a story of nefarious China duping the innocent, guileless constitutional democracies. China was only doing what the United States and other countries had done as a matter of course: shaping its environment to its advantage, so that it could flourish without having to modify its domestic regime. The George W. Bush administration tried to stack the deck against China's model, and China—aided by the 2008 financial meltdown—outplayed the Americans.

OBAMA'S MOVE:
THE TRANS-PACIFIC PARTNERSHIP

The Obama administration's response was the Trans-Pacific Partnership (TPP). The TPP was designed to take international commerce to another level by reducing informal barriers to trade for which China was notorious, such as government favoritism of domestic producers and lax environmental and labor standards. China was not a part of the negotiations, and the TPP would intentionally disallow the kind of state intrusion into industry exemplified by China's large SOE sector.[72]

Obama was explicit that the TPP was aimed at China's attempt to make the international environment friendlier to its domestic model. "We can't let countries like China write the rules of the global economy," said the U.S. president. "We should write those rules." In the early stages of TPP negotiation, China was hostile to the pact, openly stating that it was a ploy to keep it from rising in the world. But as the TPP neared completion, Beijing took a more neutral tone, and U.S. National Security Advisor Susan Rice said that all countries meeting the TPP's standards, including China, would be welcome to join.

But becoming a Trans-Pacific partner would have weakened key components of socialism with Chinese characteristics. In what were informally called the "anti-China" provisions, SOEs would not be allowed to discriminate in favor of national companies; if China joined the TPP, it would need to let data flow freely across its borders; its antitrust laws would need to serve efficiency and consumer welfare; and decision procedures would need to be transparent.[73] China could either stay out and suffer, allowing some of its neighbors to draw closer to the United States; or it could join and adapt, submitting to rules that would alter its domestic political economy and restore the international environment to its old liberal state.

In January 2017, in one of his first acts as U.S. president, Donald Trump relieved Xi of his dilemma by withdrawing the United States itself from the TPP. Trump was making good on his campaign commitment to pull out of trade treaties that, in his view, did not serve American interests. His constituents were hostile to economic openness in general, and that hostility made some sense. In Chapter 4 we saw how hyper-globalization has not been kind to vast portions of the U.S. population, nor to millions in other mature democracies. America's withdrawal from the treaty eased China's worries not only about reduced exports and foreign investment, but about ecological pressure to liberalize.[74]

Most TPP signatories carried on without the United States. In March 2018 Australia, Brunei, Canada, Chile, Japan, Malaysia, Mexico, New Zealand, Peru, Singapore, and Vietnam signed the Comprehensive and Progressive Agreement for Trans-Pacific Partnership (CPTPP)—a cumbersome moniker even by the standards of international organizations. The CPTPP was much like the TPP, except less favorable to pharmaceutical companies and other producers in which the United States enjoys a comparative advantage. In other words, members continued to want to bias the international environment in favor of more market-driven economies and away from the China model. Signatories made clear their openness to welcoming more members, including the United States. Taiwan, Malaysia, Indonesia, and South Korea expressed interest in joining.[75]

China, meanwhile, exploited Trump's move by embracing and cosponsoring the world's largest free-trade area. The Regional Comprehensive Economic Partnership (RCEP) included fifteen countries, among which are Japan, South Korea, Indonesia, Thailand, Australia, and New Zealand. Predictably, the RCEP is much friendlier to China's domestic system than the TPP. It neither touches government subsidies to SOEs nor protects independent labor unions, the environment, or intellectual property.[76] It does not press China to adapt to its environment, but instead rewards China for being the way it is and tells other states that they could prosper by imitating China.

Making the World Select for Autocracy

At least since 1989, successive leaders of the Chinese Communist Party have been alert to ways in which participating in the international order built by the United States and other constitutional democracies moves China both toward and away from its vision. Moving deeply into the liberal international ecosystem has brought China breathtaking economic growth, power, and prestige. The country has well and truly put its Century of Humiliation behind it. But as Deng saw back in May 1989, the liberal ecosystem exacted a price. Moving an authoritarian society into this system lets in new ideas and shifts power around. It puts pressure on single-party rule. It helped end the Soviet Union, and it could do the same to China.

Xi Jinping has followed his predecessors in refusing either to close China up again or to sit passively while the liberal niche selects for democracy. Convinced that the greatest external ideological threat to "socialism with Chinese characteristics" is "Western constitutional democracy," Xi has not been slack in countering that ecological pressure. He has dialed up China's "go out" strategy so as to reshape the environment to the party's advantage. In the terms of Alexander Cooley and Daniel Nexon, he shifted China from a strategy of order contestation to one of alternative order-building.[77]

To date, China's ecosystem reengineering has not imitated some of the most important tools the Americans used in their own ecosystem engineering after World War II. China has built no formal military allies, and the only two countries it could be argued to have informal alliances with are North Korea and Pakistan. China has not used force or (so far as open sources reveal) covert means to promote autocracy or overturn liberal democracy in other countries. Indeed, Beijing is willing to work with states of whatever domestic regime so long as they respect China's own system of government.

But China's effect on the international environment is not neutral with respect to democracy and autocracy. Lately the party been using its "discourse power" (*huayu quan*), introducing ideas from Xi Jinping Thought into the language of global institutions—particularly the "community with a shared future for mankind" (*renlei mingyun gongtongti*).[78] The beneficent language calls to mind the insipidness of an Olympic Games opening ceremony. But it signifies principles designed to replace the liberal bias from the international order with one that allows China's autocracy, and autocracy in general, to flourish.

In deliberalizing the international environment, China has help from its large northern neighbor. Russia is a risky partner, no doubt, but the two authoritarian giants have found much room for cooperation. In the next two chapters we examine Russia and its strategy to keep liberal democracy at bay, sometimes partnering with China to do so.

6

Russia

If You Can't Join Them, Beat Them

No one feels safe. I want to emphasize this: no one feels safe!

—Vladimir Putin, 2007

Putin among the Liberals

Vladimir Putin, Russia's president, is known to like surprises. On February 10, 2007, he caught off guard hundreds of delegates at the annual Munich Security Conference, a regular gathering of diplomats, politicians, and other elites from the wealthy democracies. Opening with a playful warning that he was going to "avoid excessive politeness," Putin set about arraigning the "unipolar world," more particularly its one "pole," the United States. "What is a unipolar world? . . . It is a world in which there is one master, one sovereign." The result, Putin continued, has only been the creation of more dire problems— "an abyss of permanent conflicts." All because "one state . . . the United States, has overstepped its national borders in every way."

Up to this point, many of America's democratic allies,

and indeed many Americans, concurred with Russia's president even as they shifted in their chairs. The Munich gathering included plenty of critics of the Bush Doctrine, which declared that the United States would act in its own interests regardless of what old allies thought. The George W. Bush administration used its doctrine to justify the war in Iraq that so many allies roundly opposed.

But Putin was hunting even bigger game: the very notion of democracy promotion, one of the pillars of the liberal international order: "Russia—we—are constantly being taught about democracy. But for some reason those who teach us do not want to learn themselves." U.S. unipolarity was a problem for "the economic, political, cultural and educational policies it imposes on other nations. Well, who likes this? Who is happy about this?" Discomfort in the room was palpable. Even those delegates to the Munich conference who rejected the Bush Doctrine shared the goal of spreading "economic, political, cultural, and educational" reform into authoritarian countries. Democracy was essential to the progress that international order had made since World War II. Constitutional self-government was as important as economic openness and international institutions to leaving behind the bad old world of great-power competition, empire, and war. The Europeans were spreading democracy with as much determination as George W. Bush.

Putin, however, was asserting that democracy promotion was widely resented and provoking a dangerous backlash. Some countries were responding by developing weapons of mass destruction; many people, by becoming terrorists.[1] For those present, the signal was unmistakable: Russia was going to push back against liberal internationalism. Putin was condemning the system that had won the Cold War a generation earlier and that the core liberal states continued to believe was the best, the only, way forward for the world.[2] He seemed to have gone off script.

"As Putin spoke," write U.S. diplomats Daniel Fried and Kurt Volker, "the atmosphere in the ballroom changed palpably."[3] While Russia had its problems—power was more centralized, the country was clearly an oligarchy, the ongoing war in Chechnya was savage—it had still seemed fundamentally oriented toward democracy and cooperation. Russia and the West had continued to become economically interdependent. Russia was negotiating for membership in the World Trade Organization (WTO). Domestically, the country seemed to be holding the line since Putin's election in 2000. He had stabilized Russia's economy. He retained a circle of liberal advisors. He insisted that Russia was on an irreversible path to democracy. Europe's leaders, in particular, thought they had made Russia an offer it could not refuse: give up autocracy and great-power politics and embrace liberal internationalism, and all of the wonders of life in the West will be open to you. Now Putin was throwing the offer back in their faces.

The following year, Putin removed any doubt that he was serious with the first of a series of military actions against liberal pro-Western governments. Russia invaded Georgia briefly and cemented the de facto secessions of its two breakaway regions. That was only the beginning. In 2014 Russia annexed the Ukrainian region of Crimea after occupying it militarily. In 2022 Russia launched a massive invasion of Ukraine, the largest military action in Europe since 1945. Ukraine's military surprised the world by repulsing Russian forces from Kyiv and other major cities, but no one could any longer doubt Putin's willingness to take enormous risks and alienate the West in order to engineer Russia's ecosystem to favor his regime.

The International Environment
versus Authoritarian Russia

Putin's 2007 Munich speech did announce a fundamental shift in Russian foreign policy. But that shift really had begun a few years before, and he had hinted broadly at it in his past critiques of liberalism. Like his predecessor, Boris Yeltsin, Putin had never intended for Russia to become just another democracy in the liberal order, a Germany with oil and gas rather than advanced manufacturing. Those European countries, to him, were under the sway of America, even if they did not want to admit it. Putin wanted Russia to be a great power again, a country that the world, including the United States itself, recognized as America's equal. Getting Russia to that point required cooperating with the West and even joining some of its international institutions. It meant offering genuine help to the George W. Bush administration after the 9/11 terrorist attacks. It even meant affecting acceptance of NATO's eastward expansion. But the point of playing along with liberal internationalism was to help Russia modernize its economy, technology, and institutions so that it could become great again.[4]

It was the so-called "color revolutions" early in the twenty-first century that changed Putin's thinking about Russia's international environment. The chain of popular uprisings in lands once under Russia's rule or influence, uprisings that replaced corrupt pro-Russian leaders with liberal pro-Western governments, convinced him that the United States did not respect Russia, in fact wanted it to be divided and weak, just another country to dominate. In November 2000 came the Bulldozer Revolution in Russia's traditional ally Serbia, which replaced Slobodan Milosevic with Vojislav Kostunica. In November 2003 came the Rose Revolution in Georgia, in which Eduard Shevardnadze resigned and Mikheil Saakashvili took office. A year later came a much more serious one, the Orange Revolution in Ukraine, which placed Viktor Yushchenko in power. What Putin saw as Russia's sphere of influence was being systematically dismembered.

And the United States was the prime mover behind the dismemberment. George W. Bush had moved the United States toward a policy of aggressive democracy promotion after 9/11. In January 2005, in his second inaugural address, the U.S. president had announced his "Freedom Agenda": "America's vital interests and our deepest beliefs are now one. . . . So it is the policy of the United States to seek and support the growth of democratic movements and institutions in every nation and culture, with the ultimate goal of ending tyranny in our world."[5] In the Slovak capital of Bratislava a few days later, Bush drove the point home: "The democratic revolutions that swept this region over fifteen years ago are now reaching Georgia and Ukraine," he declared, adding that Moldova and Belarus were next, and that "one day, freedom's promise will reach every people and every nation."[6]

After the color revolutions, Putinists had gone on high alert. "Yesterday: Tblisi. Today: Kiev. Tomorrow: Moscow," is how one writer put it.[7] The dots seemed to connect themselves. The revolutions were not spontaneous. The West, with its activist diplomats and foundations and NGOs, was engineering them.[8] Or so it looked from the Kremlin.

Russia is a wounded country. Historically the great power that repulsed Napoleon, broke the back of Nazi Germany, and then held a third of the world in its grasp as the Soviet Union, it has been taken lightly since the collapse of the Soviet Union in 1991. Democracies respect wealth, technology, and cultural innovation. With an economy smaller than that of Canada, Russia elicits pity, contempt, and sometimes fear—fear that its instability and autocratic history will combine with its possession of several thousand nuclear warheads to menace the world again. Russians are aware of how their country is viewed in the West. Putin and his regime blame Russia's predicament partly on communism, but mostly on malevolent foreign entities and their actions and rules and discourse. His message, which increasingly has drowned out all others in Russia, is that the West wants Russia to fail and that the particular culprit is the United States, with its self-assigned mission of imposing its values and institutions on Russia and the rest of the world.

The Soviet collapse more than three decades ago freed Russia from institutional and ideological pathologies that were holding it down, including the burden of a decaying empire. It gave Russia the opportunity to follow the evidence—to become a liberal democracy and prosper within the liberal international order. In the early days of Boris Yeltsin's presidency, when liberal reformers held the high cards in Moscow, it was not hard to discern a bright democratic future for Russia. But in the ensuing decades, things have gone badly wrong, and the government lays most of the blame on the international order and its architect and enforcer.

When they survey their international environment, Russia's leaders see a bias, unacknowledged but clear, against their country. The bias appears in the perpetual harping about Russian violations of human rights and its backsliding from democracy. It appears in the established international rules and institutions that enforce this discourse, from the United Nations to NGOs to mainstream international journalism. It shows up in the narrative that liberal democracy is the only legitimate way to order society and the only route to success. Most of all, the bias is evident in the aim that the West has taken at Putin's own regime by sponsoring color revolutions and rolling NATO and the European Union up to Russia's border.

The bias is even more severe than that, for it is not clear to Putinists that the West would ever allow a stable, liberal-democratic Russia to join it. In 2022 Putin alleged that he had once asked U.S. President Bill Clinton how America viewed the possibility that Russia might eventually join NATO: "The reaction to my question was, let us say, quite restrained." Putin drew the conclusion: "There can be only one answer—this is not about our political regime or anything like that. They just do not need a big and independent country like Russia around. This is the answer to all questions. This is the source of America's traditional policy towards Russia."[9] Indeed, the subject was much discussed in the 1990s, and many in Europe and North America did dismiss out of hand Russian membership in NATO.[10]

Putin's government wants to change this international environment, to remove its anti-Russian bias. The Kremlin lacks the grand vision of China of a "shared future for mankind." Instead, Russia's rulers want a world that lets Russia assume again its rightful place as a shaper of international order. There is no doubt that for Putin, Russia, the true Russia, cannot be anything but a country with heft in its own region and other parts of the world, respected by the other great powers. It cannot be the mere "regional power" acting "out of weakness" that Barack Obama called it.[11] It is Great Russia, big brother to Little Russia (Ukraine and Belarus), a nuclear-armed empire with a permanent veto on the UN Security Council, able to do as it pleases without any other power's permission—a nation with such mass that Central Asia, Eastern Europe, and parts of the Middle East fall within its gravitational pull, which enjoys an equal place with America and China at the great-powers' table.[12]

Also clear is that Putin and his many supporters believe sincerely that for Russia to be great, it must have a regime capable of imposing and maintaining domestic order, a regime that concentrates power in the center, the Kremlin.[13] And for now, at least, it must be Putin himself at the head, for he alone has the vision, the competence, and the ruthlessness to maintain order and make Russia great again. Russia's current authoritarian regime has become what political scientists call a "personalist" one (see Chapter 2), in which the regime and the dictator are merged.[14]

But Russia's leadership is equally convinced that America, the West, and the international order they run will not let that happen voluntarily. Russia did try liberal democracy out in the early 1990s, and it was a disaster. For Putinists, that period showed that this alien Western regime type would be their country's undoing, a poison that would incapacitate it and render it fit only to be another colony of the United States. And, says official Russia, that is exactly why the West tries to impose its system on Russia and around the world—not to bring the blessings of liberty to faraway people they will never meet, but to bring Russia and the rest of the world under American control. The eastward spread of democracy by a liberal-imperial complex of the U.S. State Department, CIA, and Western-based NGOs is part of a larger U.S. strategy to keep Russia down.[15]

Russians, then, are alive to the ideas-power nexus, the entanglement of democracy and U.S. influence and power. Western leaders describe the situation in more benign terms, emphasizing that their societies are extending freedom, opportunity, and human rights. But they too understand that the interests of European democracies and ultimately American influence is at play. "I viewed NATO expansion as a powerful tool to advance the freedom agenda," Bush himself wrote in his memoir.[16] Putin would simply reverse the terms: the expansion of freedom was a tool to advance NATO (and hence American power).[17]

Thus Russia openly calls and works for a "multipolar world," or one in which the United States has some peer states to which it must sometimes defer.[18] Thus too Russia's support of China's assertions of power: China is eroding America's global position. Liberal westerners who believe that the world has moved on from power politics sometimes say that Putin is a man out of time, a nineteenth-century statesman in the twenty-first-century world, who still believes the big states can carve up the small ones for the sake of security and stability. Putin, however, believes that the world never really left the nineteenth century, and never can do so. Liberal powers disguise their domination through humanitarian rhetoric and soft power—a package that Russians call "hybrid warfare," which marries kinetic force with soft power, subversion, and economic inducements to extend one's influence and power.[19] Russia's leaders believe that the West is the pioneer of this full-spectrum warfare, and they are determined to match and beat it, particularly in former Soviet lands and satellite states and in parts of the Middle East. They use whatever means they have, from communications technology to the Russian army, to divide and weaken the West by sowing confusion and assisting anti-liberal politicians and parties.[20] They have coalesced with other countries opposed to liberal internationalism; the most important of these is China.[21]

Russia is not trying to overturn the liberal international order altogether. Its leaders, like those of China, know that their country depends on exporting, foreign investment, and technology transfer, things that can only happen if their economies are to some degree open to the West. Prior to the war in Ukraine, international trade made up one-quarter of Russia's economy, and more than half of Russia's exports were in energy—oil, natural gas, and coal.[22] Nor is Russia is trying to build an autarkic formal empire. As Robert Horvath has written, "Instead of playing according to the post-Cold War rules of the game, the Putin regime is seeking to change those rules. . . . [It is] spearheading a campaign to make the world safe for authoritarianism."[23]

As with China, understanding what Russia is trying to do to the international environment requires understanding its internal system of government.

Russia's Domestic Regime

Like China, Russia has an internal political order tolerably captured by the phrase "authoritarian-capitalist." But behind that phrase are Putin and his United Russia party. It is difficult to conceive of the country's current regime without the man who built it from the capsizing system that he inherited from Boris Yeltsin in 1999. Now in his third decade in power, Putin has over time constructed what political scientist Henry Hale calls a "power pyramid," in which all actors and institutions with leverage support him, and all are confident that everyone else will continue to do so in the foreseeable future.[24]

Russia offers a textbook case of why a written constitution alone is a poor guide to a country's domestic regime. Its constitution of 1993 is a fairly standard liberal-democratic document. The document upholds individual rights and freedoms as paramount, establishes the rule of law, mandates regular competitive elections for government officials, and lays out the distribution of power between the national and regional governments (mostly republics).[25] Yet, even as the constitution was being drafted, Yeltsin took steps to strengthen the presidency at the expense of the national legislature; in September 1993 he dissolved the body, which promptly impeached and deposed him, leading Yeltsin to call out the army, shell the parliament building, and arrest his enemies. Ever since, Russia's president has been strong in practice and difficult to counter. Yeltsin effectively named Putin his successor in 1999.

Putin has steadily moved the country further from liberal democracy by weakening or eliminating other centers of power in government and society.[26] He has been in power continuously since 1999, either as president (1999–2008 and after 2012) or prime minister (2008–12). In 2020, as his fourth presidential term neared its end, the constitution was amended to allow him two additional six-year presidential terms; in principle, Putin could serve until 2036. He has collected more and more of the levers of power, giving himself great control over the national government, local governments, and civil society.

A major mechanism of Putin's aggrandizement has been the growing power of the United Russia party. In the early years he built the party as a complex to co-opt regional and local elites who enjoyed more independence than he liked. United Russia is an ongoing bargain, a "bundle of rules, norms, and agreements" under which elites at all levels of government receive spoils in exchange for loyalty to Putin.[27] The party dominates both chambers of the national legislature: in 2022 it held nearly three-quarters of the seats in the State Duma (lower house) and around 90 percent of the seats in the Federation Council (upper house, whose members are all appointed by governors or legislatures). In 2004 Putin eliminated the popular election of governors; he appoints them through a representative.[28] Freedom House finds that elections in Russia are neither free nor fair. Putin has extended control over broadcast media; irregularities in vote tabulations are now regular. In the 2018 presidential election, opposition leader Alexei Navalny was disqualified for "a politically motivated criminal conviction." The party's funding sources are opaque.[29]

Putin has riveted United Russia to the Russian state

through a number of means.[30] He has struck bargains with law enforcement, the Federal Security Service (FSB), the military, and the Russian Orthodox Church. Any potential threats that he could not co-opt he has weakened, exiled, or killed. Oligarchs who made their billions in the go-go early 1990s and who dared to challenge Putin have been sidelined: two of the richest, media magnate Boris Berezovsky and oil executive Mikhail Khodorkovsky, ended up in London.[31]

As with China, the Russian state's entanglements with commerce are so deep and extensive that the country's economy is best called "semi-capitalist." The Russian economy was heavily privatized in the 1990s, but according to the International Monetary Fund it has roughly 32,500 directly state-owned enterprises (SOEs), with many thousands more indirectly owned by the state. The Kremlin wants ownership or at least a large measure of control over Russia's key energy sector; that is one reason why Khodorkovsky, who was head of Yukos, an immense private oil company, had to be gotten rid of. Putin has called Gazprom, the state-owned natural gas firm, "a powerful political and economic lever of influence over the rest of the world."[32] About 19 percent of employed Russians work for SOEs, a figure well ahead of the European norm. A World Bank study shows that SOEs create inefficiencies in Russia's economy by, for example, paying excess compensation and siphoning efficient labor from private companies.[33] Clearly, Putin believes that the benefits to his regime outweigh the costs to Russia's economy.

All in all, the standard array of Western regime rating entities give Russia low marks for democracy. Freedom House labels it "not free," with a score of 19 out of a possible 100.[34] V-Dem places it in the second-lowest decile, between Laos and Congo.[35] The Economist Intelligence Unit ranks the country 124th out of 152.[36]

OFFICIAL IDEOLOGY

A central guiding ideology that makes sense of and justifies Russia's political system is elusive. The days of Soviet ideological precision and heresy-hunting are long gone. Putin's regime is adept at picking up ideas here and there, plastering them to the regime, and shifting them about as needed. Journalist Anne Applebaum writes that "Putinism" is a story of centralized control and distrust of spontaneity or self-organization. Putin and his coterie "deeply believe that the rulers of the state must exert careful control over the life of the nation. . . . Markets cannot be genuinely open, elections cannot be unpredictable and [dissidents] must be carefully controlled through legal pressure, public propaganda and, if necessary, carefully targeted violence."[37] Another emphasis is national independence, captured in the favored phrase "sovereign democracy." The government presents itself as serving the people of Russia and no one else, and Russia has the right to decide for itself what democracy means.[38] The result looks much more sovereign than democratic.[39]

Behind this set of principles is a strong notion of Russian exceptionalism, as laid out by an array of thinkers. The country, these thinkers argue, is by nature authoritarian. Putin's onetime advisor Vladislav Surkov argues that geography and demography make it so: "The tremendous internal stress of holding enormous heterogeneous expanses, and the continuous state of being in the thick of geopolitical struggle, make the military and police functions of the state important and decisive. We have almost never been governed by merchants who consider military affairs less important than commerce, or by the liberals who accompany the merchants and whose teaching is built on the negation of everything even slightly related to police." The brief exceptions to the autocratic rule noted by Surkov are revealing: in 1917, after the fall of the monarchy but before the Bolshevik putsch, and the early 1990s, following the collapse of the Soviet Union. When Russia is governed by liberals and liberalism, it is divided and vulnerable. Strong rule then emerges to save the country. Today, Putin fills the role, a man uniquely able "to hear and understand the people, to see the people through to its depths."[40]

The eccentric Alexander Dugin, declared "Putin's brain" by *Foreign Affairs* magazine, grounds Russia's regime in his "fourth political theory," sometimes called "neo-Eurasianism." The first three political theories, writes Dugin, were liberalism, communism, and fascism. Liberalism vanquished the other two in the late twentieth century, but now faces a historical moment of failure. Drawing on the German philosopher Martin Heidegger, Dugin argues that Western liberalism's technology-driven nihilism is producing "nothingness." But that very nothingness will call for a return of "Being," which Dugin says entails a rediscovery of traditional religion. Russia has a special role in this moment, as a country that has struggled with Western ideas and identity for many centuries. It is the crucial constraint on America's voracious liberal hegemony.[41]

Historian Nataliya Narochnitskaya, who has enjoyed enormous influence over the Russian right wing in the Orthodox Church and State Duma, presents an exceptional Russia sharply distinct from the rationalistic West. Russia is its own civilization, she writes, based in Orthodox Christianity; it places morality above rationality and aspires to a "state of truth" rather than a "state of laws." It has suffered under the encroachments of Western rationalism—communism after 1917, liberalism since 1991. Russian civilization has its own notion of human rights, one that stresses duties and the need for the individual to choose good over evil.[42]

The Main Threat: Liberal Democracy

Russian ideologists speak with one voice about the regime's general enemy: it is liberalism. They appreciate that participation in the liberal international order has brought wealth and modernization to Russia. The country joined the WTO in 2012. Prior to its invasion of Ukraine, Russia's two biggest foreign customers were the European Union and the United States. Putin has stated repeatedly his desire for more foreign investment in his country. But it is equally clear that Russia's leaders and their apologists believe that liberalism undermines the country's authoritarian regime and is hence entangled with U.S. influence and power.[43] A liberal-democratic Russia would have weak leaders whom the West would find more pliable. America's drive to universal empire is, in this view, why it tries to spread democracy to other countries: U.S. leaders know that liberal self-government is effectively a carrier of American influence and power. And for Russia's leaders, the threat is not abstract. It is in fact coming their way.[44]

For the first decade or more of Putin's time in power, it could be easy to miss this antipathy to liberalism because official Russian discourse stressed democracy and personal liberty for the Russian people. Yet, the democracy talk cloaked the centralization of power in the Russian state. Putin's 2005 State of the Union address was a master class: "I consider the development of Russia as a free and democratic state to be our main and political and ideological goal," the president declaimed at the outset. Yet, he went on to outline how the central state needed to do more to tame greed, "excessive zeal," broadcast television, and even bureaucratic inertia. The speech called for the presidential appointment of governors and a state group of "qualified specialists" to "help [the television networks] with their work."[45] In other words, democracy meant more power for the Kremlin and less for other institutions, including the news media.

For Surkov, liberalism is a cheat. Behind its promise of individual choice hides the liberal "deep state," which drives the globalization that in reality removes individual choice. The Russian state is at least honest about itself; "all its parts and manifestations [are] in view." Disillusioned westerners are beginning to see their own states' hypocrisy.[46] Dugin and Narochnitskaya take aim in particular at twenty-first-century liberalism—what I call in this book "open liberalism." Dugin asserts that liberalism's triumph over communism transformed it into "postliberalism," a non-ideology of the global market that removes individual freedom.[47] Narochnitskaya attacks today's liberalism as a sham. The culprit is the current "third system of [liberal] rights," "those very libertarian rights, in which the human personality is proclaimed completely auton-omous of any system of values, independent of whatever civi-lization he or she inhabits." The result is that freedom is denied to adherents of traditional religions who object to these new libertarian rights.[48]

Liberalism, then, would emasculate Russia, and hence the Putinists' fear of the color revolutions. On the surface, much of the fear pointed to the pro-Western orientation of these new governments; comparisons to "banana republics" in Latin America were drawn.[49] But it is not only American power that Putinists fear, for that power is inseparable from the Western ideas that the United States and Europe are imposing on Rus-sia and its neighborhood. Putin put it this way to a French tele-vision network in 2006:

> If we go back 100 years and look through the news-
> papers, we see what arguments the colonial powers

of that time advanced to justify their expansion into
Africa and Asia. They cited arguments such as playing a civilizing role, the particular role of the white
man, the need to civilize "primitive peoples." We all
know what consequences this had. If we replace the
term "civilizing role" with "democratization," then
we can transpose practically word for word what the
newspapers were writing 100 years ago to today's
world and the arguments we hear from some of our
colleagues.[50]

Putin was speaking at the end of a Group of 8 summit in
St. Petersburg, a meeting in which the other leaders—all rep-
resenting wealthy democracies—challenged him on Russian
backsliding away from democracy. Sergei Ivanov, then Russia's
minister of defense, claimed that Russia was boldly presenting
an alternative to Western liberalism: "By declaring its own
ideological project, Russia has entered a harsh and uncompro-
mising competitive struggle."[51]

Russia and the West:
Competitive Ecosystem Engineering

For its leaders, then, Russia must be a great power again, and
for Russia to be a great power, it must be an autocracy run by
Putin. The United States, the EU, and the liberal international
order, however, are trying to make Russia into a democracy.
They are presenting the country with a choice it cannot accept:
either remain authoritarian and continue to be handicapped,
denied the prestige you crave, vulnerable to economic sanctions and even regime change; or, become a liberal democracy
and join Europe in a late-modern liberal paradise under Amer-

ican hegemony. Not only is the choice intolerable, but Russians doubt that they would be allowed in the club even if their country were to become a giant version of Sweden.

As they have come to see liberalism as the enemy that is everywhere, even inside their own house, Putin and his coterie have not sat back passively. They have used whatever agency they can muster to reengineer the ecosystem. Putin's government has tried to deliberalize Russia's international environment so as to relieve the democratizing pressure. In Chapter 7 we will see how the Kremlin has done so indirectly, acting alone and in concert with China to alter international rules and institutions on human rights and internet governance, and to show the world that authoritarian capitalism is superior to liberal democracy in the twenty-first century.

Russia's chief method, however, has been to address one particular element of its international environment: the balance of power among regime types, especially to its immediate west and south. Russia's war of aggression in Ukraine that began in February 2022 is only the most obvious case. That shock-and-awe invasion did not come out of nowhere. It only took to another level the Kremlin's long-standing effort to engineer Russia's international ecosystem. It is only the most lethal and risky phase in a long hybrid war—involving subversion, propaganda, economic leverage, election interference, and intimidation—against the United States and the West, a war to keep Russia authoritarian.[52] Most democracy promoters, particularly those who work for NGOs, believe they are simply promoting freedom and human rights and safeguarding fragile democracies from Russian mischief. Russia's leadership sees the matter differently: Western democracy promotion is a tool of American power against Russia.[53] As political scientist Oisín Tansey writes of autocracy promotion in general, Russia's hybrid war is defensive. Putin knows that Russia cannot remake the world in Russia's image. His chief goal is more modest: to keep liberalism out of Russia's neighborhood.[54] The project is difficult, partly because it means Russia and the West are trying to engineer the same part of the ecosystem in Eastern Europe. As Vitali Silitsky has written, for Putin the "survival of autocracy at home increasingly depends on the failure of democracy abroad."[55]

REPULSING DEMOCRACY
BY EXPORTING AUTOCRACY

In the 1990s, Russia—itself groping toward democracy yet rife with corruption—competed with the European Union for economic commitments in some former Soviet lands. Russia was poor and needed trading partners. The example of Belarus, a former Soviet republic north of Ukraine, suggested that the best partners were autocrats. Alexander Lukashenko, elected Belarus's president in 1994, quickly moved to make himself president-for-life. Under Boris Yeltsin's administration, Russia helped broker a deal in 1996 under which Lukashenko gained the power to appoint half of the country's parliament. In his 2001 reelection campaign, Lukashenko received favorable coverage from the Russian media (popular in Belarus). Russian officials praised Lukashenko and refused to meet with opposition candidates. Putin's government did the same in subsequent elections.[56]

At the same time, Russian subsidies bolstered the legitimacy of Lukashenko's rule by keeping standards of living stable and comparable to what its citizens had in the Soviet era. Most significant were energy subsidies, worth at least $1 billion per annum.[57] Meanwhile, throughout these years, Western entities have worked to undermine Lukashenko. The U.S. government and American NGOs have cultivated civil society in

Belarus and spent funds to strengthen opposition political parties. The Organization for Security and Cooperation in Europe
(OSCE), dominated by the mature democracies, has condemned
Lukashenko's fraudulent elections repeatedly. The West's efforts
have had little effect. In Belarus, Russia has prevailed.[58]

In the early 2000s, Putin began to expand his goal for
Russia's other western neighbors: it would no longer be simply
economic partnership, but keeping liberal democracy away. As
he saw the United States joining the Europeans in promoting
democracy in Serbia, Georgia, and Ukraine, it became clear to
Putin that the threat to Russia was not simply lost commercial
opportunities. It had become the more direct threat of regime
change. Lukashenko knew this threat full well and used it to
his advantage. He and Putin have not always gotten on well,
but Belarus's president knows he can count on Putin's fear of
spreading revolution. As Lukashenko likes to say, "A revolution in Belarus is a revolution in Russia."[59]

Georgia and Ukraine have proven more troublesome than
Belarus, however. Georgia's nonviolent Rose Revolution of
November 2003 put the liberal reformer Mikheil Saakashvili
in power and showed that it would be difficult to fix elections
for pro-Russian candidates in that country. Saakashvili openly
called for Georgia to be admitted to NATO. Rather than try
to overthrow him, the Kremlin imposed economic sanctions
to bring him to heel. Those had no effect, and the United States
warmed to Saakashvili's idea. In a telephone call in early 2008,
George W. Bush told Putin that he need not fear if Georgia
joined NATO, because "NATO is an organization that helps
democracies flourish. Democracies are good things to have on
your border." Putin would have none of it. Shortly thereafter
he was telling NATO leaders that these former Soviet republics were not real countries.[60]

Russia still had cards to play. Its chief assets in Georgia

were two breakaway regions, Abkhazia and South Ossetia, that had fought against the Tbilisi government in the early 1990s. Putin weakened Georgia by enabling the de facto independence of these breakaway regions.

Moscow had brokered an agreement between Tbilisi and the two regions in 1994. In 2008, with hundreds of Russian peacekeepers still in both, Russia began to trade directly with the breakaway regions, in violation of an old agreement. Saakashvili responded by moving troops near the Abkhazian border. Russian planes shot down Georgian drones. In August ten thousand Russian troops conducted exercises just over the border in Russia. Saakashvili sent troops into South Ossetia's provincial capital who then attacked the Russian peacekeepers. Russia responded with force, invading Georgia proper and even sinking several Georgian ships on the Black Sea. The Russo-Georgian War lasted five days and was an utter defeat for Georgia. Russia immediately recognized South Ossetia and Abkhazia as independent republics.[61] Saakashvili remained in power, but Georgia was weakened and further from meeting the criteria for NATO membership. Putin had made his point.

Ukraine, with its population of forty million, was the most important prize of all, and Putin has used every tool available to keep it from becoming a stable liberal democracy. Leonid Kuchma, president from 1994 to early 2005, tried to avoid leaning toward Russia or the West. The election of Kuchma's successor was scheduled for 2004, a year after Georgia's Rose Revolution. This time, Putin would not be caught off guard. The candidates were Viktor Yanukovych, the prime minister, who tilted toward Russia, and Viktor Yushchenko, a pro-Western former prime minister, who was a reformer married to a U.S. citizen.[62] As the election campaign in Ukraine got underway, the Kremlin set to work to fix the election for Yanukovych. It pressed Kuchma to help his campaign, funneled tens of millions of dollars that Yanukovych used to bribe local election officials, and sent its crack "political technologists" to Kyiv to work their magic.[63] Russian state television, seen in most of Ukraine, propagandized relentlessly for Yanukovych; Putin visited the country, endorsed Yanukovych's economic policy, and signed a five-year contract for natural gas delivery at a quarter the price paid in Western Europe.[64]

The first round of the election, held on October 31, gave Yushchenko a razor-thin lead—39.87 percent to 39.32 percent for Yanukovych. As the country prepared for the runoff between the two men, Putin raised his bet. He urged Yanukovych to make more use of his power as prime minister to boost turnout. In eastern districts that favored Yanokovych, lists of voters swelled with names of dead people.

Yanukovych won the November 21 runoff by three points, 49 percent to Yushchenko's 46 percent. The turnout in Donetsk, in the east, had risen by 20 percentage points, to an impressive but suspicious 96.7 percent. Hundreds of easterners were caught voting twice—first in their home districts and then in Kyiv, where fleets of buses had taken them during the day. As rumors of such cheating circulated, thousands of orange-clad Yushchenko supporters took to Kyiv's streets and built a tent city. International election observers questioned the official tally. Exit polls funded by Western NGOs showed an eleven-point lead for Yushchenko—a fourteen-point difference from the official result. Some journalists began to question the result openly.[65]

Putin pushed on, telephoning congratulations to Yanukovych. Ukraine's election commission declared him the winner. When most leaders of EU countries refused to recognize the result, Putin charged them with inciting street riots. On December 2 he summoned outgoing President Kuchma to Moscow to press him to send tanks to Kyiv. But Kuchma instead called for a second runoff. Ukraine's parliament agreed, as did Ukraine's highest court. This second second round was held on December 26, and Yushchenko triumphed by 52 to 44 percent. The pro-Western reformer took the oath of office a month later.

What became known as the Orange Revolution was a humiliation for Putin. Not only had he lost Ukraine; he also had been outplayed by the West in his own backyard. Yulia Tymoshenko, a prominent liberal Ukrainian politician, announced that Russia was next.[66] Democracy and American power entwined to form a kind of a noose meant for him and for Russia. It was a turning point in Russia's relations with the West and how Putin's Russia saw its place in the international order.[67] Putin denounced the Orange Revolution as unconstitutional and undemocratic.[68]

Russia's president may have been paranoid, but he did have enemies.[69] In all of the color revolutions, the National Endowment for Democracy and the International Republican Institute—both funded by the U.S. government—and private NGOs such as the Open Society Institute—funded by George Soros—had trained civil society activists. Lincoln Mitchell, an American foreign policy analyst, writes that in 2003 he led a group of Georgian activists to Serbia to learn about the Bulldozer Revolution; some of these activists participated in the Rose Revolution there.[70] As Samuel Charap and Timothy Colton write: "Moscow could no longer distinguish (what the West couched as) democratic change from loss of influence. Geopolitics and geo-ideas were now hopelessly entangled."[71] It was the ideas-power nexus: democracy carried U.S. influence, autocracy carried Russian.

From Ukraine's Orange Revolution, Putin concluded that the liberal international order was not going to allow Russia to regain its rightful international status. The order allowed only one great power—the United States—and relegated all other states to subordinate status: they must be liberal democracies with open economies and agendas set by Washington. Indeed, the events in Ukraine in 2004 showed that the United States was very good at ecosystem engineering, and especially good at covering what it was doing with "beautiful, pseudo-democratic phraseology."[72]

The regime-power dilemma pressed hard on Russia. It could not simply withdraw from the liberal international order and isolate itself from the West. It could not become an immense North Korea, impoverishing itself through autarky and blackmailing the world with nuclear and missile tests. Russia's economy relied heavily on exports, and in 2004 more than two-thirds of those exports went to wealthy democracies.[73] Making Russia great again also meant technological modernization, and that too required openness to the West.

The best available remedy was to continue to try to neutralize the liberalizing pressure from Russia's environment but to use more potent weapons. That meant changing the terms of Russia's participation in the international order. Because the most acute threat to his regime, and hence to Russia's great-power status, was Western-driven regime change to Russia's west and south, blocking those changes was an urgent task. If Russia could place and keep friendly autocrats in power in its neighborhood, this would help it accrue the power and security necessary to become an independent great power again. The West would then have to deal with it on its own terms.

Moscow's early reaction to the Orange Revolution was mild. Putin and Yushchenko even exchanged visits, and Russia's government suggested that Ukraine might be able to integrate with both the EU and Russia's newly formed customs union, although in that case Russia would end its heavy subsidies on its natural gas exports to Ukraine. In late 2005 negotiations over a new gas contract broke down, and in January 2006 Russia cut Ukraine off; Ukraine responded by siphoning gas meant for the rest of Europe; the Europeans accused Russia of weaponizing energy, and Putin backed down.[74]

Ukraine held another presidential election in 2010, with Yanukovich, the pro-Russian, running against the pro-Western Yulia Tymoshenko. The Kremlin correctly judged that it need not intervene so much this time. Yanukovych defeated Tymoshenko 49 percent to 45.5 percent. Official Russia was pleased: the chairman of the State Duma's foreign affairs committee, Konstantin Kosachyov, remarked that the outgoing Yushchenko had interpreted Ukraine's interests in a "false way," that "they consisted of getting as far away from Russia as possible and quickly moving toward the West." Yanukovych, by contrast, had "a significantly more precise and adequate understanding of Ukraine's interests." The new president quickly announced that Ukraine would not seek NATO membership after all and signed a twenty-five-year extension of Russia's lease for its Black Sea fleet. Yet, Yanukovich also tried to continue his predecessor's attempts to have good economic relations with both the EU and Russia.[75]

Neither side was inclined to allow him to do that. Under the EU's European Neighborhood Policy, if Ukraine wanted full economic access to EU customers, merchants, and investors, it had to make concrete moves toward liberal democracy, had to join an EU customs union called the "Eastern Partnership," and had to stay out of any customs unions outside of the EU—that is, any Russian economic bloc. In 2009 Ukraine joined Georgia and Moldova in signing up for the EU's Eastern Partnership. Russia's government was not pleased. Said Sergei Lavrov, the foreign minister, "We are accused of having spheres of influence. But what is the Eastern Partnership, if not an attempt to extend the EU's sphere of influence, including to Belarus?" Russia responded in 2010 with its own customs union, including Belarus and Kazakhstan.[76]

The two economic blocs—the EU and Russia—were now playing a zero-sum game, with Ukraine the greatest prize. Putin announced that he foresaw Russia's customs union—which became the Eurasian Economic Union (EEU) in 2015—"becoming one of the poles of the modern world." Armenia and Kyrgyzstan signed up for the EEU. Putin and Dmitry Medvedev, then Russia's president, pressed Ukraine hard to abandon the Eastern Partnership and join the EEU. Yanukovich, knowing that Ukraine exported roughly equally to the EU and Russia, tried to avoid the choice. In July 2013 Moscow turned the screws with an embargo on most imports from Ukraine. The sanctions lasted only a week, but Yanukovych received the message. Moscow sweetened the offer with large bond purchases and gas subsidies. Putin and Yanukovych announced a deal in Moscow in December 2013: Ukraine would join the EEU and say goodbye to the Eastern Partnership.[77] It would lean to the east, to Russia, not to the west.

What followed is well known: another Ukrainian revolution, this one named for the Maidan, the central square in Kyiv where the enraged protesters gathered. Police violence brought more protesters to the streets. Urged on by Putin, Yanukovych cracked down. In February 2014 police and protesters clashed, killing one hundred. As Parliament prepared to impeach Yanukovych, he fled to Russia. Parliament named an interim government that quickly signed the agreement with the EU and withdrew from the EEU, the Russian customs union. As Western diplomats celebrated, the Kremlin saw the hand of Washington at work, the same hand it saw in the Orange Revolution of 2004. This time, however, Putin was ready. Hundreds of Russian commandos without insignia—dubbed "little green men"—appeared in Crimea, Ukraine's strategically vital peninsula on the Black Sea. The interim government in Kyiv refused to back down, and pro-Russians in Crimea voted overwhelmingly in a referendum to secede from Ukraine and join Russia. Moscow proposed that the United States and EU guarantee a new constitutional order in Ukraine, including neutrality. The West dismissed the proposal, and Russia responded by supporting separatist militias in Ukraine's eastern region of Donbas. The EU offered Ukraine a new trade deal. As the Donbas war continued, NATO began training and supplying the Ukrainian military, effectively making it into a twenty-first-century force—the so-called "Comprehensive Assistance Package."[78]

Eastern Europe is a field of competitive ecosystem engineering. The balance of power between democracy and autocracy in the region is delicate, and leaders in Russia, EU countries, and the United States all know it. At stake for Putin and his regime are their own power and, to their minds, Russia's chance to become a great power again. In Georgia and Ukraine, in particular, the Kremlin has been outplayed by the West, with its greater wealth, its NGOs, and its liberal soft power. That is why Russia has turned to violence in both countries. In the Ukrainian case, Russia has launched the largest and most dangerous war Europe has had since 1945. Efforts to steer evolutionary selection seldom take such lethal form, especially in a nuclear-armed world. But that they have in this case should remove any doubt that great powers take ecosystem engineering seriously.

Altering the balance of power among domestic regimes is not the only way that Putin's Russia is trying to remove the liberal bias in the international environment. The Kremlin is aware of how international rules and institutions, and information about regime types, also affect the prognosis for authoritarian, great-power Russia. It also is aware that its vast and substantially more powerful southern neighbor, authoritarian China, faces the same threat. In Chapter 7 we examine how the two authoritarian giants, separately and together, are laboring to make the world stop selecting for democracy.

7

Authoritarian Internationalism

Russia and China stand against attempts by external forces to undermine security and stability in their common adjacent regions, intend to counter interference by outside forces in the internal affairs of sovereign countries under any pretext, oppose color revolutions, and will increase cooperation in the aforementioned areas. . . . Friendship between the two States has no limits.

—Joint statement by Russia and China,
Beijing, February 4, 2022

At his first press conference as America's president, Joe Biden summed up his thinking about relations between the United States and China: "This is a battle between the utility of democracies in the 21st century and autocracies. We've got to prove democracy works."[1] A few weeks later China's ruling party made clear that it was unimpressed: "In the face of rising competition from emerging markets and the calls of developing countries for a fairer international governance system, Biden is seeking to do what his predecessor sought to do, which is to bend the international system to serve the US hegemony."[2]

Round Two quickly followed: China, said U.S. Secretary of State Antony Blinken in May 2021, "is the one country in the world that has the military, economic, diplomatic capacity to undermine or challenge the rules-based order that we—we care so much about and are determined to defend." Again, China's leaders waited a few weeks to unleash their response. Wrote Chen Weihua, chief of the European Bureau of *China Daily:* "What [Blinken] really meant is that China is the one country that could challenge the US's global hegemony."[3]

The contest between democracy and autocracy was to become a leitmotif for the Biden administration. And in editorial after editorial, social media post after post, China's response has been consistent: the United States wants to keep China down but is afraid that it can no longer do so. That is why Washington hectors Beijing on human rights, treats the South and East China Seas as if they were owned by the U.S. Navy, and tried (and failed) to create an Indo-Pacific trading order that would exclude China. America talks freedom and openness but thinks and feels power. And it is feeling China today.

The Americans and the Chinese are both correct, of course. Since the 1940s, U.S. leaders—with the exception of some officials in the Trump administration—have all wanted to maintain the liberal international order because it achieves their goal of keeping the United States a superpower *while* remaining a market-based liberal democracy. The order is part of a broader liberal ecosystem that enables the United States to avoid either having to adapt to external pressure by becoming more authoritarian or to sacrifice international power so as to remain democratic. The Americans like to emphasize democracy and rules; the Chinese focus on American hegemony.

Americans sometimes point out that if they wanted to

keep China down, they certainly went about it in an odd way: they reached out to the country in 1971, pushed its admission to the World Trade Organization (WTO) in the 1990s, and for many years were China's largest customer. To be sure, Washington did these things for reasons of self-interest, first to counter Soviet power in the Cold War, and later to reap the gains from trade. But that is how liberal internationalism works: all grow rich together when they worry less about the sizes of navies and armies and more about following comparative advantage. Besides, the risks to the United States seemed low for many years. From the late 1980s through only a few years ago, it was a commonplace in democratic capitals that open, market-oriented China was on the well-worn path from autocracy to democracy.[4]

Few in Washington still believe that. It is evident that China's ruling party figured out how to sustain economic growth and popular support while fending off democratic reform. Now the conventional wisdom in democratic capitals is that China is challenging the international "rules-based order." In truth, China's leaders want a rules-based international order too. They just want to change some of the rules and to have a much greater say in interpreting and enforcing those rules. China is what political scientist Stacie Goddard calls a "bridging revisionist" power: having risen through the U.S.-dominated international order, it has begun to construct new institutions with an eye to, in the words of Chinese politician Fu Ying, "reshape the order structure."[5]

Russia's leaders, too, routinely lambaste the United States for pretending to bring freedom to a world that it really wants to dominate and rule. The Russians want something similar to what the Chinese want: an international order open enough to enable their country to thrive, but that does not press them to make Russia democratic. Moscow's position, however, is weaker than Beijing's. With an economy ranked only eleventh in the world in 2021, less than 8 percent the size of America's and 10 percent of China's, and heavily dependent on oil and gas exports, Russia has less leverage over the international environment.[6] It cannot buy as many friends nor set as many agendas. Russia is driven to more coercive means of revisionism, using election manipulation, blackmail, and war to get its way.[7]

No doubt the Chinese and Russians are correct that the Americans want their country to remain the world's most powerful. In that, Americans are no different from citizens of any great power in modern history. The more difficult problem is that the United States is a liberal democracy and China and Russia are not, and do not seem fated to become democracies any time soon. Hence their power is an indirect but real threat to democracy everywhere, including in the United States itself, and American power is an indirect but real threat to the Chinese and Russian regimes.

That is why the rulers in Beijing and Moscow are taking various steps to make the world select for autocracy. Xi Jinping and Vladimir Putin intuitively grasp the regime-power dilemma, that the ecosystem cannot be rigged to advantage both of these regime types. The ecosystem's decades-old bias toward liberal democracy has handicapped Russia and China and will do so as long as they are authoritarian states. It is time, Beijing and Moscow believe, to turn the coevolutionary table—to reengineer the ecosystem into one that lets them flourish as they are and makes the United States the country that feels the pressure to adapt.

Fixing Evolution

For the Chinese Communist Party's leadership, the regime-power dilemma was manifest in 1989, when the West's harsh reaction to the Tiananmen Square massacre revealed a much lower ceiling to China's rise than it had expected. Between that year and roughly 2008, Beijing managed the dilemma by nodding agreeably or changing the subject when human rights or democracy were discussed in diplomatic settings. Since 2008 China's leaders have changed strategies, facing the problem directly and mobilizing their foreign-policy apparatus to turn the tables on the wealthy democracies. Analysts of China's international moves tend to focus on threats to Taiwan, military assertiveness in the South China Sea, and the aggressive "wolf-warrior" diplomacy that has become familiar in recent years. China's more subtle actions to alter the three components of the international environment—the balance of power among regime types, international rules and institutions, and information—may have a more profound lasting impact on democracy in the world, however.

That Russia likewise suffers from a Western-imposed regime-power dilemma only became clear to Putin in 2003 and 2004, a few years into his rule. He had just taken steps he believed absolutely necessary to stabilize Russia and his own government. The West's response was scathing criticism for human rights violations and, worse, aid to the color revolutions in Georgia and Ukraine. Since 2004 the Kremlin has worked to weaken and divide the West and to undermine the global narrative about liberal democracy's superiority; to alter discourse and practice concerning human rights; and to cast doubt on the West's claim that the liberal international order is liberal or "rules-based" at all. It wants to show that the world is better off with a multipolar international system, and that Russia is leading the way in bringing about that world.

The two autocratic powers have made common cause on several fronts.[8] By no means do they form a tight bloc. Still, the two powers are working together in limited but consequential

ways to safeguard their own authoritarian-capitalist regimes.[9]
Between 2012 and 2022 Xi met with Putin three dozen times.[10]

THE BALANCE OF POWER AMONG REGIMES

Beijing and Moscow have attempted to weaken democracy and
strengthen autocracy in the world in various ways. Neither
government is on a crusade to remake the world in its image.
The chief aim of each is to preserve its own regime. But autocracy preservation involves keeping liberal democracy out of
the neighborhood. In practice, that sometimes mean enabling
autocracy in other countries.[11] Chapter 6 showed that Russia's
rulers have been much more aggressive autocracy promoters
because democracy is in Russia's immediate western neighborhood, where the United States and its allies have actively
been promoting it. Putin and his circle see themselves in a
contest with the United States over what is rightfully Russia's
sphere of influence. Moscow evidently has written off the Baltic states of Estonia, Latvia, and Lithuania, now members of
NATO. But it has poured resources into keeping constitutional
self-government at bay not only in Ukraine, Georgia, and Belarus, but also in Moldova, Armenia, Kyrgyzstan, and elsewhere, using money and propaganda to help autocrats win
elections and stay in power, and to undermine liberals when
they governed.

In 2014 Russia began using another tool by trying to divide the Western democracies and weaken their commitment
to liberal internationalism. It extended its battle-tested political interference operations beyond former Soviet republics
into the West itself, widening rifts, deepening the demoraliza-
tion, and easing the rise of anti-NATO populism. Putin's United
Russia party lent France's National Front party €9 million. Russian hackers attacked the website of Poland's electoral commis-

sion.[12] In 2015 United Russia signed a five-year "cooperation agreement" with Austria's far-right Freedom Party.[13] Russians hacked into the German parliament to steal election documents, spread disinformation during Scotland's referendum on independence, and created fake accounts purporting to be in the Finnish parliament.

In 2016 the Kremlin picked up the pace by reaching into the Brexit vote in the United Kingdom and the presidential election in the United States. Russian operatives stole documents and spread disinformation to favor Brexit and Trump and sow confusion. They supported a failed coup d'état in Montenegro. In 2017 they hacked into French presidential candidate Emmanuel Macron's campaign and propagated anti-immigrant messages. They flooded German social media and the internet with messages hostile to Angela Merkel's government. In 2018 Russians used fake social media accounts to spread political messages in Italy, the Netherlands, and Spain; Russian cyberattacks hit Dutch and Spanish parties and Swedish newspapers, and Russian disinformation campaigns hit Bulgaria and Macedonia.[14]

China has interfered in democratic elections on a smaller scale. A study at the University of Cardiff finds that a video of a man burning ballots cast for Trump at Virginia Beach—a video that went viral after Eric Trump posted it—may have originated in China; it turned out that the ballots were samples, not actual votes. Another Cardiff study finds that several high-quality videos using footage of the January 6, 2021, Capitol attack to discredit U.S. democracy came from Chinese sources.[15] In an irony familiar to the democracies, the Chinese are using open liberal internationalism to undermine the democratic regime that built it—that of the United States.[16]

China's main efforts to weaken democracy have been less direct. Its rulers have long professed tolerance of all regime types so long as their governments are pragmatic—that is, willing to do business with China on terms that China can accept. China's chief method of buttressing authoritarianism abroad is to invest heavily in countries that need infrastructure. The Belt and Road Initiative (BRI), once known as the "New Silk Road" and then as "One Belt, One Road," is a sprawling and decentralized project, stretching across scores of countries from Southeast Asia to Southwest Asia, Africa, Latin America, and even Europe. The BRI is the largest infrastructure project in history. Its announced goal of $1 trillion is more than seven times the value of America's postwar Marshall Plan in real (2020) dollars. Chinese companies are building seaports, airports, railways, highways, pipelines, power grids, optical cables, satellite communication facilities, and more in countries without the financial or technical means to build their own. The BRI includes six overland corridors connecting regions to China.[17] (Some of these have encountered difficulties with local politicians and practices.)[18]

It is clear the BRI is partly about making money for the Chinese companies involved, which have surplus capacity, and equally clear that the economies of many host countries can benefit from the investment.[19] But more is at stake than corporate profits. Although private lenders have increased loans in recent years, the chief BRI funders, and sometimes lead planning agencies of its projects, have been the state-owned China Development Bank and Export-Import Bank.[20] State-owned enterprises are more likely than private firms to carry out BRI projects.[21] The party-state clearly sees a strategic interest in the grand project. Its flagship project is the $70 billion China–Pakistan Economic Corridor. It starts at the port of Gwadar, Pakistan, less than four hundred miles from the mouth of the Persian Gulf, source of a third of the world's oil. A planned highway and pipeline would transport gulf oil through Pakistan into China's Xinjiang province. If completed, the Pakistan project would reduce China's exposure to energy disruption: at present, its immense oil imports pass through the Strait of Malacca in the territorial waters of Malaysia, with which the United States has close naval cooperation, and Singapore, whose naval base grants the U.S. Navy various privileges. The China–Pakistan corridor is smart statecraft.[22]

But China is also using the BRI to export tools to many countries that make autocracy easier.[23] Adam Segal writes that Beijing "promote[s] [its] model of internet management to China's BRI partners and strengthen[s] their capability to exercise control over their own cyberspace." China provides authoritarian governments with surveillance hardware and training in techniques. Employees of Huawei—by far the biggest exporter of this technology—are reported to have aided security officials in Uganda and Zambia track regime opponents.[24] As of 2019, thirty-six of the eighty-six BRI countries had received artificial intelligence surveillance infrastructure from China. Huawei had exported seventy-five "smart city-public security projects." In many cases, recipients have benefited from low-interest loans from China's Export-Import Bank. Huawei itself appears to have closer ties to the party than it admits, including with China's security and intelligence bureaus.[25] China's own example shows that twenty-first-century digital technology makes authoritarian control easier.[26]

The BRI has made the international environment friendlier to authoritarian capitalism in less direct ways. As the United States and European powers themselves have demonstrated abundantly over centuries, credit gives wealthy countries leverage over poor countries. Countries that owe China large sums or want more BRI investment have reason to shield China from criticism at the UN, to criticize China's rivals.[27] The Chinese message that their goal is a world in which all states are treated

equally, not like the anachronistic, hierarchical world built by
the imperialistic West, resonates in poorer and younger states.[28]
The BRI validates China's development model of using state
assets to build infrastructure.[29] The BRI also can encourage corruption; countries such as Argentina and Kenya have changed
or possibly broken their laws to accommodate China, making
them less transparent and more hostile to labor.[30]

Like Moscow, Beijing has labored to peel democracies
away from the United States. In 2017 a scandal erupted in Australia when it came to light that Chinese businessmen with ties
to the Chinese Communist Party were contributing large sums
of money to both main Australian political parties; in return,
the parties were to soften their positions on China's assertiveness in the South China Sea.[31] Most dramatic is the long-
running tension over Taiwan (the Republic of China), a democracy with which the United States has long had special, if
complex, relations. One of the Chinese Community Party's chief
goals is reunification with Taiwan. A report funded by the Taiwanese government accuses the Beijing government of "cognitive warfare," a mix of intimidation and misinformation aiming
to undermine pro-independence politicians and sentiment.[32]

Not content to act alone, China and Russia have joined
forces in trying to constrain and reverse the spread of democracy. In the early months of the Russo-Ukrainian war, China's
government amplified Russia's official message that the war
was not about Ukraine defending its sovereignty and democracy against Russian aggression, but rather about Russia defending its sovereignty against American imperialism. (Yet,
China heeded U.S. warnings not to provide material support
to Russia's war efforts by subverting the deep economic sanctions imposed by the West.)

More generally, through the Shanghai Cooperation Organization (SCO)—examined more closely below—Moscow and

Beijing have built broad foreign support for authoritarian regimes to counter international democratic institutions. "Sovereignty," "non-interference," "diversity," "stability"—these words
figure prominently in the SCO's founding documents, and
they clearly signal a united opposition to Western democracy
promotion. "Stability" evidently means warding off color revolutions; "diversity" means that each country can find its own
path to development, be it democratic or not; "human rights"
are relative to a country's traditions.[33]

The two authoritarian powers have also led the way in
countering Western NGOs that promote democracy. Believing that NGOs drove the color revolutions of the 2000s and
the Arab Uprising of 2011, Russia and China have hobbled
NGO activity in their own regions and have created their own
pseudo-NGOs, with the curious label "government-organized
non-governmental organizations" (GONGOs). When Western
NGOs send monitors to observe elections, the SCO sometimes
follows suit and sends monitors of its own. To no one's surprise, the assessments of what Alexander Cooley calls "zom-
bie monitors" nearly always differ from those of the Western
NGOs.[34]

INFORMATION ABOUT REGIME TYPES

Both authoritarian giants are running complex information
campaigns to blunt the appeal of democracy and build authoritarianism's reputation for competence and global momentum.[35]
Russia's notion of "hybrid warfare" (see Chapter 6) includes a
heavy component of information warfare. The Kremlin firmly
believes that the West has been trying to keep Russia down
for many years by persuading elites around the world that liberal democracy is the only real route to national development.
China's leaders agree. In 2012 Hu Jintao warned that "hostile

foreign powers are using methods of soft power to Westernize and divide China."[36]

New information can enter the environment without any special effort by challengers. Elites around the world pay attention to the successes and failures of authoritarianism and democracy because they want to know what contributes to national power, wealth, and stability in today's world. China has enjoyed gravitational pull among foreign elites by virtue of its astonishing performance as a country over the past four decades. Its generation of wealth, economic development, enduring political stability, and other widely recognized marks of national success have built the reputation of a loosely defined "China Model." From 1979 to 2019 China's economy grew from $315 billion to $11.54 trillion; that is more than 356 percent, or an average of nearly 9 percent growth per annum, doubling in size every eight years.[37] The World Bank calls this "the fastest sustained expansion by a major economy in history." In the process, eight hundred million Chinese have escaped from poverty. Depending on how national economies are measured, China's either became the world's largest in 2016 or should do so around 2030. China today is the world's largest exporter and holder of foreign exchange reserves.[38]

The country also has managed the inevitable societal disruptions that come from such rapid economic growth. In 1979, 18.6 percent of the population lived in urban areas; in 2019 the figure was 60.3 percent.[39] In 1979 just under one million Chinese were enrolled in universities; the 2019 figure was 53.8 million.[40] Swift urbanization and educational progress often bring civil unrest and the threat of revolution. China had a close run with revolution in 1989, but since then the party's rule has been remarkably stable. As shown in Chapter 5, citizens have reported high satisfaction with their government's performance.

Political scientist Michael Miller has found that democracy spreads in periods when democracies' incomes grow rapidly. In similar fashion, he argues, China's recent economic success relative to democracies should spur a diffusion of its authoritarian-capitalist model.[41] Stefan Halper sees Chinese economic success as the chief driver of the spread of its system. On an official visit to Washington, a Mongolian official said that while his country remained committed to democratic reform, "we really like what we see in China. . . . You get the benefit of 10 percent annual growth, a middle class, and leaders know that they have a job for more than four years . . . but without the 'side-effects' of democracy."[42] Luiz Inácio Lula da Silva, president of Brazil, has expressed admiration for the Beijing model based on its ability to develop an economy without sacrificing national sovereignty.[43]

China's Ministry of Propaganda broadcasts the virtues of its regime to Chinese and foreigners alike. It has been especially burdened to "tell China's story well," as Xi put it in his 2017 speech before the Nineteenth Party Congress. "Socialism with Chinese characteristics," Xi asserted, is "blazing a new trail for other developing countries to achieve modernization. It offers a new option for other countries and nations who want to speed up their development while preserving their independence; and it offers Chinese wisdom and a Chinese approach to solving the problems facing mankind."[44] Fudan University professor Zhang Weiwei has published bestselling books—all translated into English, the global *lingua franca*—making the case that the American model has failed and the Chinese model is both novel and a great success.[45]

Beijing has harnessed television and digital technology for its public diplomacy efforts. China Central Television has studios in dozens of countries—chiefly recipients of its aid—and broadcasts in local languages. Platforms such as Facebook and Twitter give the party a more tailored and seemingly intimate way to reach foreign publics than was possible before the internet. A 2021 report from the University of Oxford finds that Chinese diplomats, usually disguised as ordinary citizens, have increased their social media statements about the superiority of China and its regime. The impact of these posts is vastly augmented by "super-spreader" accounts, possibly run by algorithms, that rapidly repost them.[46]

China's ability to suppress the COVID-19 pandemic in 2020 further burnished its regime's image at home and abroad. The SARS-CoV-2 virus evidently originated in Wuhan, and at first party officials tried to suppress information about its nature and spread. But as the disease leapt to other countries, the party pivoted and acted ruthlessly to halt its spread within China. It mobilized regional and local cadres to enforce severe lockdowns and monitor the illness's spread; noncompliance would damage a citizen's social-credit score and hence prospects for educational and professional advancement. China essentially went on a war footing.[47] By December 15, 2020, China's rolling seven-day average of new cases was 108, while that in the United States was 214,735.[48] The party has made the most of the prowess China has shown in managing the pandemic, telling its own people and the world that COVID-19 reveals the vigor of the China Model and the decrepitude of the American model and Western liberal democracy. "Time to wake up from blind faith in the Western system," announced the *China Education News* in December 2020. "Vicious partisan fighting has worsened in certain Western countries, social fissures have deepened, and a severe social crisis is brewing."[49]

Beijing has brought thousands of officials of less developed countries to China to train them in how to develop an economy while maintaining a single party in power. The Baise Executive Leadership Academy in Guanxi province, founded in 2017, has trained more than one thousand Association of

Southeast Asian Nations officials in such topics as "how to 'guide public opinion' online when there are emergencies, and how to alleviate poverty in a 'targeted' way." Beijing has focused particular attention on Cambodia. The Chinese government also trains judges and police officers from member states in the SCO.[50] Hundreds of African officials have made the pilgrimage to China for instruction in how to extend state control over civil society through censorship of social media.

Like the United States before it, China works to build and use soft power, or the ability to get others to want what China wants. Beijing has constructed a narrative of benevolence around the BRI, depicting it as an immense, wise plan to bring the world's peoples together for the benefit of all—a "shared future for mankind," as Xi likes to put it.[51] The party is working through higher educational institutions overseas to burnish the image of its brand of autocracy. With cooperation from university campuses, Beijing has established hundreds of Confucius Institutes in dozens of countries to educate people in Chinese languages, culture, and history. These institutes have been perceived on some campuses as propaganda engines uninterested in the free exchange of ideas, however, and many have been shuttered.[52]

Recent surveys of Chinese scholars and officials suggest a lack of confidence in the country's ability to outdo the United States in terms of soft power.[53] The consumer goods that China exports—particularly digital hardware—enable individualism as much as anything the United States exports, and they reinforce the norms that buttress liberalism, particularly in its twenty-first-century open form. China's cultural exports, particularly in music, film, and sport, do not come close to rivaling those of the United States. China is, however, using its market leverage to alter U.S. movies and coerce foreign athletes, team owners, and celebrities to favor a Chinese point of view.[54] The year 2021 saw a victory for Chinese efforts, as eighty countries expressed support for the party's repressive policies in Xinjiang province.[55]

Russia's domestic regime may seem to have less to recommend it than does China's. That has not deterred the Kremlin from hammering away at the aging narrative that liberal democracy is the final and best regime for the human race. "The liberal idea," Putin told the *Financial Times* in 2019, has "outlived its purpose" as publics in democracies have soured on international openness, particularly immigration. "[Liberals] cannot simply dictate anything to anyone just like they have been attempting to do over the recent decades," he added.[56] Sergei Lavrov, Russia's foreign minister, has blamed disorder and terrorism on the West's attempt to spread liberalism: "The reverse side of the 'West-centric' globalization model, the persistent desire to measure others by one's own pseudo-liberal values, impose changes from the outside with no consideration for local traditions and even use force to remove undesirable regimes, has been a surge in international terrorism."[57]

Moscow has posed Russia as the great alternative. In former Soviet republics it has taken advantage of ethnic Russians— many of whom favor Russian-language media and feel partial to Russia already—to drive home its notions about political legitimacy. In the former Soviet republics in Central Asia, it has used its soft power to buttress the notion of "sovereign democracy" (see Chapter 6), already congenial to the autocrats in place there.[58] Dozens of Russian GONGOs propagate the message in these countries and find Russian-speakers particularly receptive.[59]

Beyond its own region, Putin has made much of Russia's claim to be the global champion of anti-liberalism. Against open borders and a single liberal social model, it defends national sovereignty and respect for cultural and historical difference. Against liberal experimentation with sexual norms and gender identities, it poses social conservatism and tradition.[60] Against the aggressive West, especially the United States, pushing these alien values onto countries that do not want them, Russia works for a more democratic world, in which societies control how they organize their own internal affairs. Russia claims to be the champion of global social conservatism, the only significant counterforce to the decadent liberalism with which the West constantly bombards the rest of the world. Intellectuals noted in Chapter 6—Nataliya Narochnitskaya, Alexander Dugin, Vladislav Surkov—and others supply theoretical material. State-run RT (formerly Russia Today) and the multimedia company Sputnik broadcast these messages across five continents.[61]

Russia and China sometimes join forces to propagandize against liberal democracy. Leaders from the two countries use their frequent summit meetings to denounce Western democracy promotion. At their July 2005 meeting in Moscow, Putin and Hu Jintao blasted those who "ignore objective processes of social development of sovereign states and impose on them alien models of social and political systems."[62]

INTERNATIONAL INSTITUTIONS AND PRACTICES

Both authoritarian powers are keenly aware of the importance of international society and global governance to the international environment. Liberal rules and interpretations have handicapped Russia and China in many ways: by leading to economic sanctions, by penalizing closed and opaque ways of doing business, by harming autocracy's international reputation. Together and separately, Moscow and Beijing have taken pains to remove liberal biases from the rules of some international organizations and by building their own. What political scientist Katherine Morton writes of Xi's China is true of Putin's Russia: it has set out to "shap[e] the system of global governance rather than simply navigat[e] around it."[63]

Political scientists have found that "Western linkages"—international exchanges of goods and money, people, and information between mature democracies and autocracies—have shifted some autocracies toward democracy.[64] It follows that shriveling those linkages and constructing new ones to authoritarian giants could have the reverse effect, moving states toward autocracy. China and especially Russia have been building authoritarian links for many years. Their most concerted attempt to build an international political organization of their own has been the SCO, created by Beijing and Moscow in 2002. The SCO's original stated purpose was to combat the "three evils" of terrorism, separatism, and extremism; members agreed to nonaggression and nonintervention in one another's internal affairs.[65] In 2017 it admitted India and Pakistan. It then contained half of the world's population but found its purposes further diluted.[66] More an aspiration than a significant element of the international environment, the SCO is still useful for generating multilateral support for Sino-Russian proposals. The two also have used the BRICS—Brazil, Russia, India, China, and South Africa—to pose a symbolic alternative to the hegemony of the liberal West. In its early months, Russia's war on Ukraine showed signs of solidifying the BRICS. Publicly they agreed that the war was more about resisting U.S. imperialism than suppressing Ukrainian democracy and independence.[67]

Russia has gone beyond China in constructing international institutions designed to bind former Soviet republics to itself. The Eurasian Economic Union (EEU), discussed in Chapter 6, aims to build economic interdependence. The Collective Security Treaty Organization (CSTO) is a military alliance comprising Russia, Belarus, Armenia, Kazakhstan, Kyrgyzstan, and Tajikistan.[68] By no means is the CSTO a latter-day Warsaw Pact, the Soviets' tightly institutionalized Cold War, anti-NATO alliance.[69] It has, however, been a way for Russia to garner multilateral support for its efforts to alter international rules.

Beijing and Moscow also have worked through existing international institutions to try to nudge discourse, rules, and practices away from their original liberal orientation toward support for autocracy. In Chapter 5 we saw how Beijing has worked through the WTO and other entities to transform norms of international trade toward giving an advantage to economies with a large state sector. Russia, too, is a member of the WTO and has profited enormously from economic openness, yet its leaders want to have more control over their country's economy without paying a penalty. Russia first applied for membership in the WTO's predecessor, the General Agreement on Tariffs and Trade (GATT), in 1993. Final accession only came two decades later. One reason for the lengthy process was the ambivalence of Russian elites who depended on state support and knew that WTO membership could jeopardize their positions.

During his first presidential term (2000–2004), Putin was keen for Russia to join the WTO because he wanted a privatized economy. In 2004, as the color revolutions darkened his view of liberalism, he began to extend greater state control over Russia's economy and seek more leverage over former Soviet republics. His interest in the WTO waned.[70] When the 2008 global financial meltdown damaged Russia's economy, Putin became even more ambivalent.[71] In 2009 came a strange episode: Moscow announced that it would only join the WTO as part of a customs union it had organized with Belarus and Kazakhstan. The WTO was adamant that only individual states could join, and Moscow reverted back to its solo application.[72]

For the next decade, Russia was a fairly typical WTO member. Its 2022 invasion of Ukraine, however, led a number of wealthy countries, including the United States, to suspend Russia's most-favored-nation status, and in May, Moscow announced its intention to withdraw Russia from the WTO.[73]

Human rights and the internet also stand out as areas where Moscow and Beijing are trying to construct alternative rules that favor autocracies over democracies. International law contains a sizable body of UN declarations and covenants on human rights that most countries have signed and ratified. Neither China nor Russia has set out to wreck the UN's elaborate human rights regime. Instead, both have worked from the inside to reshape the discourse that directs the regime's goals and methods.

With help from the Russian Orthodox hierarchy, Moscow has labored to replace the open liberal discourse of individual rights with language that upholds tradition and cultural difference. In 2006 Nataliya Narochnitskaya (see Chapter 6), a leading Russian anti-liberal thinker, joined a group of clergy and laity in producing a "Declaration of the Rights and Dignity of the Human Being." It read: "We recognize the rights and freedoms of the person to the extent that they facilitate the ascent of the personality towards good, protect him from internal and external evil, and permit him to realize himself positively in society." Rights correctly understood aimed at helping the individual achieve dignity, and dignity entailed duties to family, local community, nation, and humanity. Rights that did not respect traditional values would endanger "the existence of the Fatherland." The UN's 1948 Universal Declaration of Human Rights, the Russian declaration said, was a recipe for moral and social chaos.[74] Elements of the Russian critique of mainstream liberal human rights were similar to some Western critiques, such as those calling for more emphasis on community and less on individual autonomy.[75] Yet Russia added a strong dose of nationalism and ultimately was using the critique to safeguard its authoritarian regime.

In 2008 the Russian government, following its strategy to become a global champion of social conservatism, began a long campaign to implant its 2006 document into official UN language and procedures. Metropolitan Kirill of the Russian church told the Human Rights Council that the UN's existing human rights discourse was marred by a "limiting range of ideas about human nature, which are not shared by most people in the world." The following year, with support from China, the council passed a Russia-sponsored resolution to hold a seminar on "how a better understanding of traditional values of humankind . . . can contribute to the promotion and protection of human rights." The seminar, held in Geneva in 2010, pitted the UN High Commissioner for Human Rights, Navi Pillay of South Africa, against Narochnitskaya herself and a draft report by Vladimir Kartashkin, a Russian law professor. Pillay and the human rights establishment warned that "traditional values" were in effect a cudgel to oppress women and sexual minorities. A 2012 resolution passed by the council split the difference, stating blandly that traditional values were important to human rights.[76]

The Chinese delegation supported the Russians, asserting that "disrespect for culture was itself a human rights violation."[77] For the Chinese Communist Party, the UN's liberal conception of human rights sullies China's reputation, exposes it to possible economic sanctions, and can even reach inside of China itself to elevate opposition to party rule.[78] Since Tiananmen Square, the party has labored behind the scenes to alter the way the UN talked about human rights. It worked with the Like-Minded Group, a coalition of two dozen developing states that shared its interest in fending off meddling liberals and their insulting human rights reports.[79] In 2005 the UN was in the process of replacing its old Commission on Human Rights with a new Human Rights Council. China, Russia, and the rest of the Like-Minded Group succeeded in opening the council's membership to all countries, including those with atrocious human rights records. They also successfully barred human rights experts and NGOs from participating in the writing of UN human rights reports, thus closing off significant sources of critical information and analysis. They failed, however, to bar the council from conducting periodic reports on specific countries.[80]

Under Xi, China has acted still more assertively. It has pressed for a particularistic norm of human rights by proposing "human rights with Chinese characteristics." As the Chinese delegation said in protesting a 2013 UN report, "Whether the shoes fit, only the person knows. . . . The Chinese are in the best position to know the situation of human rights in China."[81] Beijing's biannual South-South Human Rights Forum has cultivated an alternative language of human rights among developing countries.[82] The 2017 forum declaration was typical in stating that human rights must take into account regional, national, and historical contexts.[83]

All of this writing, talking, and lobbying has met with some success. The UN Human Rights Council has passed resolutions introduced by Beijing that "suggest that human rights depend on 'people-centered' development." The UN, it said, should stop "naming and shaming" alleged rights violators. Instead, economic development of the nation must come first; "'mutually beneficial cooperation,' constructive dialogue, technical assistance, and capacity-building should be the primary tools for promoting human rights." The Like-Minded Group has defended China's actions in its Xinjiang province in the name of national sovereignty and attacked U.S. and European countries for hypocrisy. Chinese media have praised the country's "growing influence and ability to set the agenda in international human rights governance."[84]

The story in the realm of global cyber governance is similar. Nowhere does the regime-power dilemma confront Beijing and Moscow more clearly than in the digital revolution. These authoritarian powers cannot do without the internet. By making information cheaper than ever, it has increased the returns to openness for countries seeking national development and competitiveness. Yet, openness brings heavy risks to both regimes because it brings an unending flood of foreign ideas that include new identities and affiliations that could challenge the power of the Chinese and Russian regimes.[85] As Xi has put the matter, "Western anti-China forces have continually tried in vain to use the internet to 'pull down' China."[86]

"Multi-stakeholderism" is the clumsy term for the original global internet norm of complete openness. A product of Silicon Valley culture as underwritten by America's open liberal regime, multi-stakeholderism is a bottom-up, decentralized norm in which "technical communities, civil society, and the private sector," rather than states, play the leading roles in governance.[87] Multi-stakeholderism envisages an internet free of governmental censorship, stretching across all national borders, bringing individuals in all nations together for unencumbered interaction, mutual benefit, and emancipation. The United States has backed the multi-stakeholder vision out of liberal principle but also because the world's major internet companies have been American.[88]

Beijing and Moscow have led what analysts call the "post-liberal challenge" to the U.S.-sponsored global internet order.[89] They both aim for a new worldwide norm of national internet sovereignty (in Mandarin, *wangluo zhuquan*).[90] Within China, the Chinese Communist Party controls, monitors, and harnesses all social media, transforming them from a threat into a support. It has used its considerable market power to prevail on U.S. internet giants to censor social media and to pressure anyone critical of Chinese policies, including foreign entertainers and sports executives. The party's 2010 "White Paper" on the internet lays out China's distinctive concepts and policies, particularly on what constitutes a threat to "security." "National situations and cultural traditions differ among countries, and so concern about internet security also differs," reads the White Paper. "Concerns about internet security of various countries should be fully respected."[91] In Russia the state has not monopolized the internet—Putin has focused more on traditional broadcast media—but has tightened its control over time and has pushed in the same direction as China.

The two countries have worked through international institutions to bring about the changes they want. The original UN group working on internet governance was dominated by Western countries. It voted down national sovereignty proposals from authoritarian powers. In 2011 Tajikistan and Uzbekistan joined China and Russia in submitting to the UN a proposal to alter global governance in the cyber realm. The stated goal was to establish a multilateral and "democratic" system of global internet governance that allowed national censorship. It failed.[92] In 2018 Russia proposed a new UN internet working group open to all countries. The new group, working in parallel to the original group, has more authoritarian members and is more receptive to the national-sovereignty norm.[93]

Moscow and Beijing also have worked through international institutions that they founded. The SCO has made clear its opposition to the use of "information communication technology" for "political purposes that . . . trigger social instability in countries."[94] In 2015 the SCO submitted a revised proposal softening some of the language but again suggesting a norm of national censorship.[95] A year earlier, the historic town of Wuzhen hosted China's first World Internet Conference. The Wuzhen Declaration stressed each country's "internet sovereignty." China's 2017 International Strategy of Cooperation on Cyberspace is similar, calling on countries not to "pursue cyber hegemony, interfere in other countries' internal affairs, or engage in, condone or support cyber activities that undermine other countries' national security."[96] China wants the UN to have a regulatory role over the internet and to give governments priority over private firms and civil society. Ironically, as foreign cyber-intervention in elections has become a high concern, more and more countries—even some liberal democracies—have moved toward China's view of internet sovereignty.[97] Russia, meanwhile, works through the Collective Security Treaty Organization, comprising a number of authoritarian former Soviet republics, to spread the norm of national internet sovereignty.[98]

Is all of this activity by the rulers of China and Russia— maneuvering to deliberalize international rules regarding trade, the internet, and human rights; elevating autocrats and undermining democrats in foreign countries; and burnishing the international image of authoritarian capitalism—really a threat to democracy in the world? Does it compromise America's own ability to remain a prosperous and powerful democracy?

Not in an immediate sense. As Chapters 3 and 4 have shown, the United States needs no outside help in damaging its own democracy. The threat to democracy from Chinese and Russian ecological engineering construction is more indirect and long-term. American self-government's stability and legitimacy were supported for many years by a pro-liberal international environment—one deliberately molded by the United

States itself. The Xi and Putin governments are patiently trying to change the environment's liberal-democratic bias into one favoring authoritarian capitalism. It is the work of decades, and is only beginning. The more that China continues to rise, the more Russia expands its influence, the more success they will have in flipping the regime-power dilemma. Autocracies will feel less pressure to democratize, unsteady democracies will lean more authoritarian, and leaders in the United States and other democracies will be tempted to edge away from democracy. An authoritarian-friendly international ecosystem would force an unwanted choice on democracies: adapt by becoming less democratic, or resign yourself to perpetual disadvantage.

Liberal internationalism has some astounding successes to its credit. One of those is today's China, a vibrant, wealthy, ambitious country, no longer picked apart by foreigners or crippling itself with ideology but sovereign, wealthy, confident, and bidding to surpass the United States as the world's greatest power. China's ruling party deserves most of the credit for its rise, particularly Deng Xiaoping and his early reformers. They set a course in the late 1970s and early 1980s that the party continues to follow. But Deng's genius consisted partly in his understanding that making China great again required adapting the country to the liberal international order only up to the point where risks to China's domestic regime became too high.

A more qualified success is today's Russia. Liberal internationalism helped cause the abrupt decomposition of the old Soviet Union, which left Russia as the biggest of the successor republics. It also pummeled Russia in the 1990s, with help from the country's own internal corruption and feeble political institutions. But Putin's authoritarian rule permitted Russia to grow in the liberal international ecosystem. Until they threw it away by attacking Ukraine with all of Russia's might in 2022,

Putin and his circle had figured out how to reap some of its benefits, including exporting to wealthy democracies and attracting investment from them, while holding democracy at bay.

After decades of thinking that all that happened after 1989 was an afterword to history, leaders in the West have come to understand that history has more chapters. The Xi and Putin governments are adapting international order to their own desires and plans. Neither Beijing nor Moscow is focused on making America or Japan or Australia or Europe authoritarian. They simply want their own countries to be rid of the regime-power dilemma that the West has placed on them for so long. They have had enough of choosing between keeping their regime and aspiring to great-power status. They want it both ways, as America has had it both ways for so long. They want the United States and the other liberal democracies to face their own regime-power dilemma: if you choose to remain a liberal democracy, be prepared to operate at a handicap in international relations.

8

Making the World
Select for Democracy

In its earlier, post–World War II form, liberal internationalism was not designed to be a system of global governance to supersede national sovereignty. It was not chiefly a scheme to enrich global capital. It was not a grandiose bid to achieve world peace or universal democracy. It was an elaborate strategy to protect constitutional self-government in the United States and for its democratic allies. Its designers understood that the international environment can favor democracy or handicap it. In building new institutions and rules and in promoting democracy and containing communism, liberal internationalist leaders aimed to enable the United States to avoid having to choose between prosperity and power, on the one hand, and democracy, on the other.

But in recent times, vast numbers of Americans have turned against liberal internationalism. That is bad news, because, as Paul Musgrave argues, for liberal internationalism to survive, it must be supported by the American public.[1] In 2016 the country elected a president who promised to end this decades-old grand strategy. Even his opponent, Hillary Clinton, a veteran internationalist, found that she had to back away from certain aspects of it. She repudiated the very Trans-Pacific Partnership that she had worked for as secretary of state—itself an elaborate attempt to take back from China the pole position in shaping the international environment. In 2020 Americans elected a president, Joe Biden, who promised to reunite the country and put it back in front of the liberal international order—tasks that he saw as related. He made some headway in reuniting the wealthy democracies. But the spur to that renewed comity was Russia's aggression in Ukraine and China's trampling of human rights. Those countries continued to loom even as polarization in the United States perpetuated itself. The pummeling of American democracy, and its weakening in much of the rest of the world, continued apace.

In a sense, the United States is most to blame for its own troubles. It has been pumping open liberalism into the international environment for more than a generation. China is a superpower in part because the United States beckoned it further and further into the liberal ecosystem. The good news is that America can still influence the future of its own democracy. As it has done before, it can strengthen its own domestic system of constitutional self-government and that of other countries as well. This book is about coevolution, and coevolution recognizes agency: countries share an international environment that is shaped by great powers. In principle, the United States can reengineer the liberal ecosystem and limit the harm from a Sino-Russian reshaping of international order. That need not mean enmity with China and Russia. It does mean that America should step back, change its ways, and infuse the international environment with a bias that supports constitutional self-government in the twenty-first century, within its own borders and elsewhere.

The Regime-Power Dilemma

The international environment tends to select for one regime type more than for others. An ecosystem that favors autocracy imposes upon democracies a trade-off between two things that they want very much: national competitiveness and liberal democracy itself. They must give up more liberty and self-government than they would like for an acceptable degree of national power and prosperity—or else give up more national power to gain an acceptable degree of liberty and self-government. Such a democracy is under pressure to adapt to the unfriendly ecosystem. If it wants more power, wealth, and security, it must become more authoritarian. If it wants to protect its domestic regime, it must accept national decline.

It is no surprise that these competing pressures have pushed analysts from various places on the political spectrum to gesture in an authoritarian direction. *New York Times* columnist Thomas Friedman, a centrist liberal, has repeatedly speculated in print about how America could solve its problems if it had China's one-party system, at least for a day. "One-party autocracy certainly has its drawbacks," wrote Friedman in 2009. "But when it is led by a reasonably enlightened group of people, as China is today, it can also have great advantages. That one party can just impose the politically difficult but critically important policies needed to move a society forward in the 21st century."[2] Making a similar point is progressive comedian Jon Stewart: "It's a remarkably inefficient system that's not agile, and I think it's why democracy . . . is in some ways on the wane in the world."[3] From the populist Right, TV personality Tucker Carlson has pushed the point further: "In China . . . leaders still think beyond the next election. They don't have real elections, so they can take a long-term view. And in China, they understand that countries in which the population is divided against itself, countries in which citizens have nothing meaningful in common with one another, are weak countries. And over time, countries like that are doomed."[4]

Certainly, the United States and its fellow democracies can learn from authoritarian countries. China's high-speed railways, for example, are greatly superior to passenger rail in the United States. The United States and its democratic partners have adapted to pressure from China's Belt and Road Initiative (BRI) by offering to find infrastructure projects in the Build Back Better World (B3W) initiative—although conventional bridge-and-tunnel infrastructure is not emphasized.[5] But B3W is financed by the private sector and does not portend a move toward autocracy.

Reaching for the other horn of the dilemma has been the so-called "Restraint school." These analysts do not want a weak America, to be sure, but they do call on the country's leaders to pull it back from many of its global commitments and allow Russia and China their spheres of influence. The Restraint school is grounded in a realist theory of international relations that focuses on material power and the perpetual insecurity of states in an anarchical international system. It makes the important claim that when one state increases its material power, even for defensive reasons, other states will feel threatened and compelled to respond in kind. That is a different dilemma, called the *security dilemma:* increasing your power to make yourself more secure can make others feel less secure, and those others will then increase their power, putting you back where you started. The Restrainers say that the United States has run afoul of the security dilemma by extending its power so far—into the Indo-Pacific, Eastern Europe, and the Middle East for good measure—that an alarmed China and Russia have no choice but to push back by increasing their own power.

These countries are not doing anything nefarious or even un-
usual; they are responding rationally to American foreign policy. Some realists point out that expanding national power can
be hazardous to democracy, too, because it means centralizing
domestic power.[6]

The Restraint school captures important facts about international relations. The security dilemma is real, and there
clearly are points beyond which an extension of national power
brings diminishing returns.[7] They are correct to caution that
going for empire can itself lead to a weakening of democracy.
Following the catastrophic terrorist attacks of September 11,
2001, the United States, under the guidance of open liberalism, followed that script. In the name of spreading democracy
abroad, it sowed disorder abroad; in the name of protecting
democracy at home, its central government gathered too much
power. Yet, this kind of realism does not recognize the coevolutionary dynamics that are at work in world politics. It does
not take seriously the international institutions and practices,
the propaganda, the domestic regime promotion that states
themselves take deadly seriously and to which they devote
enormous resources. Academic realism fails to see that there
is more going on in international relations than states jostling
against one another and eyeing one another's material gains and
losses. Countries' internal properties can be changed by certain properties of the international environment. In response,
rational autocratic great powers will try to shape that environment to select for their own regime type. Democracies can let
them do that, but will not like the price they must pay later. As
John Ikenberry has written, "The uncomfortable counterfactual, reminiscent of the interwar years, would be that once a
Westphalian order comes to be dominated by illiberal states
rather than liberal states, the very viability of liberal democracies may be compromised."[8]

Time for Ecosystem Reengineering

In what follows, I grasp neither horn of the regime-power dilemma. Instead, I follow the American tradition, laid out in earlier chapters, of trying to minimize it. I assume that Americans continue to want both a robust liberal democracy and sustainable international competitiveness. I do not lay out a precise or comprehensive program. No rigorously derived new version of liberalism, no grand new program for international trade and finance, and no new strategy for U.S. or international security lie in the pages ahead. History shows that ecosystem engineering is the work of generations and involves no central guiding intelligence. It emerges as ideas are proposed, tried, succeed, and fail. Instead, I point to a few directions in political thought and policy that the current peril seems to call for and note where departures from open liberalism have already become visible.

PRAGMATISM, NOT DOGMA

One thing that the history presented in Chapters 3 and 4 reminds us of is that the United States has survived crises of legitimacy before. The country has worked through problems in the past that seemed so intractable that leaders feared for democracy itself. Then, too, remedies required ecosystem engineering, or new sets of protections for democracy through fundamental reform of public policy and philosophy. In the 1930s classical liberalism gave way to welfare liberalism. In the late 1970s welfare liberalism gave way to open liberalism. These were not revolutions but anti-revolutions. They were pragmatic, not ideological, requiring leaders to relax some dogmas about how economy and society worked. Conserving self-government necessitated fresh thinking about the changed situation and about what self-government now entailed. In FDR's words, they required "new terms of the old social contract."[9]

It was the intractability of these historic crises—the inability of the overall orientation of law and policy at the time—that prodded leaders to reengineer the ecosystem. Classical liberalism could not save democracy in the 1930s. In the 1970s welfare liberalism had run out of ideas. Leaders saw that fundamental reform was needed, which meant new articulations and understandings of the principles of liberty and majority rule. For the first century and a half of their country's existence, Americans generally thought of personal freedom as the ability of adult white men to move west and make their fortunes. The crisis of the 1930s changed that: it became mainstream to think of personal freedom not so much as the capacity to migrate and become wealthy and more as liberation from the vicissitudes of capital and the exploitation of capitalists. The legitimacy crisis of the 1960s and 1970s pushed into the mainstream the notion that personal freedom was emancipation from old traditions and boundaries.

Those changes were not to everyone's liking. They had their failures and hypocrisies. They did what they were supposed to do at the time, however. Welfare liberal internationalism had solidified democracy in the industrial age and kept the Soviet menace at bay. Open liberal internationalism renewed economic growth, buried the Soviet Union, and helped press liberal democracy outward into regions of the world that had not known it before.

Following the trauma of the Trump years, it might be tempting to try to renew open liberalism. Some believe that things were going so well until the orange-hued con man from New York's outer boroughs cheated his way into the White House. His departure from office in 2021 freed us to revert to the way things were before, with a few tweaks. Such thinking may inform Robert Zoellick's comment: "It is a fool's game—and a loser's strategy—to compete with authoritarians by restricting America's openness, whether to people, goods, capital, inventions, or ideas. Fortress America retreats to defense, instead of going on offense to reshape the competition."[10] Others, such as Rebecca Lissner and Mira Rapp-Hooper, call for a reformed open liberalism—one without the misadventures in the Middle East but that counters Chinese and Russian efforts to seal off areas of the world from the liberal order.[11]

Some favor instead a restoration of welfare liberalism. There remains a hardy band of academics and intellectuals who have always rejected open liberalism root and branch, who loathed the Reagan-Thatcher project and its Third Way offspring from the start. They have long pressed for a return to a time when unionized workers earned their fair share of society's income and democratically elected governments could respond to the needs of their people without answering to foreign capital or multilateral institutions. Bernie Sanders, who nearly won the Democratic nomination for the presidency in 2016 and 2020, greeted the successful Brexit vote with a warning in the *New York Times:* "Let's be clear. The global economy is not working for the majority of people in our country and the world. This is an economic model developed by the economic elite to benefit the economic elite. We need real change."[12] Across the wealthy democracies, welfare liberals have been hostile to globalization and have gotten traction since the 2008 financial meltdown. Former British Labour Party leader Jeremy Corbyn never liked the European Union, seeing it as a neoliberal project to enrich capital at the expense of the workers. Centrists in his party accused him of not fighting hard enough against Brexit in 2016.[13]

Open liberalism and welfare liberalism both enjoy backing from smart academics and are grounded in impressive theories. There are economic theories that say deregulation and privatization are always best, and political theories that say the best society is one that aims for expressive individualism. There are economic theories that say state regulation is always needed for markets to work properly, and political theories that say that the best society protects employment and the family. Advocates for these theories tend to be adamant and can be persuasive.

Their error is to assert that their preferred policies are valid for all time. The bold assertions they make, however, presuppose that they understand far better than they possibly can how societies, national and global, work. The truth is that we cannot explain the cycle of liberal success and failure recalled in Chapters 3 and 4. We do not really know what caused classical liberalism to work in 1895 but not in 1935, why welfare liberalism did its job in 1950 but not 1975, and why open liberalism revived the West in the 1980s but desiccated it after 2008. We might offer an explanation of one of these success-to-failure stories, but not of all three.

We do know, however, that the United States has succeeded over time by shifting from one variety of liberalism to another when circumstances demanded. It has known when to shed dogma and put on pragmatism. In each transition period, leaders saw correctly that safeguarding democracy required a deep change in policy orientation. Welfare liberalism replaced classical liberalism not only because the left-wing Franklin Roosevelt somehow happened to win four presidential terms. He won those terms in large part because welfare liberalism seemed to majorities of voters to be far superior to classical liberalism at the time. Open liberalism became predominant later not only because right-wing politicians happened to take power in a number of countries in the 1970s and 1980s. The center-Right and center-Left alike adopted open liberalism, and continued to be elected to power, because welfare liberalism's narrative and policies were clearly exhausted. In the third decade of the twenty-first century, with a new crisis facing American democracy and many decades of liberal internationalism behind us, a more pragmatic approach is again called for.

A FOURTH STAGE: PLURALISTIC LIBERALISM?

The polarization spiral that elevated Trump in America was caused in part by open liberal internationalism. So was populism in Europe. One cannot solve a problem by doubling down on the thing that helped cause it. Nor is a simple reversion to welfare liberalism possible. Manufacturing is a much smaller part of the U.S. economy than it was in the 1930s; labor unions are far weaker. The culture of welfare liberalism cannot be retrieved, not entirely. The 1960s happened.

The imperative in this moment is to build a fourth-stage liberalism, a new political articulation of individual freedom and a new strategy for its defense that address the challenges of life in the middle decades of the twenty-first century and that can travel across countries. A new type of liberalism is necessary if liberal democracy itself—the delicate and cherished tension between majority rule and individual rights—is to be preserved. It is time to reshape democracy's international ecosystem, to infuse it with new ideas and practices, to alter the environment in ways that reinforce rather than undermine democracy in America and elsewhere. It may seem that a country whose people fall into two tribes that fear and loathe one another is incapable of mustering sufficient consensus to do this. The chief reason to believe it can happen is because the alternatives are so grim.

In the past, a new version of liberalism has arisen when

enough influential thinkers and politicians have identified a new enemy to personal liberty that the old liberalism was unable to remedy or even articulate. For classical liberals, the enemy was the old regime; for welfare liberals, unfettered capital; for open liberals, old norms, boundaries, and institutions. Today's chief barrier to individual freedom must be identified over time through the same process: by a consensus of thinkers and politicians grappling with why so many do not experience or enjoy liberty under the current regime.

It is impossible to discern precisely what the new liberal consensus will look like or by which winding path it will be reached. It will certainly need ideas that have already been thought of and proposals that have already been written. FDR, Carter, Reagan, and their administrations put the country on a different path using materials handed down from previous generations. Not all of these materials cohered at first. Early welfare liberals did not all agree on the right policies or even orientation. Early open liberals could even be enemies: as governor of California (1967–75), Ronald Reagan suppressed antiwar protests by New Left activists; only later did Reagan's economic agenda and the New Left's cultural agenda join forces. In both cases, there was a swirl of ideas about policy and public philosophy, and it took politicians in power to cobble them together into a program.

That said, the pathologies of open liberalism suggest that the leading threat to personal freedom today is *the imperative to multiply all options perpetually for everyone*—to effectively discourage people from settling in, to make everyone into a free chooser of more and more things throughout life, up to the point of death. That being the case, a more adequate notion of individual freedom would be *the power to choose to commit for the long-term to people and work and institutions and communities without suffering unfair consequences.* It would mean being able—not forced—to choose a life in which one can thrive without being confronted with endless choices in perpetuity. Call it *pluralistic liberalism:* it would be more pluralistic than open liberalism because it would not punish those who choose to limit their own choices through robust commitment.

Such a critique of open liberalism might draw charges of Orwellian doublethink. Freedom is constraint? Liberty is to choose a lack of choice? But having perpetual choices across an endless set of issues is, for many people on the Right and Left alike, an unwanted and indeed an unchosen burden. The "ethic of authenticity"—in Charles Taylor's words, "the understanding of life . . . that each one of us has his/her own way of realizing our humanity, and that it is important to find and live out one's own, as against surrendering to conformity with a model imposed on us from outside, by society, or by the previous generation, or religious or political authority"—has been to some extent self-defeating.[14] The goal of this 1960s ethic has been to weaken traditional institutions and norms, and the goal has been reached thanks to its alliance with neoliberalism. But open liberalism's very success makes it harder for people freely to choose to commit to any institutions or norms, traditional or otherwise, precisely because those institutions and norms are now weaker and scorned. Open liberalism expanded one kind of choice by limiting another. It has brought on a paradox, which must be answered with the opposite paradox.

Infinite choice is linked to the ideology of meritocracy, which tells people they will be rewarded for making the right choices and that those who fail or disappoint have only themselves to blame. Even if meritocracy worked as advertised—and, as discussed in Chapter 4, it is more a heritocracy—it would reward its winners with a version of the good life that not all want: a life of still more choices, of no reliable resting places. Open liberalism does not really offer mastery of one's fate, because what is chosen is always temporary and commitment must always be weak, if only because one can never know if one's partners are truly committed. New choices among options yet unknown, at times only to be guessed, always lie ahead. The choice to escape choice is either unavailable or brings penalties: not abandoning one's small town or one's trade, not returning to school to learn to write software code, means no job.

Classical liberalism, at its best, delivered on its promise to let the free individual determine his (and it applied only to men, mostly propertied white men) life's course. Open liberalism allows more choices over a much wider array of goods—to live stream from Netflix or Amazon, to travel nearly anywhere in the world (at least virtually), to try on various identities, to shed one's marriage or religion—but makes long-term commitment to a career, a neighborhood, a family, and other groups and institutions more difficult. Welfare liberalism reduced individual choice in the classical sense but provided greater security for individuals so that the choices to have a family and become loyal to a community were less risky. Open liberalism has taken away that security and restored the risks to well-being of long-term commitment. Hyper-globalization, the economic face of open liberalism, has hurt not only individuals but entire communities and regions.[15] The culture of open liberalism has derided and disdained such places, compounding the injury. Some people thrive on the pressure of late-modern life in liberal society and want perpetual choice. Yet, even among the putative winners, the meritocrats, large numbers suffer from anxiety and depression and seek relief from permanent medication.[16]

A pluralistic liberalism would recognize the paradoxical threat to individual freedom from an imposed regime of boundless, perpetual choice. It would not seek to eliminate the life of perpetual choice for those who want it. Rather, it would seek to create conditions under which citizens who do not want that life would not be penalized. Pluralistic liberalism would aim to support the formation and endurance of institutions that help stabilize individuals' lives. These include the family, an institution that has suffered disproportionately among the working classes and the poor—urban and rural alike—under open liberalism.[17] They also include what social scientists call "civil society"—the bottom-up associations, such as clubs, sports leagues, unions, and religious congregations, that mediate between the individual and government. The nineteenth-century social theorist Alexis de Tocqueville argued that these associations were essential to democracy in America.[18]

A pluralistic liberalism will need to attend much more closely to the millions of citizens and thousands of communities that have been cheated by open liberalism. That could mean a kind of revival of some of the features of welfare liberalism that protected labor's share of national income. That, in turn, would likely mean less intrusive, less homogenizing international institutions. It might entail a World Trade Organization (WTO) and international financial institutions that allow national governments more leeway in responding to the needs of their citizens over against the imperatives of efficiency. It also probably will mean a revival of classical liberalism's reluctance to promote democracy abroad by force.

One encouraging development is that proposals for new policies to replace open liberal internationalism are already gaining currency on both the Left and the Right. The progressive economist Dani Rodrik argues that countries face a trilemma: they cannot have democracy, national sovereignty, and hyper-globalization all at the same time; they all need to choose two of these three. If they choose democracy, they must relax either sovereignty, as members of the European Union have done, or de-globalize to some extent. Rodrik favors the latter.

"The hyperglobalization agenda, with its focus on minimizing transaction costs in the international economy," he writes, "clashes with democracy for the simple reason that it seeks not to improve the functioning of democracy but to accommodate commercial and financial interests seeking market access at low cost."[19] Notwithstanding, Rodrik makes clear that he sees a significant degree of openness as essential to democracy in today's world. That leads to what he calls the "paradox of globalization": to sustain economic openness among nations, democratic governments must limit it.

Backing away from total openness does not mean shutting down trade, foreign investment, or immigration. It does mean recognizing that openness is a means to an end and that democratic governments should be permitted to limit trade when it threatens popular practices. Among other things, Rodrik calls for a WTO that allows governments leeway to safeguard national self-government. Restoring more national sovereignty over finance would complicate transactions, but would be worth the loss in capital mobility.[20] Regarding immigration, reform-minded economists disagree: Rodrik actually favors opening borders up to more unskilled labor, whereas labor economist George Borjas is skeptical, pointing out that such a move would lower both the wages of native unskilled labor and migration within the United States. Unskilled immigrants also have a more difficult time integrating into their new society.[21]

Similar ideas are found on the Right. Oren Cass calls for a conservatism oriented toward workers and families rather than consumers and maximum efficiency. The drive to increasing economic openness achieved much good in past generations, but it has begun to dissolve the bonds of democratic society. High inequality, the disappearance of small, locally owned businesses, value chains that span multiple countries—all of these can be laid at the feet of open liberalism and require reform and correction.[22]

Sections of the Right and Left also agree that the days of forcible democracy promotion and nation-building should end. Opposition to foreign wars is a staple of the far Left. Bernie Sanders, the Justice Democrats (a political action committee), and others in the progressive wing openly criticize the "forever wars." In that, they are not far from Donald J. Trump, one of whose talking points in his 2016 campaign was to lambaste U.S. wars and attempts to impose democracy in the Middle East.[23] Trump's incoherence obscured his unerring sense of the discontents within his constituencies. Parts of the political Right, particularly the libertarian wing, are perennially skeptical of military intervention.

A pluralistic liberalism that takes on board these concerns would not simply be an appeasement of white populism that ignores racial and ethnic disparities. As noted in Chapter 4, black and Latino Americans have not particularly thrived under open liberalism. As of 2016, the wealth of the average black American was roughly what it had been in 1992, and that of the average Latino, about what it was in 1995. Both averages were less than one-eighth the wealth of the average white American.[24] All working and poor Americans are due for a change.

Any new liberal international ecosystem engineered by the United States will need significant support in other democracies. From the start, welfare liberal internationalism had powerful advocates in other wealthy democracies. In 1930s Britain, the Labour Party wanted to move the country at last to a welfare state, as did John Maynard Keynes himself; leftist parties elsewhere in Europe had similar goals. These communicated with their U.S. counterparts, and indeed Keynes headed the British delegation at the 1944 Bretton Woods Conference that birthed the International Monetary Fund and World Bank.

The origins of open liberalism tell a similar story. In the 1970s officials from Germany and France worked with U.S. counterparts to coordinate tighter monetary policy to tame inflation. That was an early step away from welfare liberalism and toward open liberalism. Without these international connections, international ecosystem engineering would not have succeeded.

Today, the zone of liberal democracies is not confined to its original post–World War II core. That is partly an achievement of open liberalism. These newer democracies, in Asia, Africa, and Latin America, must be part of a new liberal ecosystem. That so many other democracies are distorted by polarization and populism, and that so many would like more sovereignty over their national economies, suggests that an agreement to replace open liberalism with a new kind of liberal internationalism is achievable. Indeed, changes of this sort are already in motion. After the Great Recession of 2008–10, international trade never recovered its preceding rate of growth. Much of the post–Cold War growth in trade up to that point was from the spread of value chains across countries, as companies took advantage of the drop in shipping prices to acquire components from whatever country could produce them most efficiently. But after 2008, companies reassessed the risks of having distant sources of components. Value chains became regionalized around the three hubs of China, the United States, and Germany.[25] At the same time, economies did not close; as manufacturing became less scattered, the knowledge and service economies became more global.[26]

U.S. forcible intervention, too, tapered off after the peak years of the George W. Bush administration. The Obama administration sent the U.S. military to join a NATO intervention to topple Muammar Qaddafi in Libya in 2011. But Obama refused to intervene in the horrific Syrian civil war, even after the Assad government used poison gas on civilians in June 2013.

Since 2011 U.S. administrations have labored to extract the country from its wars rather than become involved in new ones. The Biden administration's rapid withdrawal in 2021 of all U.S. forces from Afghanistan in the face of a likely Taliban takeover drives the point home. The move to pull back from foreign commitments has strengthened among academics as well. The Restraint school calls for the United States to reduce or end its military commitments in Europe, the Middle East, and East Asia. A few voices continue to call for a resumption of full open liberalism. But it is telling that many who once wanted robust American global engagement are trying to find a middle ground.[27]

The imperative to retire open liberal internationalism—to acknowledge our debt to it, to celebrate its late twentieth-century achievements, but send it off to pasture—is clear. Protecting constitutional self-government will require another historic reformulation of what individual freedom is for and how it might be secured. One possible direction is toward pluralistic liberalism, a formulation that recognizes that individuals should find it easier to commit long-term to careers, communities, people, and ways of life. That, in turn, would require a greater measure of national autonomy over against the forces of global markets. Out of the swirl of discontent and creativity in the United States and other democracies, ideas and policies are taking shape for a such a pluralistic liberal internationalism.

One International Order, or Two?

Should the United States succeed in reengineering its eco-system, protecting democracy from the outside would still be complicated by the related challenges of China and Russia. Together, those countries have as much influence over the outcome as does America. Realists generally favor a divide-and-conquer strategy: the West should try to peel Russia away from China. Some analysts argue that the need is so urgent that the United States ought to de-emphasize the contest between democracy and autocracy.[28] But the war in Ukraine has pushed rapprochement with Russia into the distant future. China and Russia have drawn closer, as have the wealthy liberal democracies.

There is no avoiding the problem. Today, the great powers differ sharply on the oldest question in politics, dating back to Aristotle: What is the best regime? Each side is determined to improve its international position while retaining its domestic system of government. Each knows that the international environment can be biased in favor of or against that system. Each is determined to shape that environment accordingly. Who shapes and interprets the rules, dominates the information realm, and has the most powerful and popular domestic regime will have a palpable advantage. By no means is limited cooperation among great powers over common challenges such as pandemics, climate change, and terrorism ruled out in such a world. China, Russia, and the United States all have large nuclear arsenals, and the consequences of great-power war would be cataclysmic.[29] But cooperation will always be handicapped by competition over the international environment and the mistrust that results. French philosopher Raymond Aron would call the international system "heterogeneous," and expect serious limits to great-power collaboration.[30]

Should America and the other democracies move to a pluralistic liberal internationalism, as sketched above, the result might be a more tolerant environment for the authoritarians. Such a reformed international ecosystem would afford more respect to national sovereignty, as did classical and welfare liberalism in their day. It might defang some of the Russian complaints about today's liberalism in particular. Still, pluralistic liberalism would be in service of liberal democracy, not against it, and hence it would be a threat to China and Russia so long as their leaders were determined to remain authoritarian. Beijing and Moscow would doubtless continue using their leverage to relieve outside pressure on them to democratize. Democratic governments, for their part, would still understand that a world ordered by China's Communist Party and Putin's United Russia would be biased against liberal democracy. The more powerful China and Russia became, the more pressure the United States and other democracies would feel to compromise some of their constitutional and democratic institutions.

The most straightforward outcome is perpetuation of the situation today: great-power competition over the content of the international environment. Thus far, China and Russia, on the one hand, and the United States and the West, on the other, have found the competition tolerable and have believed they can either triumph or at least prevent the other side from triumphing. If the competition continues to be mutually tolerable, this equilibrium should continue. A pluralist liberal internationalism like that sketched above—that allows national governments more autonomy over their economies and that is less militant about promoting democracy abroad—might be more acceptable to the Chinese and Russian governments precisely because it would be less open and more respectful of state sovereignty.

Ongoing competitive engineering of a single international environment—one side trying to make it friendlier to liberal democracy, the other to authoritarian capitalism—also would mean a relatively low risk of a cold war. All parties would have continuing incentives to invest in common rules and institutions, and those rules and institutions would pay enough dividends to members that they would not want to wreck them.

Trade, investment, and overall cooperation between the United States and China would be limited but significant.[31]

On the other hand, for the democracies a single, contentious international order would perpetuate the risk that the authoritarians would derange democratic politics and come to dominate the international environment. The risk is real because China continues to rise and Russia is not shy about maximizing what leverage it has. In 2022 Russia began to use Europe's dependence on it for energy to blackmail it and empower populists. More illiberal international institutions and practices, more information about the superiority of authoritarianism to democracy, more autocracies in the world: these would impose a tightening regime-power dilemma on the democracies, pressing them to become more autocratic or be less competitive. (China and Russia, of course, would incur the converse risk that the democracies could reverse the tide and win, as they did in the 1980s.)

A different global equilibrium is conceivable and may already exist in its early stages: two separate but overlapping international ecosystems within a single global environment. We can call one the "liberal international order" (LIO)—shaped by pluralist liberalism and underwritten by the United States—and the other an "authoritarian-capitalist international order" (ACIO), underwritten by China.[32] Chapter 2 noted that we can think of the international environment as a single thing, but each state interacts with it in its own way. The United States and China share an environment: the two belong to many of the same international institutions, deal with the same states, and are exposed to information about the relative performance of democracy and authoritarianism. But they are geographically distant and interact with different institutions with different intensities. China has much more interaction with Vietnam, the Shanghai Cooperation Organization, and the BRICS

(Brazil, Russia, India, China, and South Africa); the United States, with Canada, the G7, and NATO. The international environment is lumpy, not smooth or uniform.

A two-order, LIO-ACIO world could emerge not because either Washington or Beijing wants it, but because their mutual desire to protect themselves from a hostile international environment leads them to focus on separate social realms and to build separate international institutions and rules. The current global trading and financial order already exhibits some of the marks of a separating equilibrium. The United States started a trade war with China in 2018 and as of 2023 most tariffs remained in place. China's leaders speak of a "dual-circulation economy," one less reliant on exporting to the West and less vulnerable to U.S. pressure.[33] Beyond those gestures toward decoupling are differences in visions for international trade agreements. Washington wants less leeway for governmental control of economies than does Beijing. Both models appear in the free-trade agreements that the two have sponsored, described in Chapter 5: the U.S.-sponsored Trans-Pacific Partnership (TPP), which Donald Trump withdrew from but a future U.S. administration may join at some point; and the China-sponsored Regional Comprehensive Economic Partnership (RCEP).[34] The TPP aimed to protect U.S.-style domestic institutions, and the RCEP protects China's domestic institutions. The Biden administration initiated the Indo-Pacific Economic Framework as a thin version of the TPP, one that does not allow greater access to the U.S. market but does press countries to raise labor and environmental standards.[35] As the Chinese political scientist Wang Jisi has written, "'Socialism with Chinese characteristics' and 'the liberal international order' appear to be increasingly incompatible."[36]

Other areas might require an even greater degree of Sino-American separation.[37] The two countries think very differently about human rights, and each emphasizes the gap more than ever. In the cyber realm, China's ruling party wants international rules that permit national censorship, whereas U.S. administrations favor relative openness. Continuing to fight at the UN level risks losing to China and Russia and having their norms pressed on democracies that are already wobbly. It might be better for the United States and the other wealthy democracies to worry less about the UN's feckless human rights system altogether and focus more resources on democratic governments, NGOs, and international organizations. That kind of move would not mean abandoning the principle of universal human rights, but it would acknowledge that at present the UN system is so flawed that it is creating more tension and long-term risk to democracy.

Most important has been the chain of events since Russia invaded Ukraine in February 2022. Europe abruptly lurched away from Russia and reversed its policy of importing large amounts of Russian oil and gas. NATO tightened and grew: Sweden and Finland suddenly asked to join, Germany announced that it would sharply increase its military spending, and the alliance, noting China's diplomatic support of Russia, declared China a "systemic challenge." The other wealthy democracies joined Europe in imposing unprecedentedly heavy economic sanctions on Russia and its banks. Those moves, in turn, gave Russia and China incentives to draw closer together. Russia needed to export more to China and other friendly countries. China, for its part, found itself with a newly urgent task of inoculating itself against future Western sanctions. If it ever wanted to attack Taiwan or a South China Sea neighbor, it did not want to be in Russia's vulnerable position.

For China to lower its exposure to Western financial sanctions, its currency, the renminbi, would need to become a global reserve currency. China's international financial transactions could proceed without the U.S. dollar, the euro, or the Japanese yen. Russia and other pariahs of the West would doubtless be pleased with this alternative financial system. Economist Barry Eichengreen notes that Beijing would need to surmount a number of barriers for the renminbi to becoming a reserve currency. Bankers and firms would need to be confident that the renminbi would hold its value, and China's authoritarian institutions, which allow the party to violate the country's laws, are a hindrance to that. Nevertheless, Eichengreen foresees the emergence of a China-based alternative international financial machinery and advises the West to prepare for it.[38]

Should an ACIO emerge alongside the LIO, no doubt many countries, perhaps most, would mightily resist affiliating exclusively with either.[39] It would be in the interests of an India or a Brazil or a South Africa to participate in both. At the same time, both the U.S.-led LIO and the China-led ACIO would want more affiliates rather than less, because more would mean greater wealth and political influence. Therein lies the risk that this two-orders system could bring on a real cold war. Instead of competing over the shape of a single global order, the United States and China might compete for members in their respective international orders. Competition over third countries is part of what constitutes a cold war. The Soviet-American Cold War had its origin in immediate postwar competition over influence in Europe, particularly Germany. It intensified as the two superpowers competed in the 1950s and 1960s for influence in the decolonized lands of Asia and Africa. It relaxed in the 1970s and again in the late 1980s when Moscow and Washington slowed competition over the "Third World."

In other words, the LIO-ACIO world would protect the great powers and other countries from the regime-power dilemma, relieving them from outside pressure to alter their do-

mestic regimes. But it could make them less secure in the traditional realist sense. It could make proxy wars more likely
and raise the risk of great-power war. Washington would promote liberal democracy everywhere feasible and undermine
pro-China and pro-Russia movements and politicians on every
continent. U.S. leaders could work to hamper Chinese and
Russian technological advancement and their ability to attract
allies and economic partners. They could curtail American
dependence on the economies of these rivals, reducing trade
with and investment in China and Russia as well as scientific
and educational exchanges; the authoritarians gain much more
from these things than does the United States. They could press
U.S. allies to do the same. They could criticize even more ro-
bustly Chinese and Russian human rights violations and not
hesitate to lead international efforts to impose sanctions when
violations are especially egregious. Washington could use all
relevant tools to prevent the renminbi from becoming an international currency.

A new cold war would be different in important ways
from the old Soviet-American one. Today, China has more
economic power by far than Russia, and so would likely be the
chief U.S. rival. Russia would be a wild card, sometimes following China's lead and sometimes launching out on its own.
China has a much smaller nuclear arsenal than the United
States and shows little interest in matching the U.S. arsenal. To
date, China has not imposed its domestic system on other countries or formed military alliances to counter America's large alliance network. Indeed, as discussed in Chapter 5, China lacks
a clear universalist ideology to export.

On the other hand, whereas Soviet wealth never came
close to equaling American, China's economy could surpass
America's before 2030. The Soviets' domestic system worked
well until the late 1960s, when it ceased growing and failed to

innovate. China's domestic system of state-directed capitalism went from strength to strength until it began mishandling the COVID-19 pandemic, but the party has continued to use the nation's resources to aim toward global leadership in artificial intelligence, quantum computing, and other technologies with military implications. The United States won the Cold War in part because the Soviet Union had a thoroughly socialist economy and was ultimately self-impoverishing. China has not had that problem. China's soft power may be less formidable than that of the United States, but it has extended its influence in other ways, especially infrastructure investment.

In sum, while history suggests that it is always safest to bet on liberal democracy, it is still a bet.

Whatever strategy the United States pursues, and whatever the shape of international order in the middle of the twenty-first century, America's leaders must recognize that the danger to the country's cherished domestic order is real and stubborn, and that much of that danger comes from its environment. It is not an environment wholly imposed on it by others, but one that America has shaped profoundly. In the past, most of that influence has buttressed liberal democracy in the United States, and in other places as well. When U.S. leaders understood during World War II that they needed to protect democracy from the outside, they went to work and engineered an ecosystem fit for this purpose. More recently, America's influence on the ecosystem, and hence on its own democracy, has been less benign. The trench that it has dug and maintained to protect democracy has begun to look more like a grave.

America's leaders and those of other democracies need to see clearly what they have done to the liberal international order, to understand what is at stake, and to grasp what they can do to change it again. Those who think that the democracies can resume open liberalism once they dispatch with the populists are wrong. The populists are there because of open liberal internationalism. A new, pluralistic liberal internationalism is needed, one that recognizes the wishes of millions of citizens to choose greater commitment and stability over perpetual motion. Those who think that Ukraine and Taiwan are only about the great game of international rivalry, and have nothing to do with democracy in the rest of the world, are wrong too. They need to grasp that the international environment becomes a bit less friendly to democracy everywhere when democracy fails anywhere.

Constitutional self-government has never been perfected, but it is one of the glories of civilization. It remains the best system for human flourishing that has been tried. Its capacity for self-correction in its quest for a just public order is unmatched. Not long ago, as it rolled across Eastern Europe toward Russia and China, it seemed inevitable, everywhere, for all people. Now we know that it is not inevitable—not in Russia, not in China, not in the United States, not anywhere. Democracy is an achievement, easier to lose than to gain.

The main lesson of the young twenty-first century so far may be that democracy does not thrive automatically. It thrives when democracies shape the international environment with a clear understanding of what individual liberty entails in the historical moment. That lesson offers some hope, for the United States is able to help reshape international order once again. But Americans should remember a paradox that their past leaders understood: self-government is not secured alone. What happens outside America affects America; and what happens in America does not stay in America.

Notes

1
Democracy under Pressure

1. Toleration and forbearance are the two virtues identified as essential to democracy in Steven Levitsky and Daniel Ziblatt, *How Democracies Die* (New York: Crown, 2018), 8–9. See also Frances E. Lee, "Populism and the American Party System: Opportunities and Constraints," *Perspectives on Politics* 18 (2019): 370–88.

2. James Davison Hunter, *Culture Wars: The Struggle to Define America* (New York: Basic Books, 1991).

3. Nicholas Jacobs and Sidney Milkis, *What Happened to the Vital Center? Presidentialism, Populist Revolt, and the Fracturing of America* (New York: Oxford University Press, 2022).

4. Greg Lukianoff and Jonathan Haidt, *The Coddling of the American Mind: How Good Intentions and Bad Ideas Are Setting Up a Generation for Failure* (New York: Penguin, 2018), 125–42.

5. David French, *Divided We Fall: America's Secession Threat and How to Restore Our Nation* (New York: St. Martin's Press, 2020).

6. Francis Fukuyama, *The End of History and the Last Man* (New York: Basic Books, 1992); Michael Mandelbaum, *The Ideas That Conquered the World: Peace, Democracy, and Free Markets in the Twenty-First Century* (New York: Public Affairs, 2004); Levitsky and Ziblatt, *How Democracies Die*; Timothy Snyder, *The Road to Unfreedom: Russia, Europe, America* (New York: Tim Duggan, 2018); Jason Stanley, *How Fascism Works: The Politics of Us and Them* (New York: Random House, 2018).

7. Samuel P. Huntington, *The Third Wave: Democratization in the Late Twentieth Century* (Norman: University of Oklahoma Press, 1991), ch. 1.

8. Roosevelt quoted in Melvyn P. Leffler, "Austerity and U.S. Strategy: Lessons of the Past," in *Safeguarding Democratic Capitalism: U.S. Foreign Policy and National Security, 1920–2015* (Princeton, N.J.: Princeton University Press, 2017), 307–8.

9. Jessica Chen Weiss, "A World Safe for Autocracy? China's Rise and the Future of Global Politics," *Foreign Affairs* 98, no. 4 (July/August 2019): 92–102; Weiss and Jeremy L. Wallace, "Domestic Politics, China's Rise, and the Future of the Liberal International Order," *International Organization* 75 (Spring 2021): 635–64.

10. John M. Owen, "Sino-Russian Cooperation against Liberal Hegemony," *International Politics* 57 (2020): 809–33.

11. See, e.g., Viktor Orbán, "Orbán's Full Speech at Tusványos," *Visegrád Post*, July 29, 2019, https://visegradpost.com/en/2019/07/29/orbans-full-speech-at-tusvanyos-political-philosophy-upcoming-crisis-and-projects-for-the-next-15-years/, retrieved on May 25, 2021.

12. For one comprehensive, data-driven treatment of the varieties of democracy, see the Varieties of Democracy (V-Dem) Project at the University of Gothenburg, Sweden: https://www.v-dem.net, retrieved on April 1, 2021.

13. Peter A. Hall and David Soskice, *Varieties of Capitalism: The Institutional Foundations of Comparative Advantage* (New York: Oxford University Press, 2001).

14. On the importance of norms and culture to democracy, see Levitsky and Ziblatt, *How Democracies Die*; Zac Gershberg and Sean Illing, *The Paradox of Democracy: Free Speech, Open Media, and Perilous Persuasion* (Chicago: University of Chicago Press, 2022).

15. Alexis de Tocqueville's *Democracy in America* remains a subtle and comprehensive starting point for considering how culture is integral to democracy. See Tocqueville, *Democracy in America,* trans. Harvey C. Mansfield and Delba Winthrop (Chicago: University of Chicago Press, 2002), esp. 274–98.

16. James Davison Hunter and Carl Desportes Bowman, with Kyle Puetz, *Democracy in Dark Times* (New York: Finstock and Tew, 2021), 9, 17.

17. Hunter and Bowman, *Democracy in Dark Times,* 27.

18. David A. Lake, Lisa L. Martin, and Thomas Risse, "Challenges to the Liberal Order: Reflections on International Organization," *International Organization* 75, no. 2 (2021): 225–57.

19. Daniel DellaPosta, "Pluralistic Collapse: The 'Oil Spill' Model of Mass Opinion Polarization," *American Sociological Review* 85, no. 3 (2020): 507–36.

20. Eli J. Finkel et al., "Political Sectarianism in America," *Science,* October 30, 2020, 533–34.

21. Hunter and Bowman, *Democracy in Dark Times,* 36.

22. Seymour Martin Lipset, *Political Man: The Social Bases of Politics* (New York: Doubleday, 1960); Ezra Klein, *Why We're Polarized* (New York: Avid Reader Press, 2020), 49–80.

23. Finkel et al., "Political Sectarianism," 535.

24. Cass R. Sunstein, "The Law of Group Polarization," *Journal of Political Philosophy* 10, no. 2 (2002): 175–95; John M. Owen, "Springs and Their Offspring: The International Consequences of Domestic Uprisings," *European Journal of International Security* 1, no. 1 (2016): 49–72.

25. Cas Mudde, "The Populist Zeitgeist," *Government and Opposition* 39, no. 4 (2004): 541–63; William A. Galston, *Anti-Pluralism: The Populist Threat to Liberal Democracy* (New Haven: Yale University Press, 2018), 36.

26. See Sheri Berman, "Why Identity Politics Benefits the Right More than the Left," *Guardian,* July 14, 2018, https://www.theguardian.com/commentisfree/2018/jul/14/identity-politics-right-left-trump-racism, retrieved on May 27, 2021.

27. Lake, Martin, and Risse, "Challenges to the Liberal Order," 238.

28. Sarah Repucci and Amy Slipowitz, *Democracy under Siege: Freedom in the World 2021* (Washington, D.C.: Freedom House, 2021), 1–2.

29. Varieties of Democracy (V-Dem) Institute, *Autocratization Turns Viral: Democracy Report 2021* (Gothenburg, Sweden: V-Dem, 2021), 6–8.

30. The Economist Intelligence Unit, *Democracy Index 2020: In Sickness and in Health?* (London: Economist Intelligence Unit, 2021), 3–5, https://www.eiu.com/n/campaigns/democracy-index-2020/, retrieved on April 5, 2021.

31. V-Dem Institute, *Autocratization Turns Viral.*

32. Mudde, "Populist Zeitgeist."

33. R. S. Foa, A. Klassan, M. Slade, A. Rand, and R. Williams, *The Global Satisfaction with Democracy Report 2020* (Cambridge: Centre for the Future of Democracy, 2020), 11–18.

34. Huntington, *Third Wave,* 14–19.

35. Kenneth N. Waltz, *Theory of International Politics* (New York: McGraw-Hill, 1979), 73–74; Beth A. Simmons, Frank Dobbins, and Geoffrey Garrett, "Introduction: The International Diffusion of Liberalism," *International Organization* 60, no. 4 (Fall 2006): 792–95.

36. Lake, Martin, and Risse, "Challenges to the Liberal Order," 247–49.

37. Michael Kofman and Andrea Kendall-Taylor, "The Myth of Russian Decline," *Foreign Affairs* 100, no. 6 (November/December 2021): 142–52.

38. Alexander Cooley and Daniel Nexon argue for a similar notion of international order as an ecosystem, although they mean only the norms and rules (architecture) and practices (infrastructure) of an order. Cooley and Nexon, *Exit from Hegemony* (New York: Oxford University Press, 2020).

39. G. John Ikenberry, *A World Safe for Democracy: Liberal Internationalism and the Crises of Global Order* (New Haven: Yale University Press, 2020), 7.

40. Kathleen Thelen, "Historical Institutionalism in Comparative Politics," *Annual Review of Political Science* 2, no. 1 (1999): 369–404; Paul Pierson, *Politics in Time: History, Institutions, and Social Analysis* (Princeton, N.J.: Princeton University Press, 2004).

41. Jeff D. Colgan and Robert O. Keohane, "The Liberal Order Is Rigged," *Foreign Affairs* 96, no. 3 (May/June 2017): 36–44.

42. John J. Mearsheimer, *The Great Delusion: Liberal Dreams and International Realities* (New Haven: Yale University Press, 2018), 61–64; Ikenberry, *World Safe for Democracy*, 277.

43. Hal Brands, "Democracy versus Authoritarianism: How Ideology Shapes Great-Power Conflict," *Survival* 60, no. 5 (2018): 70–72.

44. Michael Zürn, *A Theory of Global Governance: Authority, Legitimacy, and Contestation* (New York: Oxford University Press, 2018).

45. Mearsheimer, *Great Delusion*.

46. Classic works include Robert Gilpin, *War and Change in World Politics* (New York: Cambridge University Press, 1981); Robert O. Keohane, *After Hegemony: Cooperation and Discord in the World Political Economy* (Princeton, N.J.: Princeton University Press, 1984); and G. John Ikenberry, *After Victory: Institutions, Strategic Restraint, and the Rebuilding of Order after Major War* (Princeton, N.J.: Princeton University Press, 2001).

47. Graham T. Allison, *Destined for War: Can America and China Escape Thucydides's Trap?* (New York: Houghton Mifflin Harcourt, 2017).

48. On Sino-American competition, see Elbridge A. Colby, *The Strategy of Denial: American Defense in an Age of Great Power Conflict* (New Haven: Yale University Press, 2021). On restoring the liberal international order, see Rebecca Lissner and Mira Rapp-Hooper, *An Open World: How American Can Win the Contest for Twenty-First-Century Order* (New Haven: Yale University Press, 2020).

2

Coevolution

1. Paul W. Schroeder, *The Transformation of European Politics, 1763–1848* (Oxford: Clarendon Press, 1994), 558–59.

2. James Monroe, "President's Message," *Annals of Congress,* Senate, 18th Congress, 1st Session (1823) (Washington, D.C.: Gales and Seaton, 1856), 23–24.

3. Monroe, "President's Message," 23–24.

4. George Canning, the British foreign minister, had suggested to Monroe an Anglo-American declaration warning the Holy Alliance to leave Latin America alone. Monroe considered the proposal, asking the advice of his predecessors, Thomas Jefferson and James Madison, but no joint declaration was made. James Monroe, letter to James Madison, 17 October 1823, U.S. National Archives, https://founders.archives.gov/documents/Madison /04-03-02-0147, retrieved on August 6, 2022.

5. Daniel H. Deudney, *Bounding Power: Republican Security Theory from the Polis to the Global Village* (Princeton, N.J.: Princeton University Press, 2008), 16.

6. In 1816 Clay told the House of Representatives that because of the system that had just been established by the Concert of Europe in Vienna, "it would undoubtedly be good policy to take part with the patriots of South America. . . . I consider the release of any part of America from the dominion of the Old World as adding to the general security of the New." Quoted in John M. Owen IV, *Liberal Peace, Liberal War: American Politics and International Security* (Ithaca, N.Y.: Cornell University Press, 1997), 113–14.

7. Monroe, letter to Madison, 17 October 1823 (see fn. 4).

8. Peter Gourevitch, "The Second Image Reversed: The International Sources of Domestic Politics," *International Organization* 32, no. 4 (Autumn 1978): 881–912.

9. Kristian Skrede Gleditsch and Michael D. Ward, "Diffusion and the International Context of Democratization," *International Organization* 60, no. 4 (2006): 911–33; Carles Boix, "Democracy, Development, and the International System," *American Political Science Review* 105, no. 4 (2011): 809–28; Seva Gunitsky, *Aftershocks: Great Powers and Domestic Reforms in the Twentieth Century* (Princeton, N.J.: Princeton University Press, 2017).

10. Richard Lewontin, *The Triple Helix: Gene, Organism, and Environment* (Cambridge, Mass.: Harvard University Press, 2002), 151–54.

11. George Modelski, "Is World Politics Evolutionary Learning?," *International Organization* 44 (1990): 1–24; Ann Florini, "The Evolution of International Norms," *International Studies Quarterly* 40 (1996): 363–89; Alexander Wendt, *Social Theory of International Politics* (New York: Cambridge University Press, 1999); Michael Barnett, "Evolution without Progress? Humanitarianism in a World of Hurt," *International Organization* 63 (2009): 621–63; Iver B. Neumann, *Diplomatic Tenses: A Social Evolutionary Perspective on Diplomacy* (Manchester: Manchester University Press, 2020); George Modelski, Tessaleno Devezas, and William R. Thompson, eds., *Globalization as Evolutionary Process: Modeling Global Change* (New York: Routledge, 2007); Herman Mark Schwartz, "An Evolutionary Approach to Global Po-

litical Economy," in *Global Political Economy: Contemporary Theories*, ed. R. Palan (New York: Routledge, 2012), 129–39; Hendrik Spruyt, *The Sovereign State and Its Competitors: An Analysis of Systems Change* (Princeton, N.J.: Princeton University Press, 1994); Miles Kahler, "Evolution, Choice, and International Change," in *Strategic Choice in International Relations*, ed. D. A. Lake and R. Powell (Princeton, N.J.: Princeton University Press, 1999), 165–98; Shiping Tang, *The Social Evolution of International Politics* (New York: Oxford University Press, 2016); Emanuel Adler, *World Ordering: A Social Theory of Cognitive Evolution* (New York: Cambridge University Press, 2019); Tarek Oraby, *A Darwinian Theory of International Conflict* (PhD diss., Stockholm University, 2019).

12. Jean-Baptiste Lamarck believed that organisms acquired and retained traits that they passed on to their offspring. Biologists abandoned Lamarckian evolution many decades ago, as it became clear that organisms that acquired new traits did not pass them on to their offspring. As Lilach Gilady and Matthew J. Hoffmann have persuasively argued, however, that is no prima facie reason why scholars of international relations should avoid Lamarckian logic. States normally do not reproduce, and their death rate is low. A state can acquire a trait, and also retain it if it continues to help the state thrive in its environment. Gilady and Hoffmann, "Darwin's Finches or Lamarck's Giraffe: Does International Relations Get Evolution Wrong?," *International Studies Review* 15, no. 3 (2013): 307–27. For other applications of Lamarckian-like adaptation to international relations, see Lars-Erik Cederman and Kristian Skrede Gleditsch, "Conquest and Regime Change: An Evolutionary Model of the Spread of Democracy and Peace," *International Studies Quarterly* 49 (2004): 603–29; Seva Gunitsky, "Complexity and Theories of Change in International Politics," *International Theory* 5, no. 1 (2013): 35–63.

13. The most common definition of "coevolution" pertains to two species, each affecting the other's evolution. Some biologists describe the environment itself as evolving, however, and hence use "coevolution" to refer to the effects that species and environment have on one another's evolution. Richard Lewontin and Richard Levins, "Organism and Environment," *Capitalism, Nature, Socialism* 8, no. 2 (1997): 95–98; Peter Godfrey-Smith, "The Subject as Cause and Effect of Evolution," *Interface Focus* 7 (2017), doi:10 .1098.rsfs.20170022.

14. Alexander E. Wendt, "The Agent-Structure Problem in International Relations Theory," *International Organization* 41, no. 3 (Summer 1987): 335–70; David Dessler, "What's at Stake in the Agent-Structure Debate?," *International Organization* 43, no. 3 (Summer 1989): 441–73, esp. on "transformational models of structure" (458–70).

15. G. John Ikenberry, *A World Safe for Democracy: Liberal Internationalism and the Crises of Global Order* (New Haven: Yale University Press, 2020), 286.

16. G. John Ikenberry and Daniel Nexon, "Hegemony Studies 3.0: The Dynamics of Hegemonic Orders," *Security Studies* 28, no. 3 (2019): 399.

17. A good introduction to coevolution is in Lewontin, *Triple Helix.*

18. David Easton, John G. Gunnell, and Michael Stein, "Introduction: Democracy as Regime Type and the Development of Political Science," in *Regime and Discipline: Democracy and the Development of Political Science,* ed. Easton, Gunnell, and Stein (Ann Arbor: University of Michigan Press, 1995), 8–9.

19. On personalist regimes, see Barbara Geddes, *Paradigms and Sand Castles: Theory Building and Research Design in Comparative Politics* (Ann Arbor: University of Michigan Press, 2003); Jessica Weeks, "Autocratic Audience Costs: Regime Type and Signaling Resolve," *International Organization* 62 (Winter 2008): 35–64; Anne Meng, *Constraining Dictatorship: From Personalized Rule to Institutionalized Regimes* (New York: Cambridge University Press, 2020).

20. The Economist Intelligence Unit, using a ten-point scale, gives similar movements for these countries from 2010 to 2020, but of different magnitudes: the United States, from 8.18 to 7.92; India, 7.28 to 6.61; Russia, 4.26 to 3.31; Tunisia, 2.79 to 6.59. Economist Intelligence Unit, *Democracy Index 2020,* 21–25.

21. Varieties of Democracy (V-Dem) Institute, *Autocratization Turns Viral: Democracy Report 2021* (Gothenburg, Sweden: Varieties of Democracy Institute, 2021), 7.

22. Daron Acemoglu and James A. Robinson, *Economic Origins of Dictatorship and Democracy* (New York: Cambridge University Press, 2006).

23. Stephan Haggard and Robert R. Kaufman, *Dictators and Democrats: Masses, Elites, and Regime Change* (Princeton, N.J.: Princeton University Press, 2017).

24. Michael Albertus and Victor Menaldo, *Authoritarianism and the Elite Origins of Democracy* (New York: Cambridge University Press, 2018).

25. Daniel Brinks and Michael Coppedge, "Diffusion Is No Illusion: Neighbor Emulation in the Third Wave of Democracy," *Comparative Political Studies* 39, no. 4 (2006): 463–89; Gleditsch and Ward, "Diffusion."

26. Frances Z. Brown and Thomas Carothers, "The US Needs a Global Anti-Coup Strategy," Just Security, June 1, 2022, https://www.justsecurity.org/81725/the-us-needs-a-global-anti-coup-strategy/, retrieved on August 6, 2022.

27. Barbara Geddes, Joseph Wright, and Erica Frantz, *How Dictatorships Work* (New York: Cambridge University Press, 2018), 25.

28. Leonardo Arriola, Jed DeVaro, and Anne Meng, "Democratic Subversion: Elite Cooptation and Opposition Fragmentation," *American Political Science Review* 115, no. 4 (2021): 1358–72.

29. Steven Levitsky and Lucan A. Way, *Competitive Authoritarianism: Hybrid Regimes after the Cold War* (New York: Cambridge University Press, 2010).

30. Steven Levitsky and Daniel Ziblatt, *How Democracies Die* (New York: Broadway Books, 2018). For an effort to adjudicate among debates over democratic backsliding, see David Waldner and Ellen Lust, "Unwelcome Change: Coming to Terms with Democratic Backsliding," *Annual Review of Political Science* 21 (2018): 93–113.

31. Gunitsky, *Aftershocks*, 22–28.

32. John M. Owen IV, *The Clash of Ideas in World Politics: Transnational Networks, States, and Regime Change, 1510–2010* (Princeton, N.J.: Princeton University Press, 2010), esp. 68–70.

33. Jørgen Møller, Svend-Erik Skaaning, and Jakob Tolstrup, "International Influences and Democratic Regression in Interwar Europe: Disentangling the Impact of Power Politics and Demonstration Effects," *Government and Opposition* 52, no. 4 (October 2017): 559–86.

34. Mark L. Haas, *Frenemies: When Ideological Enemies Ally* (Ithaca, N.Y.: Cornell University Press, 2022), 32–35; Etel Solingen, "Of Dominoes and Firewalls: The Domestic, Regional, and Global Politics of International Diffusion," *International Studies Quarterly* 56 (2012): 631–44; Stephen E. Hanson and Jeffrey S. Kopstein, "Regime Type and Diffusion in Comparative Politics Methodology," *Canadian Journal of Political Science* 38, no. 1 (March 2005): 69–99; Brinks and Coppedge, "Diffusion Is No Illusion"; Zachary Elkins, "Diffusion and the Constitutionalization of Europe," *Comparative Political Studies* 43, nos. 8–9 (2010): 969–99; Thomas Risse and Tanja Börzel, eds., "From Europeanisation to Diffusion," special issue, *West European Politics* 35, no. 1 (January 2012).

35. Gleditsch and Ward, "Diffusion," 916.

36. Thomas Ambrosio, "Constructing a Framework of Authoritarian Diffusion: Concepts, Dynamics, and Future Research," *International Studies Perspectives* 11 (2010): 375–92; Rachel Vanderhill, *Promoting Authoritarianism Abroad* (Boulder: Lynne Rienner, 2013), 14–17; Thomas Risse and Nelli Babayan, "Democracy Promotion and the Challenges of Illiberal Regional Powers," *Democratization* 22, no. 3 (2015): 381–99.

37. Jeffrey S. Kopstein and David A. Reilly, "Geographic Diffusion and the Transformation of the Postcommunist World," *World Politics* 53, no. 1 (October 2000): 1–37.

38. This according to the standard gravity model of trade. See Jan Tin-

bergen, *Shaping the World Economy: Suggestions for an International Economic Policy* (New York: Twentieth Century Fund, 1962).

39. Robert O. Keohane, *After Hegemony: Cooperation and Discord in the World Political Economy* (Princeton, N.J.: Princeton University Press, 1984).

40. Alexander Cooley and Daniel Nexon, *Exit from Hegemony: The Unraveling of the American Global Order* (New York: Oxford University Press, 2020), 57–58.

41. The literature on institutions and international cooperation is large. The best starting place remains Keohane, *After Hegemony*.

42. Gleditsch and Ward, "Diffusion," 918–20.

43. Samuel P. Huntington, *The Third Wave: Democratization in the Late Twentieth Century* (Norman: University of Oklahoma Press, 1993), 33.

44. Michael K. Miller, "Democracy by Example? Why Democracy Spreads When the World's Democracies Prosper," *Comparative Politics* 49, no. 1 (2016): 83–116.

45. Joseph S. Nye, Jr., *Soft Power: The Means to Success in World Politics* (New York: Public Affairs, 2005); Hendrik W. Ohnesorge, *Soft Power: The Sources of Attraction in International Relations* (Cham, Switz.: Springer, 2020).

46. Tanja A. Börzel and Thomas Risse, "From Europeanisation to Diffusion: Introduction," *West European Politics* 35, no. 1 (January 2012): 7.

47. Scholarship on the democratic peace is vast. See, e.g., Michael W. Doyle, "Kant, Liberal Legacies, and Foreign Affairs, Part I," *Philosophy and Public Affairs* 12, no. 3 (Summer 1983): 205–35; Doyle, "Kant, Liberal Legacies, and Foreign Affairs, Part II," *Philosophy and Public Affairs* 12, no. 4 (Autumn 1983): 323–53; Bruce M. Russett, *Grasping the Democratic Peace* (Princeton, N.J.: Princeton University Press, 1994); Thomas Risse-Kappen, "Democratic Peace—Warlike Democracies? A Social Constructivist Interpretation of the Liberal Argument," *European Journal of International Relations* 1, no. 4 (1995): 491–517; Owen, *Liberal Peace*; James Lee Ray, *Democracy and International Conflict: An Evaluation of the Democratic Peace Proposition* (Columbia: University of South Carolina Press, 1998); Michael C. Williams, "The Discipline of the Democratic Peace: Kant, Liberalism and the Social Construction of Security Communities," *European Journal of International Relations* 7, no. 4 (2001): 525–53.

48. Bruce M. Russett and John R. Oneal, *Triangulating Peace: Democracy, Interdependence, and International Organizations* (New York: W. W. Norton, 2001). Kant speculated about a league of peace comprising trading republics. See, e.g., Immanuel Kant, "To Perpetual Peace, a Philosophical Sketch" (1795), in *Kant's Political Writings,* trans. Ted Humphrey (Indianapolis: Hackett, 1983), 107–44.

49. Jon Pevehouse, "Democracy from the Outside-In? International Organizations and Democratization," *International Organization* 56, no. 3 (Summer 2002): 515–49. On socialization in particular, see also Brian Greenhill, "The Company You Keep: International Socialization and the Diffusion of Human Rights Norms," *International Studies Quarterly* 54, no. 1 (March 2010): 127–45.

50. Acemoglu and Robinson, *Economic Origins,* 323.

51. Mark L. Haas, *The Ideological Origins of Great Power Politics, 1789–1989* (Ithaca, N.Y.: Cornell University Press, 2005); also John M. Owen IV, "When Do Ideologies Produce Alliances?," *International Studies Quarterly* 49, no. 1 (2005): 73–100.

52. John M. Owen, "The Ideas-Power Nexus," *Yale Journal of International Affairs* 7, no. 2 (September 2012), https://www.yalejournal.org/publications /the-ideas-power-nexus-by-john-m-owen-iv, retrieved on June 12, 2022.

53. As seen in Chapter 4, Franklin Roosevelt's administration tried a few of these tools in the 1930s to ward off fascism.

54. Quoted in Hal Brands, "Democracy versus Authoritarianism: How Ideology Shapes Great-Power Conflict," *Survival* 60, no. 5 (2018): 65.

55. Kevin Laland, Blake Matthews, and Marcus W. Feldman, "An Introduction to Niche Construction Theory," *Evolutionary Ecology* 30 (2016): 191–202; Jeremy Kendal, Jamshid J. Tehrani, and John Odling-Smee, "Human Niche Construction in Interdisciplinary Focus," *Philosophical Transactions of the Royal Society B* 366 (2011): 785–92.

56. "Ecosystem engineering" originally simply meant modification of habitat by one species so that the well-being of other species was affected. See Clive G. Jones, John H. Lawton, and Moshe Shachak, "Organisms as Ecosystem Engineers," *Ecosystem Management* (1994), doi: 10.1007/978-1 -4612-4018-1_14. Following Godfrey-Smith, "Subject as Cause and Effect," I apply the term to coevolution.

57. L. Scott Mills, Michael E. Soulé, and Daniel F. Doak, "The Keystone-Species Concept in Ecology and Conservation," *Bioscience* 43, no. 4 (April 1993): 219–24.

58. On coevolution in general, see Lewontin, *Triple Helix.*

59. Foundational works include Charles Kindleberger, *The World in Depression, 1929–1939* (Berkeley: University of California Press, 1973); Stephen D. Krasner, "State Power and the Structure of International Trade," *World Politics* 28, no. 3 (1976): 317–47; Robert Gilpin, *War and Change in World Politics* (New York: Cambridge University Press, 1981).

60. Alexander E. Wendt, "The Agent-Structure Problem in International Relations Theory," *International Organization* 41, no. 3 (Summer 1987): 335–70.

61. Levitsky and Way, *Competitive Authoritarianism,* esp. 40–46.

62. Risse and Babayan, "Democracy Promotion."

63. Tina Freyburg and Solveig Richter, "Local Actors in the Driver's Seat: Transatlantic Democracy Promotion under Regime Competition in the Arab World," *Democratization* 22, no. 3 (2015): 496–518.

64. Lindsey O'Rourke, *Covert Regime Change: America's Secret Cold War* (Ithaca, N.Y.: Cornell University Press, 2018); Michael Poznansky, *In the Shadow of International Law: Secrecy and Regime Change in the Postwar World* (New York: Oxford University Press, 2020).

65. Owen, *Clash of Ideas,* 161–63, 181–88; John M. Owen IV, *Confronting Political Islam: Six Lessons from the West's Past* (Princeton, N.J.: Princeton University Press, 2015), 58–62, 75–79; C. William Walldorf, *To Shape Our World for Good: Master Narratives and Regime Change in U.S. Foreign Policy, 1900–2011* (Ithaca, N.Y.: Cornell University Press, 2019).

66. Poznansky, *Shadow of International Law;* O'Rourke, *Covert Regime Change.*

67. Levitsky and Way, *Competitive Authoritarianism,* 47–49.

68. Vyacheslav Molotov, Stalin's foreign minister, stormed out of a conference on the Marshall Plan in Paris in July 1947 and declared that the plan would consign the countries of Eastern Europe to permanent agrarian status, make them dependent on the United States, and dissolve their economic relations with the Soviets. Scott D. Parrish and Mikhail M. Narinsky, "New Evidence on the Soviet Rejection of the Marshall Plan, 1947: Two Reports" (working paper No. 9, Cold War International History Project, Woodrow Wilson International Center for Scholars, March 1994), 31–36, https://www.wilsoncenter.org/sites/default/files/media/documents/publication/ACFB73.pdf, retrieved on March 9, 2021.

69. Yuri Zhukov and Brandon Stewart, "Choosing Your Neighbors: Networks of Diffusion in International Relations," *International Studies Quarterly* 57 (2013): 271–87; John M. Owen IV, "The American Way of Seeking Security: Ideology and Pragmatism," in *America, China, and the Struggle for World Order,* ed. G. John Ikenberry, Wang Jisi, and Zhu Feng (New York: Palgrave-Macmillan, 2015), 299–326.

70. Martha Bayles, *Through a Screen Darkly: Popular Culture, Public Diplomacy, and America's Image Abroad* (New Haven: Yale University Press, 2014).

71. For authoritarian regimes, the most helpful technologies are probably those of surveillance and punishment. I examine such things in Chapter 5.

72. Oisín Tansey, *The International Politics of Authoritarian Rule* (New York: Oxford University Press, 2016); Jakob Tolstrup, "Black Knights and Elections in Authoritarian Regimes: Why and How Russia Supports Author-

itarian Incumbents in Post-Soviet States," *European Journal of Political Research* 54 (2015): 673–90; Risse and Babayan, "Democracy Promotion," 389–900.

73. Owen, *Clash of Ideas*, 181–96.

74. John M. Owen IV and Michael Poznansky, "When Does America Drop Dictators?," *European Journal of International Relations* 20, no. 4 (2014): 1072–99.

75. Jason Brownlee, *Democracy Prevention: The Politics of the U.S.-Egyptian Alliance* (New York: Cambridge University Press, 2012).

76. Beth A. Simmons, *Mobilizing for Human Rights: International Law and Domestic Politics* (New York: Cambridge University Press, 2009).

77. Charles Kindleberger, *The World in Depression, 1929–1939* (Berkeley: University of California Press, 1974); Keohane, *After Hegemony*. On public goods, see Mancur Olson, *The Logic of Collective Action* (Cambridge, Mass.: Harvard University Press, 1965).

78. Krasner, "State Power"; Gilpin, *War and Change*. For a comparison of the benevolent and coercive theories of hegemony, see Duncan Snidal, "The Limits of Hegemonic Stability Theory," *International Organization* 39, no. 4 (Autumn 1985): 579–614.

79. G. John Ikenberry, *After Victory: Institution, Strategic Restraint, and the Rebuilding of Order after Major Wars* (Princeton, N.J.: Princeton University Press, 2001).

80. Kyle M. Lascurettes, *Orders of Exclusion: Great Powers and the Strategic Sources of Foundational Rules in International Relations* (New York: Oxford University Press, 2020), 39–42.

81. At the U.S. Army's School of the Americas in Fort Benning, Georgia. See Lesley Gill, *The School of the Americas: Military Training and Political Violence in the Americas* (Durham, N.C.: Duke University Press, 2004).

82. Zhukov and Stewart, "Choosing Your Neighbors"; Owen, "American Way of Seeking Security."

83. Daniëlle Flonk, "Emerging Illiberal Norms: Russia and China as Promoters of Internet Content Control," *International Affairs* 97, no. 6 (2021): 1927.

84. Benjamin O. Fordham and Victor Asal, "Billiard Balls or Snowflakes? Major Power Prestige and the International Diffusion of Institutions and Practices," *International Studies Quarterly* 51, no. 1 (2007): 31–52.

85. Bayles, *Through a Screen Darkly*.

86. Daniel W. Drezner, "Counter-Hegemonic Strategies in the Global Economy," *Security Studies* 28, no. 3 (2019): 505–31.

87. Charles Lipson, *Reliable Partners: How Democracies Have Made a Separate Peace* (Princeton, N.J.: Princeton University Press, 2005).

88. Kelly M. Kadera, Mark J. C. Crescenzi, and Megan L. Shannon, "Democratic Survival, Peace, and War in the International System," *American Journal of Political Science* 47, no. 2 (2003): 234–47; Brinks and Coppedge, "Diffusion Is No Illusion"; Jan Teorell, *Determinants of Democratization: Explaining Regime Change in the World, 1972–2006* (New York: Cambridge University Press, 2010), 86–89.

89. Lewontin, *Triple Helix,* 88.

90. For a similar argument, see Cooley and Nexon, *Exit from Hegemony,* 73–77.

91. Cooley and Nexon, *Exit from Hegemony,* 65–70.

3
Liberalism

1. Karl Polanyi, *The Great Transformation: The Political and Economic Origins of Our Time* (New York: Farrar and Rinehart, 1944).

2. Jonathan Kirshner, "Keynes, Capital Mobility and the Crisis of Embedded Liberalism," *Review of International Political Economy* 6, no. 3 (1999): 313–37; Dani Rodrik, *The Globalization Paradox: Democracy and the Future of the World Economy* (New York: Norton, 2011), 67–68.

3. John Gerard Ruggie, "International Regimes, Transactions, and Change: Embedded Liberalism in the Postwar Economic Order," *International Organization* 36, no. 2 (1982): 393–96.

4. Ruggie, "International Regimes," 396–97; Rodrik, *Globalization Paradox,* 68–74.

5. Judith Goldstein and Robert Gulotty argue that from the 1940s U.S. trade policy, for domestic political reasons, did not favor U.S. workers as much as Ruggie's thesis would have it; in particular, Washington favored exporters and made inadequate provision for people who lost jobs due to cheap imports. Goldstein and Gulotty, "America and the Trade Regime: What Went Wrong?," *International Organization* 75 (Spring 2021): 524–57.

6. G. John Ikenberry, *A World Safe for Democracy: Liberal Internationalism and the Crises of Global Order* (New Haven: Yale University Press, 2020).

7. For an important revisionist history of liberalism, see Helena Rosenblatt, *The Lost History of Liberalism* (Princeton, N.J.: Princeton University Press, 2018). Rosenblatt focuses on the word "liberalism," rather than a fixed set of concepts over time. She argues that the word today is centered on individual rights and is identified with the "American Creed"; but that its origins are in the French Revolution of 1789, and that "liberalism" until recently

always meant generosity and the public welfare, as opposed to individual selfishness.

8. See Robert P. George, *Making Men Moral: Civil Liberties and Public Morality* (New York: Oxford University Press, 1993). I grapple with this kind of alternative in "Retrieving Christian Liberalism," *Providence* 11 (Spring/Summer 2018), https://providencemag.com/2019/09/retrieving-christian-liberalism/, retrieved on August 13, 2022.

9. In composing this section on autonomy, I have benefited from discussions with Malloy Owen.

10. Oñora O'Neill, "Autonomy: The Emperor's New Clothes," *Aristotelian Society Supplementary Volume 77*, no. 1 (2003): 3.

11. Heiner Bielefeldt, "Autonomy and Republicanism: Immanuel Kant's Philosophy of Freedom," *Political Theory* 25, no. 4 (August 1997): 524–58.

12. John M. Owen IV, *Confronting Political Islam: Six Lessons from the West's Past* (Princeton, N.J.: Princeton University Press, 2015), 117–20.

13. Mark Blyth, *Great Transformations: Economic Ideas and Institutional Change in the Twentieth Century* (New York: Cambridge University Press, 2002).

14. Daron Acemoglu and James Robinson, *Why Nations Fail: The Origins of Power, Prosperity, and Poverty* (New York: Crown, 2012), esp. 187–90.

15. This was a major complaint of Immanuel Kant against the despotic state: the (alleged) ability of the ruler to declare war and impose war taxes on a whim. See Kant, "To Perpetual Peace, a Philosophical Sketch" (1795), in *Kant's Political Writings,* trans. Ted Humphrey (Indianapolis: Hackett, 1983), 107–44.

16. Thomas Paine, *The Rights of Man and Common Sense* (New York: Knopf, 1994), 131.

17. John Locke, "Of the Beginning of Political Societies," in *Second Treatise on Government* (1689), repr. in *Two Treatises on Government and a Letter Concerning Toleration,* ed. Ian Shapiro (New Haven: Yale University Press, 2003), 141–54.

18. Rosenblatt, *Lost History,* 93–94.

19. John Stuart Mill, *Thoughts on Parliamentary Reform* (London: John W. Parker, 1859), 23–25. On classical liberalism's opposition to democracy in the nineteenth century, see Jon Roper, *Democracy and Its Critics: Anglo-American Democratic Thought in the Nineteenth Century* (New York: Routledge, 2011), 141–93.

20. H. G. E. Grey, "Evils and Dangers of Parliamentary Government" (1858), in *Perspectives on Political Parties,* ed. Susan E. Scarrow (New York: Palgrave-Macmillan, 2002), 133–34. Like Mill and other British liberals of

the time, Grey was influenced by Alexis de Tocqueville's observations about the "tyranny of the majority" in American democracy.

21. Thomas Jefferson, letter to John Holmes, 22 April 1820, in *Works of Thomas Jefferson,* ed. Paul Leicester Ford (New York: G. P. Putnam, 1905), 12:159.

22. Eric Foner, *Free Soil, Free Labor, Free Men: The Ideology of the Republican Party before the Civil War* (New York: Oxford University Press, 1995), xii–xx.

23. Abraham Lincoln, speech at Lewiston, Illinois, August 17, 1858: "In the enlightened belief" of the founders, "nothing stamped with the Divine image and likeness was sent into the world to be trodden on, and degraded, and imbruted by its fellows"; "Collected Works of Abraham Lincoln," University of Michigan Library, https://quod.lib.umich.edu/l/lincoln/lincoln2/1 :567?rgn=div1;view=fulltext.

24. Foner, *Free Soil,* xxviii–xxxii.

25. See the website of the Monty Pelerin Society: https://www.montpel erin.org, retrieved on March 8, 2022.

26. Quoted in George Klosko, *The Transformation of American Liberalism* (New York: Oxford University Press, 2017), 95.

27. Rosenblatt, *Lost History,* 83–84, 103–4.

28. Rosenblatt, *Lost History,* 158–59, 182–85.

29. Klosko, *Transformation,* 36–57.

30. Quoted in Immanuel Wallerstein, *The Modern World System,* vol. 4, *Centrist Liberalism Triumphant, 1789–1914* (Berkeley: University of California Press, 2011), 146.

31. Rosenblatt, *Lost History,* 222–29.

32. James Traub, *What Was Liberalism? The Past, Present, and Promise of a Noble Idea* (New York: Basic Books, 2019), 61–77.

33. Klosko, *Transformation,* 71.

34. Traub, *What Was Liberalism?,* 78–84.

35. Elizabeth Kier, *War and Democracy: Labor and the Politics of Peace* (Ithaca, N.Y.: Cornell University Press, 2021).

36. Sidney M. Milkis, "Franklin D. Roosevelt, the Economic Constitutional Order, and the New Politics of Presidential Leadership," in *The New Deal and the Triumph of Liberalism,* ed. Milkis and Jerome Mileur (Amherst: University of Massachusetts Press, 2002), 37–38.

37. Biaggio Bossone and Stefano Labini, "Macroeconomics in Germany: The Forgotten Lesson of Hjalmar Schacht," Vox EU, July 1, 2016, https:// voxeu.org/article/macroeconomics-germany-forgotten-lesson-hjalmar -schacht, retrieved on April 10, 2021.

38. Paul Dickson and Thomas B. Allen, *The Bonus Army: An American Epic* (New York: Walker, 2004).

39. Quoted in Milkis, "Franklin D. Roosevelt," 39. The speech was FDR's Commonwealth Club speech of September 23, 1932.

40. Milkis, "Franklin D. Roosevelt," 31–72.

41. Kirshner, "Keynes, Capital Mobility, and the Crisis of Embedded Liberalism," 319–21.

42. William E. Leuchtenburg, "FDR and the Kingfish," *American Heritage* 36, no. 6 (October/November 1985), https://www.americanheritage.com/fdr-and-kingfish#1, retrieved on April 7, 2021; Annika Neklason, "When Populism Swings Left," *Atlantic*, March 3, 2019, https://www.theatlantic.com/politics/archive/2019/03/huey-long-was-donald-trumps-left-wing-counterpart/583933/, retrieved on April 8, 2021.

43. Milkis, "Franklin D. Roosevelt," 42–46.

44. Melvyn P. Leffler, "Victory: The 'State,' the 'West,' and the Cold War," in *Safeguarding Democratic Capitalism: U.S. Foreign Policy and National Security, 1920–2015* (Princeton, N.J.: Princeton University Press, 2017), 227–30.

45. Stephen A. Marglin, "Lessons of the Golden Age: An Overview," in *The Golden Age of Capitalism: Reinterpreting the Postwar Experience*, ed. Marglin and Juliet B. Schor (New York: Oxford University Press, 1992), 1.

46. Traub, *What Was Liberalism?*, 117–26.

47. Traub, *What Was Liberalism?*, 117–26.

48. In the U.S. case, see Samuel P. Huntington, *American Politics: The Promise of Disharmony* (Cambridge, Mass.: Belknap Press, 1981).

49. Mary Dudziak, *Cold War Civil Rights: Race and the Image of American Democracy* (Princeton, N.J.: Princeton University Press, 2011).

50. Philip Zelikow and Condoleezza Rice, *To Build a Better World: Choices to End the Cold War and Create a Global Commonwealth* (New York: Twelve, 2019), 37.

51. Leffler, "Victory," 234–37.

52. Francis Fukuyama, *Liberalism and Its Discontents* (New York: Farrar, Straus and Giroux, 2022), 19–64.

53. Charles Taylor, *A Secular Age* (Cambridge, Mass.: Harvard University Press, 2007), 475.

54. Robert Bellah et al., *Habits of the Heart: Individualism and Commitment in American Life* (Berkeley: University of California Press, 1985), esp. 32–34.

55. Ronald Inglehart, *Cultural Evolution: People's Motivations Are Changing, and Reshaping the World* (New York: Cambridge University Press, 2018), 16–17. As critics have noted, "postmaterialism" is an odd label; material con-

sumption in Western societies is higher than ever, if also more laundered with references to fair trade and climate change. John Tomasi has linked what I call "open liberal values" to classical liberalism; the latter, he argues, is the best kind of liberalism because it best serves "self-authorship." Tomasi's defense does not match historical classical liberalism's justification by most of its defenders. Tomasi, *Free Market Fairness* (Princeton, N.J.: Princeton University Press, 2012), 94–95.

56. Traub, *What Was Liberalism?*, 23.

57. Stephen G. Brooks, *Political Economy of International Security* (Princeton, N.J.: Princeton University Press, forthcoming).

58. Quoted in Thomas Sowell, *A Conflict of Visions: Ideological Origins of Political Struggles*, rev. ed. (New York: Basic Books, 2007), 90. The original is from Adam Smith, *The Theory of Moral Sentiments* (1759).

59. Craig Calhoun, "The Class Consciousness of Frequent Travelers: Toward a Critique of Actually Existing Openism," *South Atlantic Quarterly* 101, no. 4 (Fall 2002): 877–79.

60. Leffler, "Victory," 238–39.

61. John J. Mearsheimer, *The Great Delusion: Liberal Dreams and International Realities* (New Haven: Yale University Press, 2018), 61–64.

62. Such was the claim of Bill Clinton in a speech at the University of Virginia's Miller Center on May 23, 2019; Clinton presented his presidency as a project to expand what was meant by the U.S. Constitution's opening phrase "We the people." See "Closing Keynote: President Bill Clinton," May 23, 2019, Miller Center, https://millercenter.org/prezfest2019/prezfest-videos /keynote-bill-clinton, retrieved on December 18, 2020.

63. Herman Mark Schwartz, "Globalisation/Welfare: What's the Preposition? And, or, Versus, With?" *Social Policy Review* 15 (2003): 71–90.

64. George Crowder, *Theories of Multiculturalism* (London: Polity, 2007), 192–98. The abandonment of welfare liberalism is what causes political theorist Brian Barry to reject multiculturalism; Crowder, *Theories of Multiculturalism*, 202.

65. Calhoun, "Class Consciousness," 890–92.

66. Quoted in John J. Mearsheimer, "Liberalism and Nationalism in Contemporary America," *PS: Political Science and Politics* 54, no. 1 (2021): 4.

67. Quoted in Christopher Caldwell, *The Age of Entitlement: America since the Sixties* (New York: Simon and Schuster, 2020), 93.

68. Immanuel Kant, "What Is Enlightenment?" (1784), http://www .columbia.edu/acis/ets/CCREAD/etscc/kant.html, retrieved on December 17, 2020.

69. Wilhelm von Humboldt, "Introduction," in *The Sphere and Duties of Government* (1792), https://oll.libertyfund.org/title/coulthard-the-sphere-and

-duties-of-government-1792-1854#lf0053_label_019, retrieved on December 17, 2020.

70. Algis Valiunas, "Ibsen's Soulcraft," *First Things* (December 2019), https://www.firstthings.com/article/2019/12/ibsens-soulcraft, retrieved on December 17, 2020.

71. John Stuart Mill, "Of Individuality, as One of the Elements of Well-Being," in *On Liberty* (1859), https://en.wikisource.org/wiki/On_Liberty/Chapter_3#cite_ref-1, retrieved on December 17, 2020. See also Traub, *What Was Liberalism?*, 37–52.

72. H. W. Siemens, "Nietzsche's Critique of Democracy (1870–1886)," *Journal of Nietzsche Studies* 38 (Fall 2009): 25.

73. Students for a Democratic Society, "Port Huron Statement," The Sixties Project, June 1962, http://www2.iath.virginia.edu/sixties/HTML_docs/Resources/Primary/Manifestos/SDS_Port_Huron.html, retrieved on December 23, 2020.

74. Todd Gitlin, *The Sixties: Years of Hope, Days of Rage* (New York: Bantam, 1987), 134–35, 321–22. Consider also Mario Savio, a leader of the Free Speech movement at the University of California at Berkeley. Savio was famous for his 1965 speech decrying the university's treatment of students as "the raw material" to be made into a "product." Like other leaders of the movement, Savio had spent the preceding summer in Mississippi as part of the Freedom Summer. W. J. Rorabaugh, *Berkeley at War: The 1960s* (New York: Oxford University Press, 1989), 21–23, 31.

75. Herbert Marcuse, "Repressive Tolerance," in *A Critique of Pure Tolerance* by Robert Paul Wolff, Barrington Moore, Jr., and Marcuse (Boston: Beacon Press, 1965), 95–137. See also Marcuse, *One-Dimensional Man: Studies in the Ideology of Advanced Industrial Society* (1964; repr., New York: Routledge, 2002). For a critique from the traditional Marxian Left, see Alasdair MacIntyre, *Marcuse* (New York: Fontana, 1970).

76. Quoted in Caldwell, *Age of Entitlement*, 78.

77. Marglin, "Lessons of the Golden Age," 17–19.

78. Michael Bleaney, *The Rise and Fall of Keynesian Economics* (New York: St. Martin's Press, 1985), 156–58.

79. John Hicks, *The Crisis in Keynesian Economics* (New York: Oxford University Press, 1974), 3.

80. Fred Hirsch, *Social Limits to Growth* (Cambridge, Mass.: Harvard University Press, 1976); Jürgen Habermas, *Legitimation Crisis*, trans. Thomas McCarthy (1973; repr., Boston: Beacon Press, 1975); originally published in German.

81. Bleaney, *Rise and Fall*, 133–34.

82. Pierre-Alain Muet, Alain Fonteneau, and Gerald Feldman, *Reflation*

and Austerity: Economic Policy under Mitterrand (London: Bloomsbury Academic, 1990).

83. Herman Schwartz, "Small States in Big Trouble: State Reorganization in Australia, Denmark, New Zealand, and Sweden in the 1980s," *World Politics* 46 (July 1994): 527–55.

84. The first prophet of the knowledge economy was Peter Drucker; see, e.g., his *The Age of Discontinuity: Guidelines to Our Changing Society* (New York: Harper and Row, 1969).

85. Robert Reich, *The Work of Nations: Preparing Ourselves for Twenty-First Century Capitalism* (New York: Vintage, 1992); Michael Lind, *The New Class War: Saving Democracy from the Managerial Elite* (New York: Penguin Random House, 2020).

86. David Brooks, *Bobos in Paradise: The New Upper Class and How They Got There* (New York: Simon and Schuster, 2001).

87. *Planned Parenthood of Southeast Pa. v. Casey*, 505 U.S. 833 (1992), https://supreme.justia.com/cases/federal/us/505/833/, retrieved on December 23, 2020.

88. Lind, *New Class War*, 1–2.

89. Thomas Frank, *Listen, Liberal! Or, Whatever Happened to the Party of the People?* (New York: Picador, 2016); Lind, *New Class War*.

90. James Davison Hunter and Joshua Yates, "In the Vanguard of Globalization: The World of American Globalizers," in *Many Globalizations: Cultural Diversity in the Contemporary World*, ed. Peter Berger and Samuel Huntington (New York: Oxford University Press, 2004), 14, 16, 18. Emphasis in the original.

91. Ikenberry, *Safe for Democracy*, 279–81.

92. Marc Levinson, *Outside the Box: How Globalization Changed from Moving Stuff to Spreading Ideas* (Princeton, N.J.: Princeton University Press, 2020).

4
Liberal Internationalism, Then and Now

1. Immanuel Kant, "Idea for a University History with a Cosmopolitan Purpose" (1784), in *Kant's Political Writings*, ed. Hans Reiss, trans. H. B. Nisbet (New York: Cambridge University Press, 1991), 47–49.

2. Kant, "Universal History," 48–49; Immanuel Kant, "Perpetual Peace, a Philosophical Sketch" (1795), in Reiss, *Kant's Political Writings*, 93–130.

3. For more on Kant and international evolution, see Wade L. Huntley, "Kant's Third Image: Systemic Sources of the Liberal Peace," *International*

Studies Quarterly 40 (1996): 45–76; Lars-Erik Cederman and Kristian Skrede Gleditsch, "Conquest and Regime Change: An Evolutionary Model of the Spread of Democracy and Peace," *International Studies Quarterly* 48 (2003): 603–29.

4. Jennifer Pitts, *A Turn to Empire: The Rise of Imperial Liberalism in Britain and France* (Princeton, N.J.: Princeton University Press, 2005).

5. Margaret Keck and Kathryn Sikkink, *Activists beyond Borders: Advocacy Networks in International Politics* (Ithaca, N.Y.: Cornell University Press, 1998), 39–78; John M. Owen IV, *Liberal Peace, Liberal War: American Politics and International Security* (Ithaca, N.Y.: Cornell University Press, 1997).

6. John M. Owen IV, *The Clash of Ideas in World Politics: Transnational Networks, States, and Regime Change, 1510–2010* (Princeton, N.J.: Princeton University Press, 2010), 148–49.

7. G. John Ikenberry, *A World Safe for Democracy: Liberal Internationalism and the Crises of Global Order* (New Haven: Yale University Press, 2020), 78–99.

8. Thomas Paine, *The Rights of Man and Common Sense* (New York: Knopf, 1994), 180.

9. Charles Kindleberger, "The Rise of Free Trade in Western Europe 1820–1875," *Journal of Economic History* 35, no. 1 (March 1975): 40–41.

10. Dani Rodrik, *The Globalization Paradox: Democracy and the Future of the World Economy* (New York: W. W. Norton, 2011), 34.

11. Robert Gilpin, *Political Economy of International Relations* (Princeton, N.J.: Princeton University Press, 1987), 180–81.

12. Payam Ghalehdar, *The Origins of Overthrow: How Emotional Frustration Shapes U.S. Regime Change Interventions* (New York: Oxford University Press, 2021), 56–76.

13. Owen, *Clash of Ideas*, 154–57.

14. Owen, *Clash of Ideas*, 175.

15. G. John Ikenberry, *After Victory: Institutions, Strategic Restraint, and the Rebuilding of Order after Major War* (Princeton, N.J.: Princeton University Press, 2001), 50–79; G. John Ikenberry, *Liberal Leviathan: The Origins, Crisis, and Transformation of the American World Order* (Princeton, N.J.: Princeton University Press, 2011), 157–220.

16. Michael M. McKoy and Michael K. Miller, "The Patron's Dilemma: The Dynamics of Foreign-Supported Democratization," *Journal of Conflict Resolution* 56, no. 5 (2012): 904–32. The academic literature on American hypocrisy during the Cold War, in the form of support for authoritarian rules and regimes, is vast.

17. Christopher Andrew, *The World Was Going Our Way: The KGB and the Battle for the Third World* (New York: Basic Books, 2006).

18. Philip G. Roeder, "The Ties That Bind: Aid, Trade, and Political Compliance in Soviet-Third World Relations," *International Studies Quarterly* 29, no. 2 (June 1985): 191–216.

19. Willie Thompson, *The Communist Movement since 1945* (New York: Wiley-Blackwell, 1998), 183.

20. Paul Krugman argues that high Soviet growth in the 1950s and 1960s was due to the mobilization of economic inputs (labor, education, and capital). Once those inputs had been mobilized, continued growth required increasing output per input, and the Soviets' command economy proved incapable of doing that. Krugman, "The Myth of Asia's Miracle," *Foreign Affairs* 73, no. 6 (November/December 1994): 62–69.

21. Tanja A. Börzel and Michael Zürn, "Contestations of the Liberal International Order," *International Organization* 75, no. 2 (2021): 282–305.

22. On international bureaucracies' harm to democracy, see Michael Barnett and Martha Finnemore, *Rules for the World: International Organizations in Global Politics* (Ithaca, N.Y.: Cornell University Press, 2004), 156–74.

23. Dani Rodrik, *The Paradox of Globalization: Choices to End the Cold War and Build a Global Commonwealth* (New York: Norton, 2011), 98–104; Marc Levinson, *Outside the Box: How Globalization Changed from Moving Stuff to Spreading Ideas* (Princeton, N.J.: Princeton University Press, 2020), 67–69.

24. Quinn Slobodian, *Globalists: The End of Empire and the Birth of Neoliberalism* (Cambridge, Mass.: Harvard University Press, 2018), 13–21.

25. Joseph E. Stiglitz, "The Post-Washington Consensus Consensus," Initiative for Policy Dialogue, n.d., http://policydialogue.org/files/events/Stiglitz _Post_Washington_Consensus_Paper.pdf, retrieved on March 17, 2021.

26. Slobodian, *Globalists*, 121–36.

27. Philip D. Zelikow and Condoleezza Rice, *To Build a Better World* (New York: Twelve, 2019), 41–52; Levinson, *Outside the Box*, 5.

28. John Williamson, "Democracy and the 'Washington Consensus,'" *World Development* 21, no. 8 (1993): 1330.

29. Levinson, *Outside the Box*, 81–95.

30. "Where Do iPhone Components Come From?," ArcGIS, https://www .arcgis.com/apps/MapJournal/index.html?appid=391276eb829344289df9bce 81e083fce, retrieved on May 20, 2021.

31. Levinson, *Outside the Box*, 162.

32. Historian Jeremi Suri argues that the Soviets, like the Western governments, were worried about political discontent in their own borders and in their satellite states in Eastern Europe. Détente was partly caused by the need for both superpowers to quell the transnational political unrest of the late 1960s, which in some countries was traumatic. Suri, *Power and Protest:*

Global Revolution and the Rise of Détente (Cambridge, Mass.: Harvard University Press, 2003).

33. Henry R. Nau, *Conservative Internationalism: Armed Diplomacy under Jefferson, Polk, Truman, and Reagan* (Princeton, N.J.: Princeton University Press, 2013), 171–201.

34. Ronald Reagan, "Address to Members of the British Parliament," June 8, 1982, Reagan Library, National Archives, https://www.reaganlibrary.gov /archives/speech/address-members-british-parliament, retrieved on March 17, 2021. Also, Thomas Carothers, "Taking Stock of Democracy Assistance," in *American Democracy Promotion: Impulses, Strategies, and Impacts,* ed. Michael Cox, G. John Ikenberry, and Takashi Inoguchi (New York: Oxford University Press, 2000), 182–83.

35. International Monetary Fund, "Country Data," https://www.imf.org /en/Countries/USA#countrydata, retrieved on March 17, 2021.

36. Melvyn Leffler argues that welfare states in democracies were essential to the West's Cold War victory; see Leffler, "Victory: The 'State,' the 'West,' and the Cold War," in *Safeguarding Democratic Capitalism: U.S. Foreign Policy and National Security, 1920–2015* (Princeton, N.J.: Princeton University Press, 2017), 221–42. It is certainly the case that in the 1980s the United States and its democratic allies did not cast off the welfare states they had built in the 1940s. The deregulation of the 1980s and subsequent renewal of economic growth without inflation that were so important to the end of the Cold War, however, were features of open liberalism.

37. David Marsh, "Haunted by the Old Demons," *Financial Times,* June 10, 1987, *Weekend FT,* 1.

38. John M. Owen and Michael Poznansky, "When Does America Drop Dictators?," *European Journal of International Relations* 20, no. 4 (2014): 1072–99.

39. See, e.g., Mary Elise Sarotte, *1989: The Struggle to Create Post-Cold War Europe* (Princeton, N.J.: Princeton University Press, 2009); Renée de Nevers, *Comrades No More: The Seeds of Change in Eastern Europe* (Cambridge, Mass.: MIT Press, 2002); Jacques Lévesque, *The Enigma of 1989: The USSR and the Liberation of Eastern Europe,* trans. Keith Martin (Berkeley: University of California Press, 1997).

40. For helpful timelines of 1989 in Eastern Europe, see U.S. State Department, "Fall of Communism in Eastern Europe, 1989," https://history .state.gov/milestones/1989-1992/fall-of-communism, retrieved on February 11, 2021; and Indiana University Bloomington Libraries, "Revolutions of 1989 Chronology," https://libraries.indiana.edu/revolutions-1989-chronology, retrieved on February 11, 2021.

41. Owen and Poznansky, "When Does America Drop Dictators?," 1072–99.

42. A sidewalk plaque commemorating Reagan's 1987 speech, unveiled in 2012, lies near the Brandenburg Gate.

43. Nau, *Conservative Internationalism,* 171–201; Andrew Busch, "Ronald Reagan and the Defeat of the Soviet Empire," *Presidential Studies Quarterly* 27, no. 3 (Summer 1997): 451–66.

44. Paul Kennedy, *The Rise and Fall of the Great Powers: Economic Change and Military Conflict from 1500 to 2000* (New York: Random House, 1987).

45. Francis Fukuyama, "The End of History?," *National Interest* 16 (Summer 1989): 3–18.

46. Samuel P. Huntington, *The Third Wave: Democratization in the Late Twentieth Century* (Norman: University of Oklahoma Press, 1991), 13–22.

47. For a treatment of the excesses of U.S. forcible intervention that sees liberalism itself as the problem, see John J. Mearsheimer, *The Great Delusion: Liberal Dreams and International Realities* (New Haven: Yale University Press, 2018), 120–51.

48. Tony Smith, *Why Wilson Matters: The Origin of American Liberal Internationalism and Its Crisis Today* (Princeton, N.J.: Princeton University Press, 2017).

49. As of early 2021, Freedom House rated both Afghanistan and Iraq as "not free," owing in large part to ongoing violence and insecurity. See Freedom House, "Freedom in the World 2021," https://freedomhouse.org/country/afghanistan/freedom-world/2021, retrieved on March 18, 2021. Both countries rated higher than they did in 2000. On Freedom House's 100-point scale, Afghanistan improved from 14 to 27 (prior to the U.S. withdrawal and rapid Taliban takeover in August 2021); Iraq, from 14 to 29. See Freedom House, "Freedom in the World: The Annual Survey of Political Rights and Civil Liberties, 2000–2001," https://freedomhouse.org/sites/default/files/2020-02/Freedom_in_the_World_2000-2001_complete_book.pdf.

50. Frank P. Harvey, *Explaining the Iraq War: Counterfactual Theory, Logic and Evidence* (New York: Cambridge University Press, 2011), 90–116.

51. George W. Bush, "President Bush's Second Inaugural Address," National Public Radio, January 20, 2005, https://www.npr.org/templates/story/story.php?storyId=4460172, retrieved on June 30, 2021.

52. North Atlantic Treaty Organization, "Membership Action Plan (MAP)," press release NAC-S(99) 066, April 24, 1999, https://www.nato.int/cps/en/natohq/official_texts_27444.htm?selectedLocale=en, retrieved on July 13, 2022. The 1949 North Atlantic Treaty does not mention democracy, and Portugal and Turkey were both authoritarian for periods of their membership. See Michael Poznansky and Keith L. Carter, "NATO Members Are Supposed

to Be Democratic. What Happens When Turkey Isn't?," *Washington Post*, October 13, 2016, https://www.washingtonpost.com/news/monkey-cage/wp /2016/10/13/nato-members-are-supposed-to-be-democratic-what-happens -when-turkey-isnt/, retrieved on July 13, 2022.

53. European Commission, "EU Policy for Cultural Heritage," https:// ec.europa.eu/culture/cultural-heritage/eu-policy-cultural-heritage, retrieved on March 22, 2021.

54. Slobodian, *Globalists,* 256–60.

55. Rodrik, *Paradox of Globalization,* 76–79.

56. World Trade Organization, "Evolution of Trade under the WTO: Handy Statistics," https://www.wto.org/english/res_e/statis_e/trade_evolution _e/evolution_trade_wto_e.htm, retrieved on March 18, 2021.

57. The World Bank moved away from the Consensus, and the Asian Development Bank, in which Japan and the United States are the largest stakeholders, never accepted it fully. See Allen T. Cheng, "Asian Development Bank: A Force of Stability," Institutional Investor, April 24, 2017, https:// www.institutionalinvestor.com/article/b1505p76sfj6x6/asian-development -bank-a-force-of-stability, retrieved on March 18, 2021.

58. Donnacha Ó Beacháin and Able Polese, "What Happened to the Colour Revolutions? Authoritarian Responses from Former Soviet Spaces," *Journal of International and Area Studies* 17, no. 2 (December 2010): 35–39.

59. Steven Levitsky and Lucan A. Way, *Competitive Authoritarianism: Hybrid Regimes after the Cold War* (New York: Cambridge University Press, 2010).

60. Ikenberry, *World Safe for Democracy,* 76–78.

61. G. John Ikenberry and Daniel Nexon, "Hegemony Studies 3.0: The Dynamics of Hegemonic Orders," *Security Studies* 28, no. 3 (2019): 417–19.

62. On right-wing populist challenges to the liberal international order all over the world, see Alexander Cooley and Daniel Nexon, *Exit from Hegemony: The Unraveling of the American Global Order* (New York: Oxford University Press, 2020), 137–58.

63. William A. Galston, *Anti-Pluralism: The Populist Threat to Liberal Democracy* (New Haven: Yale University Press, 2018), 33–40.

64. Thomas Frank, *Listen, Liberal! Or, Whatever Happened to the Party of the People?* (New York: Henry Holt, 2016), 2.

65. J. Lawrence Broz, Jeffry Frieden, and Stephen Weymouth, "Populism in Place: The Economic Geography of the Globalization Backlash," *International Organization* 75, no. 2 (2021): 470–71.

66. Daron Acemoglu and Pascual Restrepo, "Robots and Jobs: Evidence from US Labor Markets," *Journal of Political Economy* 128, no. 6 (2020): 2188–244.

67. Thomas M. Flaherty and Ronald Rogowski, "Rising Inequality as a Threat to the Liberal International Order," *International Organization* 75 (Spring 2021): 495.

68. Broz, Frieden, and Weymouth, "Populism in Place," 476, 465.

69. Catherine E. De Vries, Sara B. Hobolt, and Stefanie Walter, "Politicizing International Cooperation: The Mass Public, Political Entrepreneurs, and Political Opportunity Structures," *International Organization* 75, no. 2 (2021): 306–32; John J. Mearsheimer, "Liberalism and Nationalism in Contemporary America" (James Madison Award Lecture, University of Chicago, September 20, 2020), in *PS: Political Science and Politics* 54, no. 1 (January 2021): 1–8.

70. Sara Wallace Goodman and Thomas B. Pepinsky, "The Exclusionary Foundations of Embedded Liberalism," *International Organization* 75, no. 2 (2021): 411–39.

71. Jonathan Wadsworth, Swati Dhingra, Gianmarco Ottaviano, and John Van Reenen, *Brexit and the Impact of Immigration on the UK* (London: LSE, 2016), http://cep.lse.ac.uk/pubs/download/brexito5.pdf, retrieved on March 23, 2021; Martin Ruys and Carlos Vargas Silva, "The Labour Market Effects of Immigration," Migration Observatory, February 18, 2020, https://migration observatory.ox.ac.uk/resources/briefings/the-labour-market-effects-of -immigration/, retrieved on March 23, 2021.

72. George J. Borjas, "Yes, Immigration Hurts American Workers," Politico, September/October 2016, https://www.politico.com/magazine/story/2016 /09/trump-clinton-immigration-economy-unemployment-jobs-214216/, retrieved on March 23, 2021. Borjas has published many papers on the topic; for a synthesis, see "The Wage Effects of Immigration: Descriptive Evidence" and "The Wage Effects of Immigration: Structural Estimates," in *Immigration Economics* (Cambridge, Mass.: Harvard University Press, 2014), 105–48.

73. David Autor, David Dorn, and Gordon H. Hanson, "The China Syndrome: Local Labor Market Effects of Import Competition in the United States," *American Economic Review* 103, no. 6 (2013): 2121–68.

74. Levinson, *Outside the Box*, 123–25.

75. Daron Acemoglu, David Autor, David Dorn, Gordon H. Hanson, and Brendan Price, "Import Competition and the Great US Employment Sag of the 2000s," *Journal of Labor Economics* 34, no. S1, pt. 2 (January 2016), https://doi.org/10.1086/682384.

76. David Autor, David Dorn, and Gordon H. Hanson, "The China Shock: Learning from Labor-Market Adjustment to Large Changes in Trade," *Annual Review of Economics* 8 (2016): 205–40; David Autor, Kaveh Majlesi, and Gordon Hanson, "Importing Political Polarization? The Electoral Conse-

quences of Rising Trade Exposure," *American Economic Review* 110, no. 10 (2020): 3139–83.

77. Rodrik, *Paradox of Globalization,* 84–88. The list includes Paul Samuelson, Paul Krugman, Alan Blinder, Martin Wolf, and Lawrence Summers.

78. See Financial Crisis Inquiry Commission, *The Financial Crisis Inquiry Report* (Washington, D.C.: Government Printing Office, 2011), which includes reports by dissenting members of the commission; Herman Mark Schwartz, *Subprime Nation: American Power, Global Capital, and the Housing Bubble* (Ithaca, N.Y.: Cornell University Press, 2011).

79. Simon Johnson, "The Quiet Coup," *Atlantic,* May 2009, https://www.theatlantic.com/magazine/archive/2009/05/the-quiet-coup/307364/, retrieved on March 23, 2021.

80. Brian Keeley and Patrick Love, *From Crisis to Recovery: The Causes, Course and Consequences of the Great Recession* (Paris: OECD, 2010), 32.

81. Christopher Caldwell, *The Age of Entitlement: America since the Sixties* (New York: Simon and Schuster, 2020), 210–11.

82. Zygmunt Bauman, *Liquid Modernity* (London: Polity, 2000).

83. David A. Lake, Lisa Martin, and Thomas Risse, "Challenges to the Liberal Order: Reflections on International Organization," *International Organization* 75, no. 2 (2021): 240.

84. Pippa Norris and Ronald Inglehart, *Cultural Backlash: Trump, Brexit, and Authoritarian Populism* (New York: Cambridge University Press, 2019), 7–8. See also Zoltán I. Búzás, who depicts the fundamental problem as a contest between multiculturalists and "racial hierarchists." Búzás, "Racism and Antiracism in the Liberal International Order," *International Organization* 75, no. 2 (2021): 440–63.

85. Emily Ekins and Jonathan Haidt, "Donald Trump Voters Think about Morality Differently than Other Voters. Here's How," Vox, February 5, 2016, https://www.vox.com/2016/2/5/10918164/donald-trump-morality, retrieved on April 12, 2021. The article builds on Haidt, *The Righteous Mind: Why Good People Are Divided by Politics and Religion* (New York: Vintage, 2012).

86. Angus Deaton and Anne Case, *Deaths of Despair and the Future of Capitalism* (Princeton, N.J.: Princeton University Press, 2020), 38.

87. W. Bradford Wilcox and Wendy Wang, "The Marriage Divide: How and Why Working-Class Families Are More Fragile Today" (research brief, Opportunity America-AEI-Brookings Working Class Group, 2017), 13.

88. James Davison Hunter and Carl Desportes Bowman, with Kyle Puetz, *Democracy in Dark Times* (New York: Finstock and Tew, 2021), 11.

89. Clint Smith, "Elite Colleges Constantly Tell Low-Income Students That They Do Not Belong," *Atlantic,* March 18, 2019, https://www.theatlantic.com/education/archive/2019/03/privileged-poor-navigating-elite-university

-life/585100/, retrieved on March 26, 2021. See also J. D. Vance, *Hillbilly Elegy: A Memoir of a Family and Culture in Crisis* (New York: Harper, 2016); Rob Henderson, "Everything I Know about Elite College I Learned from 'Fresh Prince' and 'West Wing,'" *New York Times*, October 10, 2020, https://www.nytimes.com/2020/10/10/opinion/sunday/television-culture.html, retrieved on March 26, 2021.

90. Richard V. Reeves, *Dream Hoarders* (Washington, D.C.: Brookings Institution, 2018).

91. David Brooks, "How the Bobos Broke America," *Atlantic*, September 2021, https://www.theatlantic.com/magazine/archive/2021/09/blame-the-bobos-creative-class/619492/, retrieved on August 9, 2021.

92. Galston, *Anti-Pluralism*, 71.

93. Francisco Herreros and Henar Criado, "Social Trust, Social Capital and Perceptions of Immigration," *Political Studies* 57 (2009): 337–55.

94. Nicole J. LeBlanc and Luana Marques, "Anxiety in College: What We Know and How to Cope," *Harvard Health* (blog), May 28, 2019, https://www.health.harvard.edu/blog/anxiety-in-college-what-we-know-and-how-to-cope-2019052816729, retrieved on May 28, 2021.

95. Center for Collegiate Mental Health, "2020 Annual Report," Pennsylvania State University, 30, https://ccmh.psu.edu/assets/docs/2020%20CCMH%20Annual%20Report.pdf, retrieved on May 28, 2021.

96. Joseph E. Davis, *Chemically Imbalanced: Everyday Suffering, Medication, and Our Troubled Quest for Self-Mastery* (Chicago: University of Chicago Press, 2020).

97. Eleonora Alabrese, Sascha O. Becker, Thiemo Fetzer, and Dennis Novy, "Who Voted for Brexit? Individual and Regional Data Combined," *European Journal of Political Economy* 56 (January 2019): 132–50.

98. German Institute for Economic Research (DIW Berlin), "AfD Received More Votes in the Parliamentary Election in Rural Areas with Aging Populations," press release, February 21, 1018, https://www.diw.de/en/diw_01.c.578521.en/topics_news/afd_received_more_votes_in_the_parliamentary_election_in_rural_areas_with_aging_populations.html, retrieved on March 26, 2021.

99. Hunter and Bowman, *Democracy in Dark Times*, 35.

100. Yascha Mounk and Wesley Yang, "What Is the 'Successor Ideology'?," November 14, 2021, in *Persuasion*, podcast, https://www.persuasion.community/p/what-is-the-successor-ideology, retrieved on May 13, 2021.

101. Hunter and Bowman, *Democracy in Dark Times*, 24–28.

102. Lee Drutman, *Breaking the Two-Party Doom Loop: The Case for Multiparty Democracy in America* (New York: Oxford University Press, 2020).

103. Levinson, *Outside the Box*.

5
China

1. Chaohua Wang, "Remembering Tiananmen," *London Review of Books,* July 5, 2007, https://www.lrb.co.uk/the-paper/v29/n13/chaohua-wang/diary, retrieved on June 9, 2021.

2. Susan Shirk, *China: Fragile Superpower* (New York: Oxford University Press, 2008), 35.

3. Shirk, *Fragile Superpower,* 35–38.

4. Orville Schell and John Delury, *Wealth and Power: China's Long March to the Twenty-First Century* (New York: Random House, 2013), 306.

5. Ezra F. Vogel, *Deng Xiaoping and the Transformation of China* (Cambridge, Mass.: Belknap Press, 2013), 617.

6. "Tiananmen Square Protest Death Toll Was 10,000," BBC News, December 23, 2017, https://www.bbc.com/news/world-asia-china-42465516, retrieved on April 27, 2021.

7. Marek Hrubec calls Deng's changes a "revolutionary transformation," which is an event "that take[s] place relatively slowly along reformist lines, often constitutionally, and usually without violence, but in the long run they may be fundamental and hence alter the entire system by revolutionary means." Hrubec, "From China's Reform to the World's Reform," *International Critical Thought* 10, no. 2 (2020): 289.

8. Vogel, *Deng,* 617.

9. Vogel, *Deng,* 640–44.

10. English text available at "Human Rights in China," Information Office of the State Council of the People's Republic of China, November 1991, http://www.china.org.cn/e-white/7/index.htm, retrieved on November 13, 2020.

11. Katrin Kinzelbach, "China's White Paper on Human Rights," Global Public Policy Institute, April 5, 2016, https://www.gppi.net/2016/04/05/chinas-white-paper-on-human-rights, retrieved on November 13, 2020.

12. In constant 2010 U.S. dollars, from $340.6 billion to $2.2 trillion, according to the World Bank: World Bank, "Data: GDP–China," https://data.worldbank.org/indicator/NY.GDP.MKTP.KD?locations=CN, generated on May 3, 2021.

13. "Will China's Economy Ever Overtake America's?," *Economist,* September 6, 2022.

14. Shirk, *Fragile Superpower,* 5.

15. For a sophisticated argument of this type, see Alastair Iain Johnston, *Social States: China in International Institutions, 1980–2000* (Princeton, N.J.: Princeton University Press, 2000).

16. Andréa Worden, "China at the UN Human Rights Council: Conjuring a 'Community of Shared Future for Mankind'?," in *An Emerging China-Centric Order: China's Vision for a New World Order in Practice*, ed. Nadège Rolland (Washington, D.C.: National Bureau of Asian Research, 2020), 36–37.

17. Ted Piccone, "China's Long Game on Human Rights at the United Nations," Brookings Institution, September 2018, 7, https://www.brookings .edu/research/chinas-long-game-on-human-rights-at-the-united-nations/, retrieved on November 13, 2020.

18. Jessica Chen Weiss and Jeremy L. Wallace, "Domestic Politics, China's Rise, and the Future of the Liberal International Order," *International Organization* 75 (Spring 2021): 637–42.

19. Alexander Saeedy and Philip Wen, "Sri Lanka's Debt Crisis Tests China's Role as Financier to Poor Countries," *Wall Street Journal*, July 13, 2022, https://www.wsj.com/articles/sri-lankas-debt-crisis-tests-chinas-role -as-financier-to-poor-countries-imf-bailout-11657735179?mod=Search results_pos8&page=1, retrieved on July 14, 2022.

20. Nadège Rolland, *China's Vision for a New World Order* (Washington, D.C.: National Bureau of Asian Research, 2020), 14–15; "An Investigation into What Has Shaped Xi Jinping's Thinking," *Economist*, September 28, 2022.

21. Sergey Radchenko, "Putin and Xi Eye the Soviet Collapse," Asan Forum, March 19, 2020, http://www.theasanforum.org/putin-and-xi-eye-the -soviet-collapse/#a19, retrieved on November 16, 2020.

22. Frank Dikötter, *Mao's Great Famine: The History of China's Most Devastating Catastrophe, 1958–1962* (London: Bloomsbury, 2011).

23. That is R. J. Rummel's estimate. Rummel, *Death by Government* (New Brunswick, N.J.: Transaction, 1994), 102.

24. Benjamin A. Valentino, "Still Standing By: Why America and the International Community Fail to Prevent Genocide and Mass Killing," *Perspectives on Politics* 1, no. 3 (2003): 83.

25. R. J. Rummel, "Table 2.1: Pre-20th-Century Democide," Power Kills, https://www.hawaii.edu/powerkills/SOD.TAB2.1A.GIF, retrieved on August 27, 2021.

26. Rosemary Foot, "Chinese Power and the Idea of a Responsible State," *China Journal* 45 (January 2001): 1–19.

27. Daniel Bell, *The China Model: Political Meritocracy and the Limits of Democracy* (Princeton, N.J.: Princeton University Press, 2015). Bell argues that meritocratic democracy is superior to liberal democracy.

28. Azar Gat, "The Return of Authoritarian Great Powers," *Foreign Affairs* 86, no. 4 (July/August 2007): 59–69.

29. Stefan Halper, *The Beijing Consensus: How China's Authoritarian Model Will Dominate the Twenty-First Century* (New York: Basic Books, 2010).

30. Kenneth G. Lieberthal and David M. Lampton, eds., *Bureaucracy, Politics, and Decision-Making in Post-Maoist China* (Berkeley: University of California Press, 1992).

31. Nicholas Kristof, "China Sees 'Market-Leninism' as Way to Future," *New York Times*, September 6, 1993; Halper, *Beijing Consensus*.

32. "Economic Watch: China Accelerates Reform to Empower Private Sector amid COVID-19," Xinhua Net, September 9, 2020, http://www.xin huanet.com/english/2020-09/09/c_139355807.htm, retrieved on April 29, 2021.

33. Shirk, *Fragile Superpower*, 39.

34. Rana Mitter, "The Everlasting Mao," Project Syndicate, October 23, 2020, https://www.project-syndicate.org/onpoint/maoism-in-contemporary -china-and-the-world-by-rana-mitter-2020-10, retrieved on October 28, 2020.

35. "Document No. 9," China File, https://www.chinafile.com/document -9-chinafile-translation#start, retrieved on October 22, 2020.

36. Chris Buckley, "China Takes Aim at Western Ideas," *New York Times*, August 19, 2013, https://www.nytimes.com/2013/08/20/world/asia/chinas-new -leadership-takes-hard-line-in-secret-memo.html?mcubz=1, retrieved on October 22, 2020. For more on the party's effort to keep liberal democracy at bay, see Rachel Vanderhill, "Active Resistance to Democratic Diffusion," *Communist and Post-Communist Studies* 50, no. 1 (2017): 41–51.

37. Roland Boer, *Socialism with Chinese Characteristics: A Guide for Foreigners* (Singapore: Springer, 2021), 32–40.

38. Boer, *Socialism with Chinese Characteristics*, 116–30; Hrubec, "From China's Reform," 290.

39. Boer, *Socialism with Chinese Characteristics*, 152–57.

40. Boer, *Socialism with Chinese Characteristics*, 176–78, 193–219.

41. Boer, *Socialism with Chinese Characteristics*, 282–84.

42. Boer, *Socialism with Chinese Characteristics*, 289–91.

43. Elizabeth Economy, *The Third Revolution: Xi Jinping and the New Chinese State* (New York: Oxford University Press, 2018), 105.

44. Barry Naughton, "China's Global Economic Interactions," in *China and the World*, ed. David Shambaugh (New York: Oxford University Press, 2020), 115.

45. Shusheng Zhao, "China's Foreign Policy Making Process," in Shambaugh, *China and the World*, 104.

46. Lingling Wei, "China's Xi Ramps Up Control of Private Sector: 'We Have No Choice but to Follow the Party,'" *Wall Street Journal*, December 10, 2020, https://www.wsj.com/articles/china-xi-clampdown-private-sector -communist-party-11607612531, retrieved on April 29, 2021.

47. Scott Livingston, "The Chinese Communist Party Targets the Private Sector" (Center for Strategic and International Studies, October 2020). This

paper reprints in its entirety the party document "Opinion on Strengthening the United Front Work of the Private Economy in the New Era," from the Chinese government's official website (September 15, 2020).

48. Jonathan R. Stromseth, Edmund J. Malesky, and Dimitar D. Gueorguiev, *China's Governance Puzzle: Enabling Transparency and Participation in a Single-Party State* (New York: Cambridge University Press, 2017), 1–25.

49. Seva Gunitsky, "Corrupting the Cyber-Commons: Social Media as a Tool of Autocratic Stability," *Perspectives on Politics* 13, no. 1 (2015): 42–54; Gary King, Jennifer Pan, and Margaret E. Roberts, "How Censorship in China Allows Government Criticism but Silences Collective Expression," *American Political Science Review* 107, no. 2 (May 2013): 326–43.

50. Jinghan Zeng, "Artificial Intelligence and China's Authoritarian Governance," *International Affairs* 96, no. 6 (2020): 1441–59.

51. Editorial Board, "The End of One Country, Two Systems in Hong Kong," *Financial Times*, July 1, 2020, https://www.ft.com/content/5d3d7d2e-bba8-11ea-a05d-efc604854c3f, retrieved on October 22, 2020.

52. Eleanor Albert and Lindsay Maizland, "Religion in China," Council on Foreign Relations, September 25, 2020, https://www.cfr.org/backgrounder/religion-china, retrieved on April 29, 2021.

53. Edward Cunningham, Tony Saich, and Jesse Turiel, *Understanding CCP Resilience: Surveying Chinese Public Opinion through Time* (Cambridge, Mass.: Ash Center for Democratic Governance and Innovation, 2020), 3, https://ash.harvard.edu/files/ash/files/final_policy_brief_7.6.2020.pdf, retrieved on October 22, 2020.

54. I thank Xiaojun Li for alerting me to these sources.

55. Quoted in Halper, *Beijing Consensus*, 133.

56. Mark Hannah, "From Democracy Promotion to Democracy Attraction: How the World Views American-Style Democracy," Eurasia Group Foundation, May 2019, 9, 14, https://egfound.org/stories/independent-america/democracy-attraction/, retrieved on November 3, 2020.

57. Chris Buckley, Vivian Wang, Chang Che, and Amy Chang Chien, "After a Deadly Blaze, a Surge of Defiance against China's Covid Policies," *New York Times*, November 27, 2022, https://www.nytimes.com/2022/11/27/world/asia/china-covid-protest.html, retrieved on November 27, 2022.

58. "Former Taiwan President Admits 'One Country, Two Systems' Is Dead," *Taiwan News*, March 12, 2021, https://www.taiwannews.com.tw/en/news/4149035, retrieved on April 28, 2021.

59. Economy, *Third Revolution*, 4–9.

60. Philip B. K. Potter and Chen Wang, *Zero Tolerance: Repression and Political Violence on China's New Silk Road* (New York: Cambridge University Press, 2022).

61. Sergey Radchenko, "Putin and Xi Eye the Soviet Collapse," Asan Forum, March 19, 2020, http://www.theasanforum.org/putin-and-xi-eye -the-soviet-collapse/, retrieved on November 16, 2020.

62. Paul Blustein, *Schism: China, America, and the Fracturing of the Global Trading System* (Waterloo, Ont.: CIGI, 2019), 22–25.

63. Quoted in Blustein, *Schism,* 26–34, 65.

64. Richard Fisher, *The Collapse of Clinton's China Policy: Undoing the Damage of the MFN Debate* (Washington, D.C.: Heritage Foundation, 1994), cited in Kevin Williamson, "The End of Whig History," *National Review,* March 1, 2022, https://www.nationalreview.com/the-Tuesday/the-end-of-whig -history/?utm_source=Sailthru&utm_medium=email&utm_campaign =TUE_20220301&utm_term=Tuesday-Smart, retrieved on March 1, 2022.

65. Blustein, *Schism,* 51–60.

66. Blustein, *Schism,* 61–64.

67. Blustein, *Schism,* 91–110.

68. Jude Blanchette, "From 'China Inc.' to 'CCP Inc.': A New Paradigm for Chinese State Capitalism," *China Leadership Monitor,* December 1, 2020, https://www.prcleader.org/blanchette, retrieved on March 20, 2021.

69. Levinson, *Outside the Box,* 168–69.

70. Blustein, *Schism,* 112–18; Naughton, "China's Global Economic Inter- actions," 119.

71. Sonal Pandya, "Democratization and FDI Liberalization, 1970–2000," *International Studies Quarterly* 58, no. 3 (September 2014): 475–88; Sonal Pandya, *Trading Spaces: Foreign Direct Investment Regulation, 1970–2000* (New York: Cambridge University Press, 2016).

72. Graham Webster, "What Will the TPP Mean for China?," Foreign Policy, October 7, 2015, https://foreignpolicy.com/2015/10/07/china-tpp-trans -pacific-partnership-obama-us-trade-xi/, retrieved on November 10, 2020.

73. Blustein, *Schism,* 207–18.

74. Earl Anthony Wayne and Oliver Magnusson, "The Death of TPP: The Best Thing That Ever Happened to China," *National Interest,* January 29, 2017, https://nationalinterest.org/feature/the-death-tpp-the-best-thing-ever -happened-china-19232?nopaging=1, retrieved on November 10, 2020.

75. Jack Caporal, "The CPTPP: (Almost) One Year Later," Center for Strategic and International Studies, November 5, 2019, https://www.csis.org /analysis/cptpp-almost-one-year-later, retrieved on November 11, 2020.

76. Keith Bradsher and Ana Swanson, "China-Led Trade Pact Is Signed, in Challenge to U.S.," *New York Times,* November 15, 2020, https://www.ny times.com/2020/11/15/business/china-trade-rcep.html, retrieved on Novem- ber 16, 2020.

77. Alexander Cooley and Daniel Nexon, *Exit from Hegemony: The Unraveling of the American Global Order* (New York: Oxford University Press, 2020), 54–79.

78. Yu-Jie Chen, "China's Challenge to the International Human Rights Regime," *NYU Journal of International Law and Politics* 51 (2018): 1193–94.

6

Russia

1. Vladimir Putin, "Speech and the Following Discussion at the Munich Conference on Security Policy," President of Russia, February 10, 2007, http://en.kremlin.ru/events/president/transcripts/24034, retrieved on June 20, 2022.

2. Daniel Fried and Kurt Volker, "The Speech in Which Putin Told Us Who He Was," Politico, February 18, 2022, https://www.politico.com/news/magazine/2022/02/18/putin-speech-wake-up-call-post-cold-war-order-liberal-2007-00009918, retrieved on June 20, 2022.

3. Fried and Volker, "Speech."

4. Allen C. Lynch, *Vladimir Putin and Russian Statecraft* (Washington, D.C.: Potomac Books, 2011), 95–103.

5. George W. Bush, "President Bush's Second Inaugural Address," National Public Radio, January 20, 2005, https://www.npr.org/templates/story/story.php?storyId=4460172, retrieved on June 20, 2022.

6. George W. Bush, "President Addresses and Thanks Citizens of Slovakia," The White House, February 24, 2005, https://georgewbush-whitehouse.archives.gov/news/releases/2005/02/20050224-1.html, retrieved on June 18, 2022. Bush and Putin met in Bratislava the next day; the press conference suggested that they had had some difficult moments concerning the state of democracy in Russia. The White House, "President and President Putin Discuss Strong Russian-U.S. Partnership," press release, Bratislava, February 24, 2005, https://georgewbush-whitehouse.archives.gov/news/releases/2005/02/20050224-9.html, retrieved on June 18, 2022.

7. Andrei Vladimirov, "An Exportable Revolution," *Itogi* 49 (December 7, 2004): 10–12, trans. Pavel Pushkin; quoted in Graeme Herd, "Russia and the 'Orange Revolution': Response, Rhetoric, Reality?" *Connections* 4, no. 2 (Summer 2005): 17.

8. Robert Horvath, *Putin's "Preventive Counter-Revolution": Post-Soviet Authoritarianism and the Spectre of Velvet Revolution* (New York: Routledge, 2013), 12–18.

9. Vladimir Putin, "Address by the President of the Russian Federation," President of Russia, February 21, 2022, http://en.kremlin.ru/events/president/news/67828, retrieved on June 25, 2022.

10. Mary Elise Sarotte, *Not One Inch: America, Russia, and the Making of Post-Cold War Stalemate* (New Haven: Yale University Press, 2021), 259.

11. Scott Wilson, "Obama Dismisses Russia as 'Regional Power' Acting Out of Weakness," *Washington Post*, March 25, 2014, https://www.washingtonpost.com/world/national-security/obama-dismisses-russia-as-regional-power-acting-out-of-weakness/2014/03/25/1e5a678e-b439-11e3-b899-20667de76985_story.html, retrieved on June 13, 2022.

12. Angela E. Stent, *Putin's World: Russia against the West and with the Rest* (New York: Twelve, 2019), 2–3.

13. Hal Brands, "Democracy versus Authoritarianism: How Ideology Shapes Great-Power Conflict," *Survival* 60, no. 5 (2018): 72–73.

14. Jens Koning, "Why Putin Is Losing—the Weakness of Personalist Dictatorship," *PRIO* (blog), March 9, 2022, https://blogs.prio.org/2022/03/why-putin-is-losing-the-weakness-of-personalist-dictatorship/, retrieved on June 13, 2022.

15. On post–Cold War regime promoting competition between democracies and autocracies, see Tanja A. Börzel, "The Noble West and the Dirty Rest? Western Democracy Promoters and Illiberal Regional Powers," *Democratization* 22, no. 3 (2015): 519–35. Börzel notes that democracies sometimes support autocracy for the sake of stability, and autocracies sometimes end up provoking a democratic backlash in target states.

16. Quoted in Samuel Charap and Timothy Colton, *Everyone Loses: The Ukraine Crisis and the Ruinous Contest for Post-Soviet Eurasia* (London: International Institute for Strategic Studies/Routledge, 2017), 83.

17. Thomas Ambrosio, *Authoritarian Backlash: Russian Resistance to Democratization in the Former Soviet Union* (Burlington, Vt.: Ashgate, 2009), 151–55.

18. Jeffrey Mankoff, *Russian Foreign Policy: The Return of Great Power Politics*, 2nd ed. (Lanham, Md.: Rowman and Littlefield, 2011), 11–52.

19. Mark Galeotti, *Hybrid War or Gibridnaya Voina? Getting Russia's Non-Linear Military Challenge Right* (Prague: Mayak Intelligence, 2016).

20. Alexander Cooley and Daniel Nexon, *Exit from Hegemony: The Unraveling of the American Global Order* (New York: Oxford University Press, 2020), 137–58.

21. John M. Owen, "Sino-Russian Cooperation against Liberal Hegemony," *International Politics* 57, no. 5 (2020): 809–33.

22. World Trade Organization, "Russia Federation," https://www.wto.org

/english/res_e/statis_e/daily_update_e/trade_profiles/RU_e.pdf, retrieved on June 13, 2022.

23. Robert Horvath, "The Reinvention of 'Traditional Values': Nataliya Narochnitskaya and Russia's Assault on Universal Human Rights," *Europe-Asia Studies* 68, no. 5 (July 2016): 889.

24. Henry Hale, *Patronal Politics: Eurasian Regime Dynamics in Comparative Perspective* (New York: Cambridge University Press, 2014).

25. English text available at "The Constitution of the Russian Federation," http://www.constitution.ru/en/10003000-01.htm, retrieved on June 8, 2022.

26. David R. Cameron and Mitchell A. Orenstein, "Post-Soviet Authoritarianism: The Influence of Russia in Its 'Near Abroad,'" *Post-Soviet Affairs* 28, no. 1 (2012): 15–19.

27. Ora John Reuter, *The Origin of Dominant Parties: Building Authoritarian Institutions in Post-Soviet Russia* (New York: Cambridge University Press, 2017), 268–69.

28. Hale, *Patronal Politics,* 271.

29. Freedom House, "Freedom in the World 2022," https://freedomhouse.org/country/russia/freedom-world/2022, retrieved on June 8, 2022.

30. Ambrosio, *Authoritarian Backlash,* 34–49; Vitali Silitski, "Reading Russia: Tools of Autocracy," *Journal of Democracy* 20, no 2 (2009): 42–46.

31. Hale, *Patronal Politics,* 272.

32. Mankoff, *Russian Foreign Policy,* 46.

33. World Bank Group, "State-Owned Enterprises in the Russian Federation: Employment Practices, Labor Markets, and Firm Performance," June 2019, https://documents1.worldbank.org/curated/en/246661562074950759/pdf/State-Owned-Enterprises-in-the-Russian-Federation-Employment-Practices-Labor-Markets-and-Firm-Performance.pdf, retrieved on June 9, 2022.

34. Freedom House, "Freedom in the World 2022."

35. Varieties of Democracy (V-Dem) Institute, *Democracy Report 2022: Autocratization Changing Nature?* (Gothenburg, Sweden: Varieties of Democracy Institute, 2022), https://v-dem.net/media/publications/dr_2022.pdf, retrieved on June 8, 2022.

36. Economist Intelligence Unit, *Democracy Index 2020: In Sickness and in Health?* (London: Economist, 2021), 12.

37. Anne Applebaum, "Putinism: The Ideology," London School of Economics, February 2013, https://www.lse.ac.uk/ideas/publications/updates/putinism, retrieved on June 8, 2022.

38. Ambrosio, *Authoritarian Backlash,* 71–76.

39. Luke March, "Nationalism for Export? The Domestic and Foreign-Policy Implications of the New 'Russian Idea,'" *Europe-Asia Studies* 64, no. 3 (2012): 408–10.

40. Vladislav Surkov, "Putin's Lasting State," trans. Bill Bowler, Bewildering Stories, http://www.bewilderingstories.com/issue810/putins_state.html, retrieved on June 15, 2022. Surkov's original article, "Dolgoye Gosudarstvo Putina," appeared originally in *Nezavisimaya [The Independent]*, February 1, 2019.

41. Alexander Dugin, *The Fourth Political Theory* (London: Arktos, 2012), 15–31; Malloy Owen, "Russia's Messianic Realism," The Gate, May 13, 2016, http://uchicagogate.com/articles/2016/5/13/russias-messianic-realism/, retrieved on June 8, 2022.

42. Horvath, "Re-Invention of Traditional Values." On the ideological emphasis on Russia's continuity with its past, see Walter Laqueur, "After the Fall: Russia in Search of a New Ideology," *World Affairs* 176, no. 6 (2014): 71–77.

43. Charap and Colton, *Everyone Loses*, 74–78.

44. Laqueur, "After the Fall," 77.

45. Vladimir Putin, "Annual Address to the Federal Assembly of the Russian Nation," The Kremlin, April 25, 2005, http://en.kremlin.ru/events/president/transcripts/22931, retrieved on June 10, 2022.

46. Surkov, "Putin's Lasting State."

47. Dugin, *Fourth Political Theory*, 18–19.

48. Quoted in Horvath, "Re-Invention of Traditional Values," 878–79.

49. Herd, "Russia and the 'Orange Revolution,'" 18–19.

50. David Holley, "In Russia, a Debate over Democracy," *Los Angeles Times*, July 13, 2006, https://www.latimes.com/archives/la-xpm-2006-jul-13-fg-otherrussia13-story.html, retrieved on June 21, 2022.

51. Sergei Ivanov, in *Izvestia*, July 14, 2006, quoted in Ambrosio, *Authoritarian Backlash*, 71.

52. Galeotti, *Hybrid War or Gibridnaya Voina?*.

53. Lincoln Mitchell, "Putin's Orange Obsession: How a Twenty-Year Fixation with Color Revolutions Drove a Disastrous War," *Foreign Affairs*, May 6, 2022, https://www.foreignaffairs.com/articles/russia-fsu/2022-05-06/putins-orange-obsession, retrieved on June 18, 2022.

54. Oisín Tansey, *The International Politics of Authoritarian Rule* (New York: Oxford University Press, 2016), 55–88.

55. Vitali Silitsky, "Contagion Deterred: Preemptive Authoritarianism in the Former Soviet Union (the Case of Belarus)" (working paper #66, Center on Democracy, Development, and the Rule of Law, Stanford University, June 2006), 5. See also Jakub Tolstrup, "Black Knights and Elections in Authoritarian Regimes: Why and How Russia Supports Authoritarian Incumbents

in Post-Soviet States," *European Journal of Political Research* 54, no. 4 (November 2015): 673–90.

56. Rachel Vanderhill, *Promoting Authoritarianism Abroad* (Boulder: Lynne Rienner, 2012), 74, 77.

57. Vanderhill, *Promoting Authoritarianism Abroad*, 66–69, 78; Ambrosio, *Authoritarian Backlash*, 110–11.

58. Vanderhill, *Promoting Authoritarianism Abroad*, 78–82.

59. Quoted in Ambrosio, *Authoritarian Backlash*, 105.

60. Quoted in Charap and Colton, *Everyone Loses*, 88–89.

61. Charap and Colton, *Everyone Loses*, 91–92.

62. Vanderhill, *Promoting Authoritarianism Abroad*, 46–47.

63. Horvath, *Putin's "Preventive Counter-Revolution*," 12–23; Vanderhill, *Promoting Authoritarianism Abroad*, 18. Timothy Snyder and Timothy Garten Ash estimate the amount at $300 million; Vanderhill, *Promoting Authoritarianism Abroad*, 48.

64. Lynch, *Vladimir Putin*, 111–14.

65. Stephen Lee Myers, *The New Tsar: The Rise and Reign of Vladimir Putin* (New York: Vintage, 2016), 272–74.

66. Horvath, *Putin's "Preventive Revolution*," 32–33.

67. Robert Person and Michael McFaul, "What Putin Fears Most," *Journal of Democracy* 33, no. 2 (April 2022): 18–27.

68. Ambrosio, *Authoritarian Backlash*, 145–46.

69. Charap and Colton, *Everyone Loses*, 71; John M. Owen IV, *The Clash of Ideas in World Politics: Transnational Networks, States, and Regime Change, 1510–2010* (Princeton, N.J.: Princeton University Press, 2010), 260.

70. Mitchell, "Putin's Orange Obsession."

71. Charap and Colton, *Everyone Loses*, 74–78.

72. Charap and Colton, *Everyone Loses*, 71.

73. Observatory of Economic Complexity (OEC), "Russia," https://oec.world/en/profile/country/rus?yearSelector1=exportGrowthYear10, retrieved on June 23, 2022.

74. Charap and Colton, *Everyone Loses*, 79–81.

75. Vanderhill, *Promoting Authoritarianism Abroad*, 61; Charap and Colton, *Everyone Loses*, 106.

76. Cameron and Orenstein, "Post-Soviet Authoritarianism," 32; Charap and Colton, *Everyone Loses*, 95–101.

77. Charap and Colton, *Everyone Loses*, 114–22.

78. North Atlantic Treaty Organization, "Comprehensive Assistance Package for Ukraine," July 2016, https://www.nato.int/nato_static_fl2014/assets/pdf/pdf_2016_09/20160920_160920-compreh-ass-package-ukra.pdf, retrieved on June 24, 2022.

7

Authoritarian Internationalism

1. Quoted in David E. Sanger, "Biden Defines His Underlying Challenge with China: 'Prove Democracy Works,'" *New York Times,* March 26, 2021, https://www.nytimes.com/2021/03/26/us/politics/biden-china-democracy .html, retrieved on May 1, 2021.

2. Quoted in "Biden Administration Can Still Choose to Set Better Example," *China Daily,* April 27, 2021, https://global.chinadaily.com.cn/a /202104/27/WS6087fb0ba31024adobabacf4.html, retrieved on May 1, 2021.

3. Chen Weihua, "Blinken's Remarks on China Ring Hollow, Will Not Convince Anyone," *China Daily,* May 7, 2021, http://global.chinadaily.com .cn/a/202105/07/WS60947c61a31024adobabc573.html, retrieved on May 18, 2021.

4. Alexander Cooley and Daniel Nexon, *Exit from Hegemony* (New York: Oxford University Press, 2020), 2. For a prescient early note of skepticism, see Harry Harding, "Will China Democratize? The Halting Advance of Pluralism," *Journal of Democracy* 9, no. 1 (January 1998): 11–17.

5. Stacie E. Goddard, "Embedded Revisionism: Networks, Institutions, and Challenges to World Order," *International Organization* 72, no. 4 (2018): 793; Fu Ying quoted in Hal Brands, "Democracy vs. Authoritarianism: How Ideology Shapes Great-Power Conflict," *Survival* 60, no. 5 (2018): 72.

6. Figures are of nominal GDP in 2021, from the World Bank's online data generator: the World Bank, "GDP (Current US$)," https://data.world bank.org/indicator/NY.GDP.MKTP.CD?most_recent_value_desc=true, retrieved on June 20, 2022.

7. Goddard, "Embedded Revisionism," 793.

8. John M. Owen, "Sino-Russian Cooperation against Liberal Hegemony," *International Politics* 57, no. 5 (2020): 809–33.

9. Christian von Soest, "Democracy Prevention: The International Collaboration of Authoritarian Regimes," *European Journal of Political Research* 54, no. 4 (2015): 623–38.

10. Erin Hale, "Personal Ties That Bind: How Xi-Putin Relationship Has Evolved," *Al Jazeera,* March 18, 2022, https://www.aljazeera.com/news/2022/3 /18/personal-ties-that-bind-how-xi-putin-relationship-has-evolved, retrieved on July 4, 2022.

11. For a summary see Brands, "Democracy vs. Authoritarianism," 75–85.

12. Maggie Tennis, "Russia Ramps Up Global Elections Interference: Lessons for the United States," Center for Strategic and International Studies (*Strategic Technologies* blog), July 20, 2020, https://www.csis.org/blogs/tech

nology-policy-blog/russia-ramps-global-elections-interference-lessons
-united-states, retrieved on July 6, 2022.

13. Matt Bradley, "Europe's Far Right Enjoys Backing from Russia's Putin," NBC News, February 13, 2017, https://www.nbcnews.com/news/world/europe -s-far-right-enjoys-backing-russia-s-putin-n718926, retrieved on July 5, 2022.

14. Tennis, "Russia Ramps Up."

15. "Hundreds of Fake Twitter Accounts Linked to China Sowed Disinformation Prior to the US Election—Report," Cardiff University News, January 21, 2021, https://www.cardiff.ac.uk/news/view/2491763-hundreds-of -fake-twitter-accounts-linked-to-china-sowed-disinformation-prior-to -the-us-election,-with-some-continuing-to-amplify-reactions-to-the-capi tol-building-riot-report, retrieved on May 18, 2021.

16. Henry Farrell and Abraham L. Newman, "The Janus Face of the International Information Order: When Global Institutions Are Self-Undermining," *International Organization* 75, no. 2 (2021): 333–58; Emanuel Adler and Alena Drieschova, "The Epistemological Challenge of Truth Subversion to the Liberal International Order," *International Organization* 75, no. 2 (2021): 359–86.

17. Barry Naughton, "China's Global Economic Interactions," in *China and the World*, ed. David Shambaugh (New York: Oxford University Press, 2020), 126.

18. David Skidmore, "How China's Ambitious Belt and Road Plans for East Africa Came Apart," The Diplomat, March 5, 2022, https://thediplomat .com/2022/03/how-chinas-ambitious-belt-and-road-plans-for-east-africa -came-apart/, retrieved on August 15, 2022.

19. Mingjiang Li, "The Belt and Road Initiative: Geo-Economics and Indo-Pacific Security Competition," *International Affairs* 96, no. 1 (2020): 169–88.

20. As of March 2019, the CDB had financed more than $190 billion in six hundred BRI projects. Reuters Staff, "China Development Bank Provides over $190 billion for Belt and Road Projects," Reuters, March 26, 2019, https:// www.reuters.com/article/us-china-finance-cdb-bri/china-development -bank-provides-over-190-billion-for-belt-and-road-projects-idUSKCN 1R8095, retrieved on November 16, 2020. Some commentators have linked the Asian Infrastructure Investment Bank (AIIB), a multilateral lender founded by China in 2013, to the BRI. Naughton, "China's Global Economic Interactions," 127–28, points out that as of 2020, AIIB lending was only 1.5 percent of CDB lending, and that the AIIB is increasingly conforming to the norms of traditional international financial institutions such as the World Bank and Asian Development Bank. As of May 2022, private Chinese lenders (never fully independent of the party-state) had begun lending to BRI

projects more. "Chinese Loans and Investment in Infrastructure Have Been Huge," *Economist,* May 20, 2022, https://www.economist.com/special-report /2022/05/20/chinese-loans-and-investment-in-infrastructure-have-been -huge, retrieved on August 1, 2022.

21. Xiaojun Li and Ka Zeng, "To Join or Not to Join? State Ownership, Commercial Interests, and China's Belt and Road Initiative," *Pacific Affairs* 92, no. 1 (March 2019): 5–26.

22. Li, "Belt and Road Initiative," 179–83. Doubt has emerged as to whether the Pakistan project will work as advertised, as the construction of the port of Gwadar has stalled. See Muhammad Akbar Notezai, "Whatever Happened to the China-Pakistan Economic Corridor?," The Diplomat, February 16, 2021, https://thediplomat.com/2021/02/what-happened-to-the -china-pakistan-economic-corridor/, retrieved on May 15, 2021.

23. Yau Tsz Yan, "Exporting China's Social Credit System to Central Asia," The Diplomat, January 17, 2020, https://thediplomat.com/2020/01/exporting -chinas-social-credit-system-to-central-asia/, retrieved on November 16, 2020; Elizabeth Economy, "Exporting the China Model," testimony before the U.S.-China Economic and Security Review Commission, Washington, D.C., March 13, 2020, 4, https://www.uscc.gov/sites/default/files/testimonies /USCCTestimony3-13-20%20(Elizabeth%20Economy)_justified.pdf.

24. Adam Segal, "China's Vision for Cyber Sovereignty and the Global Governance of Cyberspace," in *An Emerging China-Centric Order,* ed. Nadège Rolland (Washington, D.C.: National Bureau of Asian Research, 2020), 97.

25. Steven Feldstein, "The Global Expansion of AI Surveillance," Carnegie Endowment for International Peace, September 19, 2019, https://carnegie endowment.org/2019/09/17/global-expansion-of-ai-surveillance-pub -79847, retrieved on November 16, 2020. Feldstein notes that liberal democracies, including the United States, use AI surveillance as well, but that democracies tend to use it far less on internal dissent.

26. Ross Andersen, "The Panopticon Is Already Here," *Atlantic,* September 2020, https://www.theatlantic.com/magazine/archive/2020/09/china-ai -surveillance/614197/, retrieved on August 27, 2021; James Kynge, Valerie Hopkins, Helen Warrell, and Kathrin Hille, "Exporting Chinese Surveillance: The Security Risks of 'Smart Cities,'" *Financial Times,* June 9, 2021, https:// www.ft.com/content/76fdac7c-7076-47a4-bcb0-7e75afoaadab, retrieved on August 27, 2021.

27. Naughton, "China's Global Economic Interactions," 126, 132–33.

28. Alisée Pornet, "Every Step Makes a Footprint: China's Aid and Development as Incremental Policies," in Rolland, *Emerging China-Centric Order,* 106.

29. Matthew D. Stephen and David Skidmore, "The AIIB in the Liberal

International Order," *Chinese Journal of International Politics* (2019): 61–91, doi: 10.1093/cjip/poy021.

30. Luke Patey, *How China Loses: The Pushback against Chinese Global Ambitions* (New York: Oxford University Press, 2021), 77, 96.

31. Amy Searight, "Countering China's Influence Operations: Lessons from Australia," Center for Strategic and International Studies, May 8, 2020, https://www.csis.org/analysis/countering-chinas-influence-operations-lessons -australia, retrieved on May 18, 2021.

32. Joyce Huang, "China Using 'Cognitive Warfare' against Taiwan, Observers Say," VOA, January 17, 2021, https://www.voanews.com/east-asia -pacific/china-using-cognitive-warfare-against-taiwan-observers-say, retrieved on May 17, 2021. VOA (Voice of America) is funded by the U.S. government.

33. Thomas Ambrosio, "Catching the 'Shanghai Spirit': How the Shanghai Cooperation Organization Promotes Authoritarian Norms in Central Asia," *Europe-Asia Studies* 60, no. 8 (2008): 1321–44; Alexander Cooley, "Authoritarianism Goes Global: Countering Democratic Norms," *Journal of Democracy* 26, no. 3 (July 2015): 52.

34. Cooley, "Authoritarianism Goes Global," 55–57; Nicole Jackson, "The Role of External Factors in Advancing Non-Liberal Democratic Forms of Political Rule: A Case Study of Russia's Influence on Central Asian Regimes," *Contemporary Politics* 16, no. 1 (March 2010): 105, 112–14.

35. Jeanne L. Wilson, "Soft Power: A Comparison of Discourse and Practice in Russia and China," *Europe-Asia Studies* 67, no. 8 (October 2015): 1178–88.

36. Quoted in Wilson, "Soft Power," 1188.

37. The Global Economy, "China: GDP, Constant Dollars," https://www .theglobaleconomy.com/China/GDP_constant_dollars/, retrieved on November 12, 2020. Values are in constant 2010 U.S. dollars.

38. "Will China's Economy Ever Overtake America's?," *Economist*, September 6, 2022; Congressional Research Service, "China's Economic Rise," RL33534, Every CRS Report, https://www.everycrsreport.com/reports/RL 33534.html, retrieved on November 12, 2020.

39. World Bank, "Urban Population (% of Total Population)–China," https://data.worldbank.org/indicator/SP.URB.TOTL.IN.ZS?locations=CN, retrieved on November 12, 2020.

40. World Bank, "School Enrollment, Tertiary (% Gross)—China," https:// data.worldbank.org/indicator/SE.TER.ENRR?locations=CN, retrieved on November 12, 2020.

41. Michael K. Miller, "Democracy by Example? Why Democracy Spreads When the World's Democracies Prosper," *Comparative Politics* 49, no. 1 (October 2016): 83–104.

42. Quoted in Stefan Halper, *The Beijing Consensus: How China's Authoritarian Model Will Dominate the Twenty-First Century* (New York: Basic Books, 2010), 129.

43. Jedidiah Kroncke, "Imagining China: Brazil, Labor, and the Limits of an Anti-Model," in *The Beijing Consensus? How China Has Changed Western Ideas of Law and Economic Development,* ed. Weitseng Chen (New York: Cambridge University Press, 2017), 52–53.

44. Xi Jinping, "Secure a Decisive Victory in Building a Moderately Prosperous Society in All Respects and Strive for the Great Success of Socialism with Chinese Characteristics for a New Era," delivered at the Nineteenth National Congress of the Communist Party of China, October 18, 2017.

45. Zhang Weiwei, *The China Wave: Rise of a Civilizational State* (Singapore: World Scientific Publishing, 2012); Zhang Weiwei, *The China Horizon: Glory and Dreams of a Civilizational State* (Singapore: World Scientific Publishing, 2016).

46. Marcel Schliebs, Hannah Bailey, Jonathan Bright, and Philip N. Howard, "China's Public Diplomacy Operations: Understanding Engagement and Inauthentic Amplification of Chinese Diplomats and Facebook and Twitter" (working paper, University of Oxford Programme on Democracy and Technology, May 2021).

47. Raymond Zhong and Paul Mozur, "To Tame Coronavirus, Mao-Style Social Control Blankets China," *New York Times,* February 15, 2020, https://www.nytimes.com/2020/02/15/business/china-coronavirus-lockdown.html, retrieved on May 14, 2021.

48. Hannah Ritchie, Esteban Ortiz-Ospina, Diana Beltekian, Edouard Mathieu, Joe Hasell, Bobbie Macdonald, Charlie Giattino, Cameron Appel, Lucas Rodés-Guirao, and Max Roser, "Coronavirus Pandemic (COVID-19)," Our World in Data, 2020, https://ourworldindata.org/coronavirus, retrieved on May 14, 2021. I thank Alice Owen for sources on China's lockdown.

49. Quoted in Chris Buckley, "China's Combative Nationalists See a World Turning Their Way," *New York Times,* December 14, 2020, https://www.nytimes.com/2020/12/14/world/asia/china-nationalists-covid.html, retrieved on May 14, 2021.

50. Chen Jia and Ding Qingfen, "Overseas Officials Head to Chinese Classrooms," *China Daily,* August 5, 2010, http://www.chinadaily.com.cn/china/2010-08/05/content_11098280.htm, retrieved on October 6, 2020; He Huifeng, "In a Remote Corner of China, Beijing Is Trying to Export Its Model by Training Foreign Officials the Chinese Way," *South China Morning Post,* July 14, 2018, https://www.scmp.com/news/china/economy/article/2155203/remote-corner-china-beijing-trying-export-its-model-training, retrieved on October 6, 2020.

51. Illuminating are Chinese propaganda videos such as this: New China TV, "Music Video: The Belt and Road Is How," Youtube, May 10, 2017, https://www.youtube.com/watch?v=MolJc3PMNIg; and this: China Daily, "What Is the Belt and Road Initiative?: Belt and Road Bedtime Stories," Youtube, May 7, 2017, https://youtu.be/uKhYFFLBaeQ, retrieved on October 6, 2020.

52. The ongoing Sino-U.S. downward spiral has included a U.S. designation of Confucius Institutes as foreign missions of the Chinese government. See Associated Press, "China Lashes Out and U.S. Deems Contentious Confucius Institutes as [sic] Foreign Missions," August 14, 2020, https://global news.ca/news/7274718/china-confucius-institute-foreign-mission/, retrieved on October 6, 2020.

53. Huiyun Feng, Kai He, and Xiaojun Li, *How China Sees the World: Insights from China's International Relations Scholars* (Singapore: Palgrave-Macmillan, 2019), 29–32.

54. Amy Qin and Audrey Carlsen, "How China Is Rewriting Its Own Script," *New York Times*, November 18, 2018, https://www.nytimes.com/in teractive/2018/11/18/world/asia/china-movies.html, retrieved on October 6, 2020.

55. Steven Lee Myers, "An Alliance of Autocracies? China Wants to Lead a New World Order," *New York Times*, March 29, 2021, https://www.nytimes .com/2021/03/29/world/asia/china-us-russia.html, retrieved on June 10, 2021.

56. Quoted in Lionel Barber and Henry Foy, "'The Liberal Idea Has Become Obsolete,'" *Financial Times*, June 28, 2019, 1.

57. Quoted in Joel Gehrke, "Russian Foreign Minister Sergey Lavrov: NATO 'Doomed to Failure,'" *Washington Examiner*, July 1, 2017, https://www .washingtonexaminer.com/russian-foreign-minister-sergey-lavrov-nato -doomed-to-failure, retrieved on June 10, 2022.

58. Jackson, "Role of External Factors," 108–11.

59. Orysia Lutsevych, "Agents of the Russian World: Proxy Groups in the Contested Neighbourhood," Chatham House, April 2016, https://www .chathamhouse.org/sites/default/files/publications/research/2016-04-14 -agents-russian-world-lutsevych.pdf, retrieved on July 7, 2022.

60. Cooley, "Authoritarianism Goes Global," 52–53; Wilson, "Soft Power," 1195.

61. Cooley, "Authoritarianism Goes Global," 60.

62. Vitali Silitsky, "Contagion Deterred: Preemptive Authoritarianism in the Former Soviet Union (the Case of Belarus)" (working paper #66, Center on Democracy, Development, and the Rule of Law, Stanford University, June 2006), 38.

63. Katherine Morton, "China's Global Governance Interactions," in Shambaugh, *China and the World*, 160–62.

64. Steven Levitsky and Lucan A. Way, *Competitive Authoritarianism: Hybrid Regimes after the Cold War* (New York: Cambridge University Press, 2010).

65. Eleanor Albert, "The Shanghai Cooperation Organization," Council on Foreign Relations, October 14, 2015, https://www.cfr.org/backgrounder /shanghai-cooperation-organization, retrieved on May 14, 2021.

66. Richard Weitz, "The Impossible Quest for Absolute Security," Yale Global Online, July 11, 2017, https://yaleglobal.yale.edu/content/impossible -quest-absolute-security, retrieved on May 14, 2021.

67. Akhil Ramesh, "An Out-of-Touch G7 Could Lose Global Leadership to BRICS," The Hill, June 29, 2022, https://thehill.com/opinion/international /3541533-an-out-of-touch-g7-could-lose-global-leadership-to-brics/amp/, retrieved on July 15, 2022.

68. Collective Security Treaty Organization, https://en.odkb-csto.org, retrieved on July 5, 2022.

69. David R. Cameron and Mitchell A. Orenstein, "Post-Soviet Authoritarianism: The Influence of Russia in Its 'Near Abroad,'" *Post-Soviet Affairs* 28, no. 1 (2012): 31–32.

70. William H. Cooper, "Russia's Accession to the WTO and Its Implications for the United States," Congressional Research Service Report for Congress, June 15, 2012, 4, https://sgp.fas.org/crs/row/R42085.pdf.

71. Dominic Fean, *Decoding Russia's WTO Accession* (Paris: Ifri Russia/ NIS Center, 2012), 13.

72. Cooper, "Russia's Accession," 5.

73. Sarah Anne Aarup and Ashleigh Furlong, "Russia Takes First Steps to Withdraw from WTO, WHO," Politico, May 18, 2022, https://www.politico .eu/article/russia-takes-first-steps-to-withdraw-from-wto-who/, retrieved on July 7, 2022.

74. Quoted in Robert Horvath, "The Reinvention of 'Traditional Values': Nataliya Narochnitskaya and Russia's Assault on Universal Human Rights," *Europe-Asia Studies* 68, no. 5 (2016): 879–82.

75. See some of the late twentieth-century communitarian critiques of liberalism, including Alasdair Macintyre, *After Virtue* (Notre Dame, Ind.: University of Notre Dame Press, 1981); and Michael J. Sandel, *Liberalism and the Limits of Justice* (New York: Cambridge University Press, 1982).

76. Horvath, "Reinvention of 'Traditional Values,'" 883–87.

77. Horvath, "Reinvention of 'Traditional Values,'" 886.

78. Rana Siu Inboden, *China and the International Human Rights Regime: 1982–2017* (New York: Cambridge University Press, 2021), 17. At the same time, the United States signed but has never ratified the 1966 International Covenant on Economic, Social, and Cultural Rights.

79. Inboden, *China and the International Human Rights Regime*, 73–76.

80. Inboden, *China and the International Human Rights Regime*, 130–58.

81. Quoted in Yu-Jie Chen, "China's Challenge to the International Human Rights Regime," *NYU Journal of International Law and Politics* 51 (2019): 1211–12.

82. A website, complete with videos and documents, is at the South-South Human Rights Forum Portal, http://p.china.org.cn/node_8001790.htm, retrieved on November 13, 2020.

83. Melanie Hart, "Beijing's Promotion of Alternative Global Norms and Standards," testimony before the U.S.-China Economic and Security Review Commission, Washington, D.C., March 13, 2020.

84. Ted Piccone, "China's Long Game on Human Rights at the UN," Brookings Institution, September 2018, 7–11, https://www.brookings.edu/research /chinas-long-game-on-human-rights-at-the-united-nations/, retrieved on November 13, 2020; Chen, "China's Challenge," 1206–7; Marc Limon, "The Return of Great-Power Politics to the Human Rights Council," Geneva Solutions, March 30, 2021, https://genevasolutions.news/peace-humanitarian /the-return-of-great-power-politics-to-the-human-rights-council, retrieved on July 7, 2022.

85. Daniëlle Flonk, "Emerging Illiberal Norms: Russia and China as Promoters of Internet Content Control," *International Affairs* 97, no. 6 (2021): 1927.

86. Jessica Chen Weiss and Jeremy L. Wallace, "Domestic Politics, China's Rise, and the Future of the Liberal International Order," *International Organization* 75 (Spring 2021): 647.

87. Mark Raymond and Laura DeNardis, "Multistakeholderism: Anatomy of an Inchoate Global Institution," *International Theory* 7, no. 3 (2015): 572–616.

88. Segal, "China's Vision for Cyber Sovereignty," 87.

89. André Barrinha and Thomas Renard, "Power and Diplomacy in the Post-Liberal Cyberspace," *International Affairs* 96, no. 3 (2020): 749–66.

90. Segal, "China's Vision for Cyber Sovereignty," 87.

91. Quoted in Segal, "China's Vision for Cyber Sovereignty," 89–90.

92. Federico Guerrini, "In Search of a Governance: Who Will Win the Battle of the Internet?," *Forbes*, October 24, 2014, https://www.forbes.com /sites/federicoguerrini/2014/10/24/in-search-of-a-good-governance-who -will-win-the-battle-for-the-future-of-the-internet/?sh=21625b6e321c, retrieved on November 13, 2020.

93. Flonk, "Emerging Illiberal Norms," 1932; Barrinha and Renard, "Post-Liberal Cyberspace," 762–63.

94. Quoted in Ambrosio, "Shanghai Spirit," 1334.

95. Henry Rõigas, "An Updated Draft of the Code of Conduct Distributed in the United Nations—What's New?," NATO Cooperative Cyber Defence Centre of Excellence, https://ccdcoe.org/incyder-articles/an-updated-draft-of-the-code-of-conduct-distributed-in-the-united-nations-whats-new/, retrieved on November 13, 2020.

96. Segal, "China's Vision," 91–92.

97. Segal, "China's Vision," 99.

98. Flonk, "Emerging Illiberal Norms," 1932–33.

8
Making the World Select for Democracy

1. Paul Musgrave, "International Hegemony Meets Domestic Politics: Why Liberals Can Be Pessimists," *Security Studies* 28, no. 3 (2019): 451–78.

2. Thomas L. Friedman, "Our One-Party Democracy," *New York Times,* September 8, 2009, https://www.nytimes.com/2009/09/09/opinion/09friedman.html, retrieved on July 22, 2021.

3. Matthew Garrahan, "Jon Stewart: 'Ain't Nothing as Agile as Authoritarian Regimes,'" *Financial Times,* October 28, 2022.

4. Quoted in Phil Owen, "Tucker Carlson Says America Needs to Be More Like China (Video)," Yahoo! Entertainment, August 6, 2020, https://www.yahoo.com/entertainment/tucker-carlson-says-america-needs-015958546.html, retrieved on July 22, 2021.

5. The White House, "Fact Sheet: President Biden and G7 Leaders Launch Build Back Better World (B3W) Partnership," June 12, 2021, https://www.whitehouse.gov/briefing-room/statements-releases/2021/06/12/fact-sheet-president-biden-and-g7-leaders-launch-build-back-better-world-b3w-partnership/, retrieved on August 17, 2022. On this particular Western adaptation to Chinese pressure, see David Skidmore, "U.S.-China Competition and Challenges to the Global Development Finance Regime" (working paper, Drake University, August 2022).

6. Barry R. Posen, *Restraint: A New Foundation for American Grand Strategy* (Ithaca, N.Y.: Cornell University Press, 2015); John J. Mearsheimer, *The Great Delusion: Liberal Dreams and International Realities* (New Haven: Yale University Press, 2018); Stephen M. Walt, *The Hell of Good Intentions: America's Foreign Policy Elite and the Decline of U.S. Primacy* (New York: Farrar, Straus and Giroux, 2018).

7. Robert Gilpin, *War and Change in World Politics* (New York: Cambridge University Press, 1981), esp. 156–85.

8. G. John Ikenberry, *A World Safe for Democracy: Liberal Internationalism and the Crises of Global Order* (New Haven: Yale University Press, 2020), 310.

9. Sidney Milkis, "Franklin D. Roosevelt, the Economic Constitutional Order, and the New Politics of Presidential Leadership," in *The New Deal and the Triumph of Liberalism,* ed. Milkis and Jerome Mileur (Amherst: University of Massachusetts Press, 2002), 35.

10. Robert Zoellick, "Reviving Conservative Internationalism," American Purpose, May 12, 2021, https://www.americanpurpose.com/articles/reviving -conservative-internationalism/, retrieved on May 13, 2021.

11. Rebecca Lissner and Mira Rapp-Hooper, *An Open World: How America Can Win the Contest for Twenty-First-Century Order* (New Haven: Yale University Press, 2020).

12. Bernie Sanders, "Democrats Need to Wake Up," *New York Times,* June 28, 2016, https://www.nytimes.com/2016/06/29/opinion/campaign -stops/bernie-sanders-democrats-need-to-wake-up.html, retrieved on May 25, 2021.

13. Tom Moseley, "In Quotes: Jeremy Corbyn and the EU Referendum," BBC, April 14, 2016, https://www.bbc.com/news/uk-politics-eu-referendum -35743994, retrieved on May 25, 2021. Also, Michael Holmes and Knut Roder, "Social Democracy and Euroscepticism: The Integration Trap," in *Europe and the Left: Resisting the Populist Tide,* ed. James L. Newell (London: Palgrave Macmillan, 2021), 19–41.

14. Charles Taylor, *A Secular Age* (Cambridge, Mass.: Harvard University Press, 2007), 475.

15. J. Lawrence Broz, Jeffry Frieden, and Stephen Weymouth, "Populism in Place: The Economic Geography of the Globalization Backlash," *International Organization* 75, no. 2 (2021): 464–94.

16. Joseph E. Davis, *Chemically Imbalanced: Everyday Suffering, Medication, and Our Troubled Quest for Self-Mastery* (Chicago: University of Chicago Press, 2020).

17. W. Bradford Wilcox and Wendy Wang, "The Marriage Divide: How and Why Working-Class Families Are More Fragile Today" (research brief, Opportunity America-AEI-Brookings Working Class Group, 2017).

18. Alexis de Tocqueville, "On Political Association in the United States," in *Democracy in America,* vol. 1, trans. Harvey C. Mansfield and Delba Winthrop (Chicago: University of Chicago Press, 2012), 180–86.

19. Dani Rodrik, *The Paradox of Globalization: Choices to End the Cold War and Build a Global Commonwealth* (New York: Norton, 2011), 206.

20. Rodrik, *Paradox of Globalization,* 241, 253.

21. Rodrik, *Paradox of Globalization*, 266–72; George Borjas, "Globalization and Immigration," in *Globalization: What's New?*, ed. Michael M. Weinstein (New York: Columbia University Press, 2005), 77–95.

22. Oren Cass, "A New Conservatism: Freeing the Right from Free-Market Orthodoxy," *Foreign Affairs* 100, no. 2 (March/April 2021): 116–28.

23. Ryan Teague Beckwith, "Read Donald Trump's 'America First' Foreign Policy Speech," *Time*, April 27, 2016, https://time.com/4309786/read -donald-trumps-america-first-foreign-policy-speech/, retrieved on May 27, 2021.

24. Kriston McIntosh, Emily Ross, Ryan Nunn, and Jay Shambaugh, "Examining the Black-White Wealth Gap," Brookings Institution, February 27, 2020, https://www.brookings.edu/blog/up-front/2020/02/27/examining-the -black-white-wealth-gap/, retrieved on March 25, 2021.

25. Marc Levinson, *Outside the Box: How Globalization Changed from Moving Stuff to Spreading Ideas* (Princeton, N.J.: Princeton University Press, 2020), 210–17.

26. Levinson, *Outside the Box*, 222–24.

27. Charles A. Kupchan, "The Case for a Middle Path in U.S. Foreign Policy," Foreign Policy, January 15, 2021, https://foreignpolicy.com/2021/01/15 /judicious-retrenchment-isolationism-internationalism/, retrieved on August 27, 2021.

28. Philip Zelikow, "The Hollow Order: Rebuilding an International System That Works," *Foreign Affairs* 101, no. 4 (July/August 2022): 107–19. Zelikow argues that the West should take the lead in building a new international order but should offer China a role.

29. A strong case for Sino-American cooperation is in Jessica Chen Weiss, "The China Trap: U.S. Foreign Policy and the Perilous Logic of Zero-Sum Competition," *Foreign Affairs* 101, no. 4 (September/October 2022): 40–58.

30. Raymond Aron, *Peace and War* (New York: Doubleday, 1966), 100–101.

31. For the path-dependent logic of international institutions, see G. John Ikenberry, *After Victory: Institutions, Strategic Restraint, and the Rebuilding of Order after Major War* (Princeton, N.J.: Princeton University Press, 2001), 50–79.

32. John M. Owen, "Two Emerging International Orders? Evolutionary Pressure and Regime Preservation in China and the United States," *International Affairs* 97, no. 5 (September 2021): 1415–31. See also Ikenberry, *Safe for Democracy*, 301–2. On the possibility of an authoritarian subsystem within a larger Western-dominated global system, see Aaron L. Friedberg, *The Authoritarian Challenge: China, Russia and the Threat to the Liberal International Order* (Tokyo: Sasakawa Peace Foundation, 2017), esp. 67–70.

33. Hung Tran, "Dual Circulation in China: A Progress Report," Atlantic Council, October 24, 2022, https://www.atlanticcouncil.org/blogs/econo graphics/dual-circulation-in-china-a-progress-report/, retrieved on November 23, 2022.

34. The RCEP was originally proposed by the Association of Southeast Asian Nations (ASEAN) in 2011, but China pushed for it, and its economy is by far the largest in the organization.

35. Andrew Restuccia and Ken Thomas, "Biden Kicks off Economic Group Linking U.S., Asia," *Wall Street Journal,* March 23, 2022.

36. Wang Jisi, "The Plot against China? How Beijing Sees the New Washington Consensus," *Foreign Affairs* 100, no. 4 (July/August 2021): 57.

37. For a somewhat different fleshing out of the "two orders" future from a Chinese perspective, see Yan Xuetong, "The Age of Uneasy Peace: Chinese Power in a Divided World," *Foreign Affairs* 98, no. 1 (January/February 2019): 40–49.

38. Barry Eichengreen, "Sanctions, SWIFT, and China's Cross-Border Interbank Payments System," The Marshall Papers, Center for Strategic and International Studies, May 2022, https://www.csis.org/analysis/sanctions -swift-and-chinas-cross-border-interbank-payments-system, retrieved on August 3, 2022.

39. Lee Hsien Loong, "The Endangered Asian Century: America, China, and the Perils of Confrontation," *Foreign Affairs* 99, no. 4 (July/August 2020): 52–64.

Index